D0028168

DAY BY ORDINARY DAY WITH LUKE

DAY BY ORDINARY DAY WITH
L U K E

Daily Reflections for Ordinary Time
Weeks 22-34

VOLUME 3

MARK G. BOYER

ALBA·HOUSE   NEW·YORK

SOCIETY OF ST. PAUL, 2187 VICTORY BLVD., STATEN ISLAND, NEW YORK 10314

ST PAULS

Quotations from the New Testament are taken from *The Alba House New Testament*, translated by Mark A. Wauck, copyright © 1997 by the Society of St. Paul, Staten Island, NY. All rights reserved.

Library of Congress Cataloging-in-Publication Data

Boyer, Mark G.
   Day by ordinary day with Luke: daily reflections for ordinary
time / Mark G. Boyer.
      p. cm.
   Contents: v. 3. Weeks 22-34.
   ISBN 0-8189-0785-1
   1. Church year meditations. 2. Bible. N.T. Luke— Meditations.
3. Catholic Church — Prayer-books and meditations — English.
I. Title.
BX2170.C55B72   1997
242'.3 — dc20   96-44890
                                 CIP

Produced and designed in the United States of America by the
Fathers and Brothers of the Society of St. Paul,
2187 Victory Boulevard, Staten Island, New York 10314,
as part of their communications apostolate.

ISBN: 0-8189-0785-1

Printing Information:

Current Printing - first digit   1   2   3   4   5   6   7   8   9   10

Year of Current Printing - first year shown

1997   1998   1999   2000   2001   2002   2003   2004   2005

Dedicated to

the members of the "Old Study Group":
James & Dorothy Askren,
Jerry & June Beck,
Thomas & Raamah Crim,
Edward & Julie Rice,
and Olive White;

and to the members
of the "Jackson Church" group:
Arthur Hobbs,
James & Brenda Jackson,
Leigh-Ann Long,
Timothy & Laura Vinyard,
Mary Wieman,
and Keith & Robin Zeka.

TABLE OF CONTENTS

INTRODUCTION

Today, in Catholic circles there is a strong emphasis on the studying and the praying of the Gospels. In part, this has been brought on by the introduction of the three-year Sunday cycle of Gospel readings and the one-year weekday cycle of Gospel readings in 1974. When a person takes a course, attends a workshop, or participates in a Bible study group, the praying of the Gospels is divorced from the study of the Gospels.

This book attempts to bring such a divorce to an end. This book joins the studying and the praying of the Gospels into a marriage of biblical spirituality that has become the foundation for the Church's proclamation and preaching of the good news during the thirty-three to thirty-four weeks of the liturgical year referred to as Ordinary Time.

According to the *General Norms for the Liturgical Year and the Calendar*, issued by the Congregation of Rites in 1969 and revised in 1975, Ordinary Time consists of those thirty-three or thirty-four weeks — distinct from Advent, Christmas, Lent and Easter — "that do not celebrate a specific aspect of the mystery of Christ. Rather... they are devoted to the mystery of Christ in all its aspects" (#43).

Ordinary Time, the longest of all the liturgical seasons, is separated into two parts. The first part usually begins on the Monday after the Sunday Feast of the Baptism of the Lord. In some years, when the Feast of the Baptism of the Lord is celebrated on the Monday following the Solemnity of the Epiphany, Ordinary Time begins on the following Tuesday; the first part ends on the Tuesday before Ash Wednesday.

The second part begins on the Monday after Pentecost Sunday and ends on the evening of the Saturday before the first Sunday of Advent. A Table of Movable Solemnities, Feasts, and Sundays, which is found at the end of this Introduction, will assist the reader in determining the beginnings and endings of the Season of Ordinary Time.

According to the 1981 Introduction to the *Lectionary for Mass,* issued by the Sacred Congregation for the Sacraments and Divine Worship, "The Sundays in Ordinary Time do not have a distinctive character. Thus the texts of... the... Gospel readings are arranged in an order of semi-continuous reading"(#67).

Except for the Second Sunday of Ordinary Time, when all three cycles of Gospel selections are from the Gospel According to John, the thirty-three or thirty-four Sundays in Cycle A consist of semi-continuous selections from the Gospel According to Matthew, in Cycle B from the Gospel According to Mark (except for the seventeenth though the twenty-first Sundays and the thirty-fourth Sunday or Solemnity of Christ the King, when selections from the Gospel According to John are read), and in Cycle C from the Gospel According to Luke.

The Introduction to the *Lectionary for Mass* states, "This distribution... provides a certain coordination between the meaning of each Gospel and the progress of the liturgical year. Thus after Epiphany the readings are on the beginning of the Lord's preaching and they fit in well with Christ's baptism and the first events in which He manifests himself. The liturgical year leads quite naturally to a termination in the eschatological theme proper to the last Sundays, since the chapters of the Synoptics that precede the account of the passion treat this eschatological theme rather extensively" (#105).

During some years, particular Solemnities and Feasts which fall on Sundays take precedence over the Sunday in Ordinary Time. These include the Solemnities of the Holy Trinity, the Body and Blood of Christ, the Birth of John the Baptist, Peter and Paul, the Assumption, and All Saints, as well as the Feasts of the Presentation, the Transfiguration, the Triumph of the Cross, the Dedication of St. John Lateran, and All Souls Day. The Gospel readings for these days are found in the Appendix.

The *Lectionary for Mass* also explains that "the weekday Order of readings is governed by... application of the principles of harmony and of semi-continuous reading" (#69). The semi-continuous reading of the Synoptic Gospels is "arranged in such a way that as the Lord's life and preaching unfold the teaching proper to each of these Gospels is presented" (#105).

During the weekdays of Ordinary time, the Gospels are arranged so that the Gospel According to Mark is read from the first through the ninth weeks, the Gospel According to Matthew from the tenth through the twenty-first weeks, and the Gospel According to Luke from the twenty-second through the thirty-fourth weeks. The Introduction of the *Lectionary for Mass* explains this schema: "Mark 1-12 are read in their entirety, with the exception only of the two passages of Mark 6 that are read on weekdays in other seasons. From Matthew and Luke the readings comprise all the matters not contained in Mark. From all three Synoptics or from two of them, as the case may be, all those passages are read that are either distinctively presented in each Gospel or are needed for a proper understanding of its progression. Jesus' eschatological discourse as contained in its entirety in Luke is read at the end of the liturgical year" (#109).

The three volumes in this series correspond to the weekday divisions indicated above. Volume I, *Day By Ordinary Day With Mark*, contains the second through the ninth Sundays of Ordinary Time Cycles A, B, and C and the first through the ninth weeks of Ordinary Time, Monday through Saturday. Volume II, *Day by Ordinary Day With Matthew*, contains the tenth through the twenty-first Sundays of Ordinary Time Cycles A, B, and C and the tenth through the twenty-first weeks of Ordinary Time, Monday through Saturday. Volume III, *Day By Ordinary Day With Luke*, contains the twenty-second through the thirty-fourth Sundays of Ordinary Times Cycles A, B, and C and the twenty-second through the thirty-fourth weeks of Ordinary Time, Monday through Saturday.

Each book in this series is designed to be used by individuals for private study of the Gospels and for prayer and by homilists for study of the Gospels, prayer and public preaching. A four-part exercise is offered for every day of the Season of Ordinary Time.

1. A few short verses of Scripture are taken from the Gospel reading provided in the Lectionary for each Mass of each day.
2. A reflective study follows the Scripture selection. The reflection attempts to critique the Gospel selection in light of contemporary source, form, redaction, literary, and historical criticism. As it offers the individual and the homilist valuable background information concerning the Gospel selection, the reflection yields new perspectives on the Scriptures for personal study and homiletic exegesis in light of contemporary biblical scholarship.
3. The reflection is followed by a question for personal meditation. The question functions as a guide for personal appropriation of the message of the Scripture selection. The homilist can use the question as a basis for a sermon or brief homily.
4. A prayer summarizes the original theme of the Scripture reading, which was studied and explored in the reflection and which served as the foundation for the meditation. The prayer concludes the daily exercise for the individual or it can be used as a fitting conclusion to the General Intercessions and the Liturgy of the Word during the celebration of the Eucharist.

Ordinary Time is the only liturgical season that leaves its mark on all four of the natural seasons of the year. Except for the Solemnity of Christ the King, the last Sunday of Ordinary Time, and a few other Solemnities and Feasts which may interrupt the Ordinary Time Sunday cycles, the color of the season is green. Green, a common color, represents stability, growth, and hope.

The woolen green plaids of January and February Ordinary Time wrap people in the winter call of Jesus and the early days of his ministry. The light green of May and June Ordinary Time are the spring buds of response to Jesus' invitation to experience the kingdom of God. The dark green of July, August, and September Ordinary Time represent the summer growth in parables, which causes the reader to see the world in different eyes. Finally, the October and November Ordinary Time fading green of fall serves as a reminder that the One who once died and was raised will come again.

It is the author's hope that through day by ordinary day study and prayer the reader will come to a deeper knowledge of and a closer relationship with the One around whom all the seasons turn — Jesus, the Christ and Lord.

Mark G. Boyer

Table of Movable Solemnities, Feasts, and Sundays
Volume III

After Pentecost

Year	Sun. Cycle	OT begins on Mon.	in week #	September 14 replaces OT Sun. #	November 1 replaces OT Sun. #	2	9	OT ends Sat. of Week 34 #
1997	B	May 19	7	24		31	32	Nov. 29
1998	C	June 1	9		31			Nov. 28
1999	A	May 24	8					Nov. 27
2000	B	June 12	10					Dec. 2
2001	C	June 1	9					Dec. 1
2002	A	May 20	7					Nov. 30
2003	B	June 9	10	24		31	32	Nov. 29
2004	C	May 31	9					Nov. 27
2005	A	May 16	7					Nov. 26

DAY BY ORDINARY DAY WITH LUKE

TRULY ALIVE

Matthew 16:21-27

Scripture: "What good will it do to gain the whole world but forfeit your life? Or what could you give in exchange for your life?" (Matthew 16:26)

Reflection: The first prediction of the passion (16:21-23) and the narrative concerning the conditions of discipleship (16:24-28) follow Peter's confession about Jesus and Matthew's unique portrait of Peter as the foundation of the Church (16:13-20). This section (16:23-28) precedes the account of the transfiguration (17:1-8).

The first prediction of the passion, as well as the second and third predictions, have been borrowed from Mark by Matthew. They are literary devices which are used to keep the story moving. Matthew already knows how his Gospel is going to end. He can internally predict the end because he, as an author, is in control of his material. These passion predictions serve to keep the reader on track throughout the last part of the Gospel.

In the second prediction Peter is called a "Satan" (16:23). This scene has been borrowed from Mark but reworked by Matthew. Peter, a sign of the Church in Matthew's Gospel, cannot accept the suffering and death which Jesus predicts. He is a "Satan" because his initial non-acceptance of this aspect of the Gospel presents "an obstacle" to Jesus (16:23).

According to Matthew, it is difficult for people (represented

1

by Peter) to think as God does. God's thinking involves suffering and death. Human beings do not think this way; human beings think of glory. Matthew is reminding his readers that discipleship is not all glory but a lot more of suffering and death.

Authentic discipleship involves a willingness to deny one's self, that is, to disown one's self as being the center of the universe. Authentic discipleship involves taking up the cross, which was a real possibility for members of Matthew's community. It also involves following Jesus to Jerusalem, where the crown of suffering and death will be given.

Matthew presents his discipleship argument in a philosophical manner by asking, "What good will it do to gain the whole world and forfeit your life?" (16:26). The point is that everyone will die some day. What point is there to having earned lots of money, a nice position, and a fancy office, if one has never lived? There is no profit in such a life. "What can you give in exchange for your life?" (16:26).

The insight of the Gospel, according to Matthew, is that discipleship permits a person to discover real life by being willing to give it up. Because a person has freely faced and dealt with the possibility of giving his or her life away, that individual is free to follow Jesus and face suffering and death. This person is truly alive and lives. He or she behaves as he or she does because it is the right way to act.

It is what God wants. In the end, such conduct will receive its due reward.

Meditation: In which ways do you judge as God judges? In which ways do you judge as human beings do?

Prayer: God of life, you gave up your only Son, Jesus, to suffering and death that you might reveal the fullness of life. Through your Holy Spirit form us into authentic disciples of Jesus. Give us an understanding of your values. Enable us to freely deny ourselves, take up our crosses, and follow in the footsteps of him who is Lord for ever and ever. Amen.

DEFILEMENT WITHIN

Mark 7:1-8, 14-15, 21-23

Scripture: [Jesus] called the crowd to himself again and said to them, "Listen to me, all of you and understand. Nothing that enters a man from outside of him can make him unclean; it's what goes forth from him that makes a man unclean" (Mark 7:14-15).

Reflection: The section of Mark's Gospel which deals with the traditions of "the Pharisees with some scribes" (7:1) comprises the first 23 verses of chapter seven. The Sunday cycle of Gospel texts, however, edits out nine of these verses. What is left (7:1-8, 14-15, 21-23) is a further redaction of an already redacted text!

The issue in this section revolves around the ritual purification of hands, cups, kettles, etc. By following the exterior ritual, a person was guaranteed interior purification — no matter what the person's motivation was for performing the ritual. Underlying and closely tied to the ritual question is the more important question of observance of Jewish purification rituals by the Gentiles.

In this passage from the Gospel of Mark, Jesus challenges the basic presupposition of the purification rituals. His disciples eat without washing their hands because it's not the ritual that makes a person clean or unclean. Just to engage in the ritual for the sake of being able to say that one has kept the ritual is not the type of worship that God wants.

This is hypocrisy. As Isaiah had written, "This people honors me with their lips, but their hearts are far from me; in vain do they worship me, teaching as doctrines mere human precepts" (Mark 7:6-7). The purpose of the ritual has been lost. "You set aside the commandment of God but cling to your own traditions" (7:8). In other words, the real intent of the law has been abandoned for the sake of merely keeping the ritual.

It is not the ritual that makes a person clean or unclean. Eating with hands that have not been washed or drinking from cups that have not been properly purified cannot make a person unclean. "Nothing that enters a man from outside of him can make him unclean; it's what goes forth from him that makes a man unclean" (7:15). "From within people, from their hearts, come evil thoughts, unchastity, theft, murder, adultery, greed, malice, deceit, licentiousness, envy, blasphemy, arrogance, and folly. All these evils come from within and they defile" (7:21-23).

Gentiles, those people who were accepting Jesus and his ways, were, according to Mark, not bound to the ritual purifications, as these had become meaningless. Faith is not concerned about washing jugs and kettles; it is concerned with the inner disposition of people. Conversion does not begin on the outside and move to the inside of a person; it begins on the inside and moves to the outside. According to Mark, those who insisted on keeping the old meaningless rituals had not been converted.

Meditation: Which old and meaningless rituals do you keep that may need to be changed or abandoned?

Prayer: God of all, you have created everything to serve the needs of your people. Nothing is clean or unclean in your sight, but all is to be used to praise your goodness. Convert our hearts to your ways. Enable us to worship you with our lives. We ask this through our Lord Jesus Christ, your Son, who lives and reigns with you and the Holy Spirit, one God, for ever and ever. Amen.

CONDUCT FOR HOSTS AND GUESTS

Luke 14:1, 7-14

Scripture: "When you are invited by someone to a wedding banquet, do not recline at table in the place of honor, lest someone more eminent than you may have been invited by him, and the host who invited both of you may approach you and say, 'Give your place to this man,' and then you would proceed with embarrassment to take the lowest place" (Luke 14:8-9).

Reflection: Luke is the only Gospel writer to provide a section on the prescribed conduct of invited guests and hosts (Luke 14:1, 7-14). This section of Luke's Gospel follows the lament over Jerusalem and precedes the parable of the great feast. It can be divided into two parts: proper conduct for invited guests and proper conduct for hosts.

Those who are invited to a wedding banquet, a favorite image of the kingdom of God, are not to "recline at table in the place of honor" (14:8), according to Luke. Since everyone is instructed to "go and take the lowest place" (14:10), no one is of any greater importance than anyone else. It is left to the host (God) to raise a person to a higher position.

By relating this parable, Luke establishes equality of all people — rich and poor alike. No one is deserving of any more or less honor. Humility consists of recognizing the equality of all people. Thus, Luke counteracts some of the social division which existed in his community.

The second part of this section deals with the duty of hosts. If all people are equal, then the person who "holds a lunch or dinner" (14:12) is instructed not to invite those of the same social rank. "Do not invite your friends or brothers or relatives or wealthy neighbors, lest they may invite you in return and thus repay you" (14:12). One of Luke's principal concerns — the poor — now emerges.

Those who are to be invited include "the poor, the crippled, the lame, the blind," who are unable to repay the host (14:13). In other words, Luke instructs the middle class members of his community in their obligation to abandon their social cliques and to take care of those less fortunate. According to Luke, those who have wealth have a responsibility to use it for the poor. Those who have a surplus have a corresponding responsibility to share with those in need.

By giving their wealth away for the sake of those who have no money, the rich enable the poor to participate in some of the good things of the earth. Furthermore, those who share their goods "will be repaid at the resurrection of the righteous" (14:14). It is by sharing goods that the rich make their path through the difficulty they have in entering the kingdom of God.

Meditation: In which ways do you share your wealth with the poor?

Prayer: God of the rich and the poor, the crippled, the lame, and the blind, in your eyes every human person is equal in dignity. Open our eyes to see our brothers and sisters in need. Open our minds to understand the equality of all people. Make us humbly equal and willing to share the goods of the earth with everyone. May we respond to the invitation to the wedding banquet in your kingdom at the resurrection of the just. We ask this through Christ our Lord. Amen.

FULFILLED IN YOUR HEARING

Luke 4:16-30

Scripture: When he had rolled up the scroll and handed it back to the attendant, he sat down, and the eyes of all in the synagogue were fixed on him. Then he began by saying to them, "Today this Scripture passage has been fulfilled in your hearing" (Luke 4:20-21).

Reflection: For twenty-one of the thirty-four weekdays of Ordinary Time, the lectionary provides selections, first, from Mark's Gospel (weeks 1-9); second, from Matthew's Gospel (weeks 10-21), and for the remaining thirteen weeks (22-34) from Luke's Gospel. The prologue (1:1-4), the infancy narrative (consisting of the announcement of the birth of John the Baptist, the announcement of the birth of Jesus, Mary's visit to Elizabeth, Mary's canticle, the birth of John the Baptist, Zechariah's canticle, the birth of Jesus, the visit of the shepherds, the circumcision, the presentation in the Temple, the finding of Jesus in the Temple) (1:5-2:52); the preaching of John the Baptist, the baptism of Jesus, the genealogy, and the temptation of Jesus (3:1-4:13) are omitted from the weekday lectionary cycle.

This section (4:16-30) consists of the beginning of the Galilean ministry of Jesus with his rejection at Nazareth.

As Luke portrays the scene, Jesus enters "Nazareth, where he had been brought up, and as was his custom he went into the synagogue on the Sabbath day" (4:16), and he stood up to read. He reads from the prophet Isaiah.

7

The words selected by Luke set the course for the rest of the Gospel. In this passage Jesus declares that the Scripture passage has been fulfilled. Luke is going to demonstrate throughout the rest of the Gospel exactly how Jesus did indeed embody Isaiah's words. Luke is interested in showing how Jesus fulfilled Old Testament hopes and expectations.

At first Jesus meets with admiration from the crowd. But as he continues his inaugural address, he mentions two incidents from Israel's past which do not please the crowd. Both incidents point back to Israel's lack of faith.

First, the reference is made to Elijah's being sent to the widow of Zarephath, a non-Israelite, during a three-year famine in Israel. Elijah was sent there because of Israel's lack of faith. Out of all the widows in Israel, none believed.

The second reference is made to Elisha, who cleansed no lepers but Naaman the Syrian, another pagan, who came to believe. Out of all the lepers in Israel none believed.

With such a reminder of their lack of faith, the crowd immediately rejects Jesus, a hint of the rejection that will continue throughout the Gospel and culminate in the rejection on the cross.

Also, by making the reference to both Elijah and Elisha, Luke is able to portray Jesus as a prophet whose mission, as that of the Church, included also the Gentiles, a theme which he will develop fully in volume two, the Acts of the Apostles.

With his first sermon completed, Jesus slips away and heads for Capernaum, where he will begin to fulfill the words of the prophet Isaiah.

Meditation: Which incidents of lack of faith from your past life make you angry when you think about them?

Prayer: God of Jesus, you poured out your Spirit on your Son and anointed him to bring glad tidings to the poor, to proclaim liberty to captives and recovery of sight to the blind, to free the oppressed, and to proclaim a year acceptable to you. Pour out your Spirit on us that we might continue his mission among those who have not hardened their hearts. We ask this through our Lord Jesus Christ, who lives and reigns with you and the Holy Spirit, one God, for ever and ever. Amen.

WITH AUTHORITY
Luke 4:31-37

Scripture: Now in the synagogue there was a man with the spirit of an unclean demon, and he cried out in a loud voice, "Ah! What do you want with us, Jesus of Nazareth? Have you come to destroy us? I know who you are — the Holy One of God!" (Luke 4:33-34).

Reflection: Following Jesus' first sermon and rejection in Nazareth, Luke, following his Marcan source, sends Jesus to Capernaum. His first act there is to cure a demoniac. This section of Luke's Gospel (4:31-37) is taken from Mark (1:21-28). Luke uses this section to introduce Jesus as a teacher and an exorcist, just as he introduced him as a prophet in the previous section of the Gospel (4:16-30).

As in Nazareth, Jesus is portrayed as teaching in the synagogue in Capernaum. Those who heard him respond with astonishment "because he spoke with authority" (4:32). The words of Jesus make a demand on the hearer/reader. Luke will demonstrate through the Gospel of what this demand consists.

The "spirit of an unclean demon" (4:33) is no match for Jesus, who has already conquered evil in the desert (cf. 4:1-13). The word with which Jesus teaches with authority is put into practice. "What sort of word is this? He gives orders to unclean spirits with authority and power, and they come out" (4:36). For Luke, those who follow Jesus must also put the word into practice.

9

Following his Marcan source and the "messianic secret" contained in that Gospel, Luke retains the notion that only the unclean spirit knows Jesus' identity. However, Luke is not interested in Mark's "messianic secret." He simply demonstrates a common belief that before the day of the Lord all evil would be overcome and God would triumph over all. By portraying Jesus as an exorcist, Luke shows that the day of the Lord is at hand.

Meditation: What has Jesus taught you? What evil needs to be exorcised from your life?

Prayer: All Holy God, you sent Jesus, your Son, to teach your people how to live according to your ways. He preached your word and freed people from all that bound them. Guide our feet into the steps of the master Teacher. Remove all that is evil in our lives. Permit us to serve you faithfully. We ask this through our Lord Jesus Christ, who lives and reigns with you and the Holy Spirit, one God, for ever and ever. Amen.

PROCLAIMING GOOD NEWS

Luke 4:38-44

Scripture: The people began to search for [Jesus], and when they came to where he was, they tried to keep him from leaving them. But he said to them, "I must proclaim the good news of the kingdom of God to the other cities, too, because for this purpose I have been sent" (Luke 4:42-43).

Reflection: Luke's source for the cure of Simon's mother-in-law, his narrative concerning other healings, and the account of Jesus leaving Capernaum is Mark's Gospel (cf. 1:29-39). Luke's own interests are revealed, however, as he edits his Marcan material.

In the narrative concerning the rejection of Jesus at Nazareth (4:16-30) Luke portrayed Jesus as a prophet. In the account of the cure of the demoniac, he portrayed Jesus as a teacher (4:31-32) and an exorcist (4:33-37). In this section (4:38-44), Luke portrays Jesus as a healer (4:38-40) and a proclaimer of God's kingdom (4:43).

Jesus enters the house of Simon and heals his mother-in-law. This action, along with the cure of "people sick with various diseases" (4:40), demonstrates that Jesus is a healer.

Luke, however, has gotten a little ahead of himself by his portrayal of Jesus going to Simon's house. In the course of the Gospel, the reader has not yet been introduced to Simon. This doesn't take place until chapter five. Since Luke has only edited a large block of Marcan material, he has not yet narrated the call of Simon, as Mark does before Jesus cures Simon's mother-in-law.

The positive reaction of the crowd in Capernaum is contrasted to the negative reaction of the crowd in Nazareth. In Capernaum, the people tried to prevent Jesus from leaving. In Nazareth, they were ready to kill him. This contrast fulfills the proverb that "no prophet is accepted in his own home town" (4:24).

For Luke, Jesus becomes the model evangelizer. He moves to other towns to "proclaim the good news of the kingdom of God" (4:43). Throughout the Gospel and the Acts of the Apostles, Luke narrates how this was to be carried on by the members of his community.

Meditation: Of what has Jesus healed you?

Prayer: God of healing, your care for people reaches all across the universe. When they are in need, you stretch forth your hand and cure them. Lay your hands on us, and heal us of our sin. Place your words in our mouths that we may announce the goodness of the kingdom, where you live and reign with Jesus and the Holy Spirit, one God, for ever and ever. Amen.

PROCESS FOR DISCIPLESHIP
Luke 5:1-11

Scripture: When [Jesus] had finished speaking, he said to Simon, "Put out to the deep and lower your nets for a catch." Simon said in reply, "Lord, we've been at it all night, working hard, and have caught nothing. But at your word I'll lower the nets." When they did so, they caught a great number of fish and their nets began to rip (Luke 5:4-6).

Reflection: Luke's account of the call of Simon the fisherman and the great catch of fish was borrowed from Mark (1:16-20), given a new place in Luke's Gospel, and rewritten with his own understanding of Simon's role in the Church. Typical of the Lucan style, the reader had already been introduced to Simon through the curing of his mother-in-law by Jesus (4:38-39). Simon's response to Jesus is thus made more credible by Luke.

The story concerning the call of Simon (Luke 5:1-11) is most likely a combination of Mark's account and a post-resurrectional narrative, such as in John 21:1-11. Simon addresses Jesus as "Lord," a post-resurrectional title which Luke has read back into this narrative.

What should interest the reader about this section of Luke's Gospel, however, is not Simon's call or the miraculous catch of fish, but the process that Luke establishes for discipleship. This process reveals some of Luke's favorite themes, which are woven throughout the Gospel.

First, there is teaching. "While the crowd was pressing in on Jesus and listening to the word of God, he was standing by the Lake of Gennesaret. He saw two boats there alongside the lake…. Getting into one of the boats… he sat down and taught the crowds from the boat" (5:1-3). Teaching involves delivering the word of God to people. One person teaches, the rest listen.

Second, a response to the word of God is necessary. In this passage Jesus tells Simon to lower the nets for a catch, even though no fish have been seen all night long. The response is obedience to the word of God. Once heard, the word must be obeyed.

Third, after obeying the word, one realizes how unworthy one really is. Simon Peter falls at the knees of Jesus and says, "Depart from me, Lord, for I am a sinful man" (5:8).

No human person is worthy or capable of making a response on his or her own; the word is God's gracious gift to his people.

Fourth, once the word is taught, heard, and obeyed, and the individual realizes how unworthy he or she is, then the person is given a mission. Simon Peter and his companions, James and John, are told, "From now on you will be catching men" (5:10). They become disciples, which means that they become teachers of the word. They leave everything (that is, they are completely detached) and follow Jesus.

Meditation: Who has been your teacher? What have you been taught? What has been your response? What is your mission?

Prayer: God of Simon, through Jesus, your Son, you teach your word to your people. At the sound of this word, we are to willingly obey and recognize our unworthiness. Your word is effective; it brings us to conversion and sends us on your mission. Make of us authentic disciples. We ask this through Christ our Lord. Amen.

FASTING FOR DISCIPLESHIP

Luke 5:33-39

Scripture: "Can you make the wedding guests fast while the bridegroom is with them? But the days will come, and when the bridegroom is taken away from them, then they will fast in those days" (Luke 5:34-35).

Reflection: Luke's narrative concerning the question of fasting (5:33-39) takes place after the call of Levi (5:27-32), while Jesus is at table in Levi's house. The weekday cycle of texts omits the cleansing of the leper (5:12-16), the healing of a paralytic (5:17-26), and the call of Levi, which follow the call of Simon and precede the discussion about fasting.

The question Luke is answering is, "Do Christians fast?"

When Jesus was with the community, he was as a bridegroom. Wedding guests do not fast with the bridegroom; they feast with him. But once the bridegroom ascends to heaven, then Christian behavior includes the discipline of fasting. This type of fasting, however, is not the same type of fasting in which the disciples of John and the disciples of the Pharisees engaged.

Gentile Christians, Luke's audience, represent a new reality; they are not tied to the Jewish past. They are not a piece of cloth taken from a new cloak and sewed onto an old cloak. They are not new wine poured into old wineskins.

Luke's community represents a dissatisfaction with the old and the emergence of the new. If one is satisfied with the old, as one who drinks old wine does not want new, then such a person cannot risk the challenge of discipleship, which does involve fasting.

Meditation: How does your fasting strengthen your discipleship?

Prayer: God of the groom, your love for your people moved you to send your Son, Jesus, the bridegroom, to announce the good news of salvation. We have heard his Gospel and responded with discipleship. Move us to fast from everything that is contrary to his way of life. Grant that we may one day come to share in the eternal wedding feast, where you live and reign with Jesus and the Holy Spirit, one God, for ever and ever. Amen.

HUMAN NEED

Luke 6:1-5

Scripture: "Have you not read what David did when he and those [who were] with him were hungry? He went into the house of God and took and ate the Bread of Offering, which only the priests could lawfully eat, and shared it with his companions" (Luke 6:3-4).

Reflection: This section of Luke's Gospel (6:1-5) presents the first of two debates about the Sabbath observance. Luke's source for the conflict concerning picking heads of grain is Mark (2:23-28).

Picking grain on the Sabbath was considered to be reaping, an action which was forbidden. However, the issue for Luke is not whether the law is broken but the intent of the law to begin with. This is represented by the example of David, who entered the sanctuary and ate the bread which he was not permitted by law to eat.

David did not violate the Sabbath rest; he did, however, violate the law. The violation of the law was permissible because David and his men were without food. Therefore, human need for food to satisfy hunger takes precedence over the law regarding what foods may or may not be eaten.

The disciples are in need of food. By picking heads of grain, they have not broken the law. "The Son of Man is Lord of the Sabbath" (6:5). Jesus has initiated a new order, wherein human need takes precedence over the keeping of the Sabbath rest.

Meditation: In which ways do you meet the needs of others while observing the Sabbath (Sunday) rest?

Prayer: God of David, when your anointed king and his companions needed food, you supplied them with the Bread of Offering from your own table. You demonstrated that it is mercy that you desire as you care for your people. Give us rest on the Sabbath, but also give us a willingness to meet the needs of those who hunger. We ask this through our Lord Jesus Christ, your Son, who lives and reigns with you and the Holy Spirit, one God, for ever and ever. Amen.

PROCESS FOR SINNERS

Matthew 18:15-20

Scripture: "Again, I say to you, if two of you agree on earth about any matter they ask for, it will come to be for them through my heavenly Father" (Matthew 18:19).

Reflection: The section of Matthew's Gospel which narrates the order to be followed in dealing with a brother or sister (fellow disciple) who sins (18:15-20) is part of the fourth sermon of Jesus. The narrative about the sinner follows Matthew's version of the parable of the lost sheep (18:10-14) and precedes the parable of the unforgiving servant (18:21-35). Its position between the two parables clearly establishes its intent and meaning concerning forgiveness.

First, if a member of the community sins against another member of the community, the one sinned against is obliged to seek out the sinner (as the shepherd does the lost sheep) and point out the fault. Reconciliation can take place between these two people; there is no need to involve anyone else in the problem.

Matthew's perspective is this: in most cases parties feel sinned against. The obligation, then, is for each one to seek out the other and come together in a reconciled union. This preserves the harmony in the community, as Matthew sees it.

However, if this does not work, then step two is to be taken. Two or three witnesses are to be involved. In Judaism, the testimony of two or three witnesses was considered reliable and necessary. It seems that the role of the witnesses is to mediate reconciliation.

If reconciliation does not occur, then the third and final step is to take it before the entire community. In this step the whole affair becomes public. The sinner is invited to repent, to mend the rift which has spread to the entire community.

Matthew invests the whole Church with the power to exclude. In this passage Jesus declares, "Whatever you bind on earth shall be bound in heaven, and whatever you loose on earth shall be loosed in heaven" (18:18). Failure to repent leaves the sinner in the state of a "Gentile or a tax collector" (18:17), a person to be avoided. According to Matthew, once the three-fold process has been tried and shown to have failed, then the community must separate itself from the sinner. This separation is validated by God.

Meditation: In which instance have you tried to employ Matthew's three-fold process for dealing with someone who has sinned against you?

Prayer: God of mercy and forgiveness, you have given the power of binding and loosing to your Church, and you have promised to remain with her until the end of time. Give us the Spirit of discernment that we may seek out those who sin against us. Give us the Spirit of mercy that we may be willing to reconcile each other. We ask this in the name of Jesus the Lord. Amen.

PROFESS FAITH OPENLY

Mark 7:31-37

Scripture: [Jesus] took [a deaf man who had a speech impediment] off alone away from the crowd and put his fingers into the man's ears and, after spitting he touched his tongue; then he looked up to heaven, sighed, and said to him, "Ephphatha!" (that is, "Be opened!") (Mark 7:33-34).

Reflection: Mark's account of the healing of a deaf man (7:31-37) occurs after the narrative of the Syrophoenician woman's faith (7:24-30) and before the feeding of the four thousand (8:1-10). The story is located in Gentile territory so that Mark can continue to validate the ministry of the Church to the Gentiles by portraying Jesus' ministry to them. The narrative is set within the form of a miracle. The issue of the inclusion of the Gentiles into the early Church is the focus, however. Like the Gentiles, the man is both deaf and dumb towards God. Once the good news is proclaimed to him, however, his ears are opened to the word and his tongue is loosed to proclaim Jesus as the Messiah.

Underlying Mark's theological perspective is the prophet Isaiah: "Be strong, fear not! Here is your God, he comes with vindication; with divine recompense he comes to save you. Then will the eyes of the blind be opened, the ears of the deaf be cleared" (Isaiah 35:4-5). For Mark, the age of the Messiah and salvation has arrived for the Gentiles.

21

Through the prophet Ezekiel God declared that on the day of the Lord, Ezekiel's mouth would be opened and he would be dumb no longer (cf. Ezekiel 24:27). "Be opened!" Jesus declares in this passage from Mark. The day of the Lord has arrived.

It is little wonder why the *Ephphatha* Rite is a part of the Rite of Christian Initiation of Adults and the Rite of Baptism for Children. The presider touches the ears and lips of the candidates and declares, "*Ephphatha*: that is, be opened, that you may profess the faith you hear, to the praise and glory of God" (RCIA #199).

Meditation: In which ways do you hear the word of God and proclaim it?

Prayer: God of hearing and speech, put your fingers into our ears that we may hear your word. Place your hand upon our lips that we may proclaim the good news we hear. May we always and everywhere praise you, the one God — Father, Son, and Holy Spirit, living and reigning for ever and ever. Amen.

TOTAL DEDICATION
Luke 14:25-33

Scripture: "If anyone comes to me and doesn't hate his father and mother, wife and children, brothers and sisters, and even his own life, he cannot be my disciple. Whoever doesn't pick up his cross and follow me cannot be my disciple" (Luke 14:26-27).

Reflection: Luke gathers together three sayings concerning Christian discipleship (14:25-33) after narrating the parable of the great feast (14:15-24) and before presenting the simile of salt (14:34-35), both of which are omitted from the Sunday cycle of the lectionary. The sayings concerning discipleship are focused on the total dedication which is necessary in being a follower of Christ. Obviously, Luke intends this section to be a guide for his community, which is struggling with a definition of the meaning of discipleship in the latter half of the first century.

First, total dedication as a Christian involves making Jesus the priority of one's life. Using hyperbolic language, Luke presents a saying from source Q about "hating" one's relatives. Hating is not to be taken literally here; it is excessive language used by Luke to point out that one's family takes second place to discipleship.

Second, total dedication involves carrying the cross. Such a possibility was real for the members of Luke's community. His middle-class church might be the subject of persecution at any time. A willingness to be put to death in order to remain faithful is required of the Christian.

Third, the Christian must renounce all possessions. "Everyone... who does not renounce all his possessions cannot be my disciple" (14:33), Jesus declares. Luke's middle-class church has wealth. The author's perspective is that wealth is given to people to be given to others — those who have none. Throughout the Gospel, Luke severely criticizes those who hoard their riches. The follower of Jesus must renounce all possessions.

These three sayings concerning discipleship are not to be taken lightly by anyone, according to Luke. Before embracing discipleship, one should calculate the cost carefully.

A person who wants to be a disciple should be like the builder of a tower who sits down and calculates the cost to see if there is enough money to complete the project. "Otherwise, after laying the foundation and finding himself unable to finish the work the onlookers should laugh at him and say, 'This one began to build but did not have the resources to finish'" (14:29-30).

A person should not set out to follow Jesus without first realizing all that discipleship entails, all that it demands. One must calculate its costs. There is no other way, according to Luke.

Meditation: What has discipleship cost you?

Prayer: God of the cross, you never cease to summon your people to follow in the footsteps of Jesus, your Servant and your Son. Mold us into authentic disciples: enable us to make discipleship the priority of our lives; give us the strength to carry the cross it entails; and move us to share our goods with all people of the earth. Do not let us be blind to the cost of following Jesus, who lives and reigns with you and the Holy Spirit, one God, for ever and ever. Amen.

A NEW ORDER

Luke 6:6-11

Scripture: [Jesus] said to the man with the withered hand, "Come up and stand in front." So he got up and stood there. Then Jesus said to them, "I ask you, is it lawful on the Sabbath to do good or to do evil, to save a life or to destroy it?" (Luke 6:8-9).

Reflection: Luke's account of the healing of a man with a withered hand is borrowed from Mark's Gospel (3:1-6). The setting is a conflict over the observance of the Sabbath regulation which forbade healing on the Sabbath. The preceding section dealt with the issue of gathering grain on the Sabbath.

Luke's Gentile community would not have been interested in such a debate about Jewish Sabbath observance. However, Luke is interested in the new lifestyle that Christianity demands. His focus is found in Jesus' question, "Is it lawful on the Sabbath to do good or to do evil, to save a life or to destroy it?" (6:9).

The answer to the question must be given by the members of Luke's community. The answer is obvious. The lifestyle of a follower of Jesus demands that human needs be placed above legal observance. Of course it is lawful to do good — not evil — on the Sabbath, to save life, not to destroy it. Works of mercy mark people as followers of Jesus. This is the new order which Jesus established.

Meditation: What deeds of mercy do you perform on the Sabbath?

Prayer: God of the Sabbath, you gave your people a day of rest that they might refrain from work and celebrate your presence. No day, however, is without its opportunity for sharing your life with others. Enable us to live the new order established by Jesus, your Son, who lives and reigns with you and the Holy Spirit, one God, for ever and ever. Amen.

FIRST, PRAY

Luke 6:12-19

Scripture: Now it happened in those days when he went out to the mountain to pray that he spent the night in prayer to God. When day came, he called his disciples to himself, and from them he chose Twelve, whom he also called apostles (Luke 6:12-13).

Reflection: Following the two debates about the Sabbath (6:1-11) in Luke's Gospel, Jesus enters into prayer and chooses Twelve apostles (6:12-16) and then ministers to a great multitude of people (6:13-19) before beginning the sermon on the plain. This selection (6:12-19) serves as an introduction to Luke's sermon on the plain, which is comparable to Matthew's sermon on the mountain.

One chief characteristic of Jesus in Luke's Gospel is that he is found at prayer before any major decision. Before choosing the Twelve apostles, "he spent the night in prayer to God" (6:12). Before the Holy Spirit descended on him at the Jordan, Luke declares that "Jesus... had been baptized and was praying" (3:21).

Later in the Gospel, Luke will portray Jesus at prayer before Peter's confession (9:18), at the transfiguration (9:28), when he teaches his disciples to pray (11:1), during the Last Supper (22:32), on the Mount of Olives (22:41) and on the cross (23:46).

For Luke, Jesus is the "first Christian." Followers of Jesus learn from him. Before any major decision in their lives, the members of Luke's community should engage in prayer.

In Luke's Gospel, the Twelve occupy a special place; they serve as the link between the ministry of Jesus and Luke's community. They serve as Luke's eyewitnesses, and they guarantee the authenticity of the Church's faith and practice. They are so important to Luke that after Judas' betrayal and death, they are reconstituted by the addition of Matthias in Luke's second volume, the Acts of the Apostles (cf. 1:15-26), before the Church begins to spread to the ends of the earth.

Only in Luke does Jesus give the Twelve the title of apostle. In Luke's community, the title "apostle" takes on a technical meaning; it refers to a person — a missionary — sent out to preach the word of God. The development of the use of the word is found in the Acts of the Apostles, wherein Paul and Barnabas are called apostles.

Once the band of apostles is formed, the author portrays Jesus as ministering to the people. "A great crowd of his disciples and a large number of the people from all Judea and Jerusalem and the coastal region of Tyre and Sidon came to hear him and to be healed of their diseases" (6:17-18).

In other words, both Jews and Gentiles come to hear Jesus and to be cured. For Luke, the ministry of Jesus reaches out to all peoples.

Meditation: Have you spent more time in prayer when you have been faced with major decisions in your life? In which ways did this intense prayer affect you?

Prayer: God of missionaries, you are always calling people to be proclaimers of your good news to all your children throughout the world. Draw us into prayer, and send us out to preach and live your word. Make us instruments of your love for the world. We ask this through our Lord Jesus Christ, your Son, who lives and reigns with you and the Holy Spirit, one God, for ever and ever. Amen.

PRESENT TO BE REVERSED

Luke 6:20-26

Scripture: "Blessed are you who are poor, for the kingdom of God is yours. But woe to you who are rich, for you have received your consolation" (Luke 6:20, 24).

Reflection: In Luke, Jesus begins the sermon on the plain (comparable to Matthew's sermon on the mount) with a set of four beatitudes and four woes (6:20-26). Luke's source is Q, but he has definitely reworked his material in light of his own theological, social, and economic perspective.

Each beatitude begins with the word "blessed," which identifies a person as being favored by God. One who is blessed shares in the characteristics of God. Such a person is favored by God. Such a person is successful.

A woe counterbalances each beatitude. The woe expresses a profound displeasure with people who are blinded by their present, fortunate situation. These are too preoccupied with the things of the world to be concerned about the kingdom of God. However, the woe declares that the present situation will be reversed in the future.

The first beatitude and its corresponding woe refer to the poor and the rich. The poor are a particular concern throughout Luke's Gospel. The poor are considered to be successful! The rich are declared to have their consolation now. Placed in the context of Luke's middle-class audience, who believed that riches were a sign of blessing from God, this beatitude and this woe would certainly have challenged and upset the hearers. Con-

29

versely, those who believed that poverty was a sign of being cursed by God would have found consolation.

The second beatitude and its corresponding woe refer to the hungry and the filled. It can be interpreted in terms of literal hunger for food and spiritual hunger for the kingdom of God. The unsatisfied will one day be filled. The satisfied will one day discover that they are not where they imagined themselves to be.

Weeping and laughing form the third beatitude-woe pair. For Luke, those who weep are those who are compassionate and care for the needs of others. Those who laugh are those who ignore the needs of others, those who are self-satisfied and indifferent.

The fourth beatitude-woe pair consist of the socially outcast and the acceptable. Those who are socially excluded and persecuted, join the ranks of the prophets, who suffered the same fate in Israel. However, those who are spoken well of should examine themselves to see if they may have rejected the Son of Man in favor of social acceptance. This is what the false prophets did.

The poor are blessed because they trust in God now, and, therefore, belong to his kingdom. Those who hunger and weep and are persecuted are blessed because they have God now and in the future they will have the fullness of the kingdom. Those persons described in the woes are to be pitied because they trust in what they have now, and, consequently, they have nothing more in which to hope. Whatever the condition in the present, it will be reversed in the future.

Meditation: In which ways are you poor, hungry, weeping, and persecuted? In which ways are you rich, filled, laughing, and spoken well of?

Prayer: "My soul proclaims the greatness of the Lord; my spirit rejoices in God my savior. For he has looked upon his handmaid's lowliness; behold, from now on will all ages call me blessed. The Mighty One has done great things for me, and holy is his name. His mercy is from age to age to those who fear him. He has shown might with his arm, dispersed the arrogant of mind and heart. He has thrown down the rulers from their thrones but lifted up the lowly. The hungry he has filled with good things; the rich he has sent away empty. He has helped Israel his servant, remembering his mercy, according to his promise to our fathers, to Abraham and to his descendants forever" (Luke 1:46-55). Amen.

RECIPROCATE WITH LOVE

Luke 6:27-38

Scripture: "To you who are listening I say, love your enemies, do good to those who hate you, bless those who curse you, pray for those who insult you. Be merciful, as your Father is merciful" (Luke 6:27, 36).

Reflection: The love of enemies section (6:27-38) of Jesus' sermon on the plain follows the four beatitude-woes. Luke's source is Q (cf. Matthew 5:43-48; 7:1-12). This part of the sermon can be divided into four units of thought, each of which attempts to break the pattern of reciprocity which is found in most human relationships.

The first unit (6:27-28) of the section exhorts the reader not to return evil for evil. Members of Luke's community are exhorted to love their enemies, to do good deeds for those who hate them, to bless those who curse them, and to pray for those who mistreat them. The way of a Christian is to return good for evil.

The second unit (6:29-31) provides four examples of what it means not to return evil for evil. These examples (striking, stealing, begging, and borrowing) are not to be taken literally but are meant to move the reader to consider the whole pattern to one's life.

"To the person who strikes you on one cheek, offer the other cheek as well, and from the person who takes your cloak, do not withhold your tunic. Give to all who ask of you, and don't de-

31

mand what's yours from the one who took it" (6:29-30). These directives are hyperboles. The members of Luke's church are being pushed to consider what nonviolent response should be made in the face of violence.

The Golden Rule states it in another way: "Do to others as you would have them do to you" (6:31). Christians are to ask themselves how they would want to be treated. Then they are to respond to violence with creative nonviolence. To respond in kind when one has been badly treated would be to compound the evil.

Section three (6:32-36) of the love of enemies portion of the sermon describes love in terms of generosity. Three questions are asked: "If you love those who love you, what credit is that to you? Even sinners love those who love them. And if you do good to those who do good to you, what credit is that to you? Even sinners do the same. If you lend money to those from whom you expect repayment, what credit [is] that to you? Even sinners lend to sinners, and get back the same amount" (6:32-34).

In this passage from the Gospel of Luke, Jesus exhorts people to move beyond love as reciprocal action. A Christian is to transcend the usual "you pat my back and I'll pat your back" mentality. The motive for doing this is to act as the Most High does. "He himself is kind to the ungrateful and the wicked" (6:35). Therefore, Christians are to "be merciful, as your Father is merciful" (6:36).

The final section (6:37-38) of this part of the sermon offers four examples of giving the usual reciprocal action of love. People are not to judge or condemn, but they are to forgive and to give. The motivation for these transcendent deeds is this: "The measure with which you measure will be measured back to you" (6:38). In other words, if Christians fail to move beyond the reciprocity of love in dealing with others, they also short-circuit God's mercy to themselves.

In this part of the sermon on the plain, Christians are exhorted to pay close attention to the principal of reciprocity, so that it does not govern their relationships.

Christians do not respond to evil with evil; they respond with the way they would want to be treated. Christians do not restrict their good deeds to those who have been good to them; they are to do good for all, just as God gives abundantly to all.

Meditation: In which ways do you respond to violence with non-violence? In which ways do you do good deeds for those who have not done anything for you?

Prayer: God of love and mercy, through the ministry of Jesus, your Son, you have taught your people to love their enemies, to do good to those who hate them, to bless those who curse them, and to pray for those who mistreat them. Enable us to share your abundant love with all men and women. Teach us to be merciful as you are merciful. Pour your good measure into our laps and move us to pour it out on others. We ask this through our Lord Jesus Christ, who lives and reigns with you and the Holy Spirit, one God, for ever and ever. Amen.

CHRISTIAN INFLUENCE

Luke 6:39-42

Scripture: "Can a blind person guide a blind person? Will not both fall into a pit?" (Luke 6:39).

Reflection: Luke's source for this section (6:39-42) of the sermon on the plain is Q (cf. Matthew 7:1-5). In order to make his point about the influence that Christians have on others, the author uses two parables.

The first parable (6:39-40) deals with metaphorical blindness. One blind person cannot lead another blind person; one person who is not fully trained in the ways of Jesus cannot train another in the ways of discipleship. The teacher, therefore, must not be blind. Furthermore, in order to help another person improve his or her life, the teacher must be always willing to improve himself or herself.

"No disciple is superior to the teacher; but when fully trained, every disciple will be like his teacher" (6:40). One who already knows the way shows it to others.

The second parable (6:41-42) employs hyperbolic language in order to make a similar point about taking stock of oneself first before making an effort to help others improve themselves. Those who fail to examine critically their own quality of discipleship walk around with a wooden beam in their eye, while those whom they are attempting to help have only a splinter in their eye.

Such persons are hypocrites concerned with the faults of

35

others but not with their own. Christians are instructed by Jesus in this passage to "remove the wooden beam" from their own eye first; then they will be capable of assisting the conversion of another person.

Meditation: In which ways does your personal transformation influence others?

Prayer: God of light, in you there is no darkness. When your people were blind, you sent your Son, Jesus, to open their eyes. Remove our blindness. Train us in the ways of discipleship. Convert our hearts to the ways of Jesus, who lives and reigns with you and the Holy Spirit, one God, for ever and ever. Amen.

LISTENING AND PRACTICING

Luke 6:43-49

Scripture: "I will show you what someone is like who comes to me, listens to my words, and acts on them. He is like a man building a house, who dug deeply and laid the foundation on rock; when the flood came, the river burst against that house but could not shake it because it had been well built" (Luke 6:47-48).

Reflection: The narratives concerning a tree known by its fruit (6:43-45) and the two foundations (6:46-49) conclude Jesus' sermon on the plain. Luke's source for this material is Q (cf. Matthew 7:16-21; 24-27).

In the section concerning a tree known by its fruit (6:43-45), Luke continues the theme of personal transformation which he began earlier in the sermon. The Christian can only give what he or she has already achieved. "A good tree does not bear rotten fruit, nor does a rotten tree bear good fruit. Each tree is known by its own fruit" (6:43-44). For Luke, each follower of Jesus must be constantly in the process of conversion, if he or she is to assist others in the same process.

"A good person out of the store of goodness in his heart produces good, but an evil person out of a store of evil produces evil; for from the abundance of the heart the mouth speaks" (6:45). In other words, persons cannot instruct others in the way of Christian discipleship, without always rediscovering its meaning for themselves.

The parable about the two foundations (6:46-49) highlights one of Luke's primary themes; listening and doing the word. In Luke's church, Christians who confess Jesus as "Lord, Lord" (6:46) are those who listen to his word and then put it into practice. People who do what they hear are stable in times of crisis.

Luke has already presented a panorama of characters who listened to the word and practiced it: Zechariah, Mary, the shepherds, Simeon, Anna, John the Baptist, and Jesus himself. For Luke, belief is grounded in listening to the word of God and practicing what was heard in daily life. In other words, faith dictates lifestyle.

"The one who listens and does not act is like a person who built a house on the ground without a foundation. When the river burst against it, it collapsed at once and was completely destroyed" (6:49).

Meditation: In which ways has the word of God changed your lifestyle? Where in your life is there harmony between listening to the word and practicing it?

Prayer: God our rock, long ago you delivered your word to your servant, Moses, and you directed your people through your prophets. Through Jesus you have shown us how to listen to your word and practice it. Through your Holy Spirit build us into a house with a sure foundation. From the store room of goodness call forth good deeds from our hearts. We ask this through our Lord Jesus Christ, your Son, who lives and reigns with you and the Holy Spirit, one God, for ever and ever. Amen.

INFINITY OF FORGIVENESS
Matthew 18:21-35

Scripture: "Then when the king had summoned him, he said to him, 'You wicked servant! I forgave you your entire debt when you begged me. Should you not have had mercy on your fellow servant, as I had mercy on you?'" (Matthew 18:32-33).

Reflection: The parable of the unforgiving servant (Matthew 18:21-35) concludes Jesus' fourth sermon in Matthew's Gospel which deals with the correction of members of the community who sin and the forgiveness that is to be extended to those who repent.

The section of the discourse begins with a question from Peter: "Lord, if my brother sins against me, how often must I forgive him? As many as seven times?" (18:21). Jesus gives a response which stresses the infinity of forgiveness: "I say to you, not seven times but seventy-seven times" (18:22). This reference is probably a contrast to Lamech's unlimited vengeance (cf. Genesis 4:24). This part of the discourse is from Q (cf. Luke 17:4).

The parable of the unforgiving servant, unique to Matthew's Gospel, follows Peter's question and Jesus' reply. The parable deals with forgiveness, but not with repeated forgiveness. In this regard, it does not illustrate Matthew's point. However, it does reveal a quality of the kingdom of heaven.

One debtor owes a king a huge amount. He is unable to pay it, but falls down, gives homage to the king, and says, "Be patient with me, and I will pay you back in full" (18:26). Now the amount owned cannot be paid back in full. Therefore, this is an empty promise. Nevertheless, "moved with compassion the master of that servant let him go and forgave him the loan" (18:27). In other words, the king canceled the entire debt; he forgave the servant everything.

The compassion of the king is contrasted to the lack of compassion of the forgiven servant. He meets a fellow servant who owes him a much smaller amount. If the first servant owed $100,000, the second servant owes only $100. The second servant imitates the first: "Falling to his knees, his fellow servant begged him, 'Be patient with me, and I will pay you back'" (18:29). The debt is repayable. This servant is not making an empty promise.

However, the first servant has no compassion. He refuses to listen to his fellow servant's promise. He has him imprisoned, wherein it is impossible for him to repay his debt. The first servant does not forgive his fellow servant, nor does he give him an opportunity to repay him (repent).

Matthew's point in telling the parable is to stress the compassion of God. When the king asks, "Should you not have had mercy on your fellow servant, as I had mercy on you?" (18:33), the reader must answer, "Yes." This is the meaning of forgiveness — forgiving others as God forgives each person. In Matthew's church, followers of Jesus who have received God's forgiveness must never refuse to offer that same forgiveness to others. Their offenses have been great and God has forgiven them; they should be more than willing to forgive the minor offenses of others. In God's kingdom, forgiveness is offered to all; all are responsible for sharing it with others.

Meditation: Whom have you recently forgiven as God has forgiven you?

Prayer: God of mercy, you never cease to show compassion to your people. You forgive us our sins; you cancel our debt; you command us to forgive our brothers and sisters from our hearts. Stir up in our lives your mercy, and make us always ready to share your compassion and forgiveness with all men and women. Bring us to the unlimited love of your kingdom, where you live and reign with Jesus, your Son, and the Holy Spirit, one God, for ever and ever. Amen.

THINKING LIKE GOD
Mark 8:27-35

Scripture: Then he [Jesus] began to teach them [disciples] that the Son of Man had to suffer greatly and be rejected by the elders, the chief priests, and the scribes, and be put to death, and rise after three days.... Peter took him aside and began to remonstrate with him. When Jesus turned around and saw his disciples, he rebuked Peter and said, "Get behind me, Satan. You are not thinking as God does, but as human beings do" (Mark 8:31-33).

Reflection: The turning or pivotal point of Mark's Gospel consists of a three-part scenario: Peter's confession regarding Jesus, the first prediction of the passion followed by Jesus' rebuke of Peter, and the conditions of discipleship (Mark 8:27-35).

With a genuine writer's skill, Mark begins to weave a new plot, which looks little like the first half of the Gospel.

The first scene is set on the way to Caesarea Philippi. Jesus asks his disciples, "Who do people say that I am?" (8:27). The answers — John the Baptist, Elijah, a prophet — all concur that Jesus has prophetic status. Then Jesus poses the question to his disciples: "Who do you say that I am?" (8:29). Only Peter knows the best answer to the question: "You are the Messiah" (8:29).

To say that Jesus is the Messiah is to proclaim what Mark has been insisting on throughout the Gospel, indeed from the very first verse. Jesus is the Christ, the Messiah, the Anointed One of God. Up to this point in the Gospel, this title has meant power — power over demons, illness, nature, etc. In this sense, then, Peter's declaration is correct.

However, this is not Mark's theological perspective. For Mark, power is powerlessness. Being the Messiah, the Christ, the Anointed One of God is to be fully human. It involves suffering and death. And so, Jesus "began to teach… that the Son of Man must suffer greatly and be rejected by the elders, the chief priests, and the scribes, and be put to death, and rise after three days" (8:31).

This is a complete reversal of the first half of the Gospel! In this new, reversed plot, (scene two) Mark gives Jesus a new title — Son of Man. It carries a number of Old Testament allusions but primarily represents the suffering, dying, and powerless Messiah for Mark. With this understanding, it is easy to see why Peter rebukes Jesus. Peter is interested in power; Jesus is interested in powerlessness.

Peter has it all wrong and Jesus calls Peter "Satan." He is thinking as people do. God thinks differently. God sees ultimate power as powerlessness. And this is the theme that Mark will develop throughout the second half of the Gospel.

The author introduces it in the third part of the scenario by detailing the conditions of discipleship. Following Jesus authentically involves denial of self and taking up the cross. Self-denial and the cross have absolutely nothing to do with human power but with human powerlessness — human vulnerability.

This perspective is best summarized by Jesus when he says: "Whoever wishes to save his life will lose it, but whoever loses his life for my sake and that of the Gospel will save it" (8:35). All is reversed. Life is gained by losing it. Life is lost by saving it. Jesus will demonstrate this on the cross. Mark's new plot is now set.

Meditation: In which experiences in your life have you discovered that authentic power is really powerlessness?

Prayer: God of the cross, through the suffering, death and resurrection of your only Son, Jesus, you have revealed your power shining through human weakness. Through the Holy Spirit guide us to self-denial and the example of the cross of your Christ. Teach us the mystery of losing life in order to save it. Remind us to think not as human beings are prone to do, but as you do. We ask this through Christ, our Lord. Amen.

LOST AND FOUND
Luke 15:1-32

Scripture: "What man among you who had a hundred sheep and lost one of them would not leave the ninety-nine in the desert and set out after the lost one until he finds it? Or what woman who had ten coins and lost one would not light a lamp and sweep the house, searching carefully until she finds it?" (Luke 15:4, 8).

Reflection: Chapter 15 of Luke's Gospel consists of three parables — the lost sheep (15:1-7), the lost coin (15:7-10), and the lost son (15:11-32), usually called the prodigal son. It is easy to see from the titles given to all three parables that they deal with what is lost. Except for the parable of the lost sheep, which Luke shares with Matthew (18:12-14) from Q, these parables are unique to this Gospel.

In these parables Luke contrasts the tax collectors and sinners with the Pharisees and scribes (cf. 15:1-2). Tax collectors and sinners are those whom Luke constantly portrays as sharing in the kingdom of God, while Pharisees and scribes find themselves shut out of the kingdom. Not only does Jesus welcome tax collectors and sinners in the Gospel of Luke, but he eats with them (cf. 15:2); that is, he becomes one with them. In the parable of the lost sheep, the owner does a very ridiculous thing — he leaves ninety-nine sheep in the desert and goes out searching for one lost sheep. No reliable shepherd would ever do such a thing. The

43

absurdly reaches an all time high when Jesus declares that there is a great celebration on the finding of the lost sheep.

The parable is not about repentance; a sheep is not capable of repenting. A sheep is found. For Luke, being found by God is to be saved. Sinners who repent are not righteous; they are sinners who have been found by God. God saves the one person for whom he has to go out looking, as well as those for whom he has no need to look. Luke's interest is that both groups — tax collectors and sinners, and Pharisees and scribes — sit down at table together.

The second parable of the lost coin moves the reader from the animate sheep to the inanimate coin, from the principal character of a man to that of a woman. The woman engages in a ridiculous action — searching for a coin that wasn't worth the time it took to look for it. Furthermore, she calls together the neighborhood and rejoices; she is excessive.

Again, Luke's point is that salvation consists of allowing one's self to be found by God. God goes out looking for people, just as the woman swept the house looking for the coin. Being saved is not something that people do; it is what God does. God is always finding people, Luke is saying. Those who are found join those who were never lost in a meal. Those who were never lost must be careful that they don't set themselves up as better than those who were lost and found.

Luke's theological perspective is made clear in the parable of the lost son. A man has two sons. One of the sons, the younger, demands his share of the inheritance and in so doing effectively declares that his father is dead. He becomes a first class sinner by squandering his money on "a life of dissipation" (15:13) and feeding the pigs — nothing more reprehensible to a Jew!

But the lost son, at a time of famine and hunger, remembers his father and the food that is on his father's table. He decides to go home, to confess his wayward life, and be accepted back as a servant of his father and not as a son.

The father looks for his son to come home. He does not act

as a man of his standing and reputation should act. He is extravagant; he runs out to meet his son, welcomes him with hugs and kisses, dresses him in his own clothes, puts a ring on his finger and shoes on his feet, and prepares to eat a festive meal with him.

The son is not welcomed back on his terms as a servant; the father welcomes him back on his terms as a son. The son has found himself; the father has found his son. Both were lost; both were found. However, there are two sons. The second son is the righteous one. He has done everything that his father commanded. He has been faithful. He refuses to enter the house and sit down at table with his younger brother. He cannot refer to him as his brother but as his father's son.

The father declares to the older son, "My son, you are here with me always; everything I have is yours" (15:31). The father wants to keep both his sons and join them with him at a table, where sinners and the righteous feast together. The older son distinguishes himself from his father and his younger brother. He wants a celebration with his own friends. The older son is lost. The father does not want to let him go. The older son creates categories and divisions.

In this parable from Luke's Gospel Jesus is declaring that salvation is present here and now and there can be no divisions between people; in God's kingdom all are equal — no matter if they are sinners who have been found, or righteous who were never lost. Salvation depends on God, and the righteous must be careful that they do not set themselves up as worthy of salvation and thus declare that they have no need for God.

For Luke, God is like the man who looks for one sheep or like the woman who searches for one coin or like the father who watches for two sons to come and share his feast. In God's kingdom sinners and righteous sit down at one table, where all are equal.

Meditation: When have you been lost and found by God?

Prayer: God of the lost, like a shepherd who searches for one lost sheep, or like a woman who looks for one lost coin, or like a father who waits for two lost sons, you continually seek your people. Remove the divisions that we create, so that we may recognize human dignity and equality. Bring all people to the banquet of your kingdom, where you live and reign with your Son, our Lord Jesus Christ, and the Holy Spirit, one God, for ever and ever. Amen.

NOT WORTHY?

Luke 7:1-10

Scripture: While Jesus… was still some distance from the
[centurion's] house, the centurion sent friends to say to
him, "Lord, do not put yourself to the trouble, for I am not
worthy to have you come under my roof. Nor, therefore,
did I consider myself worthy to come to you; just say a
word and my servant will be healed" (Luke 7:6-7).

Reflection: The narrative concerning the healing of a centurion's
slave (7:1-10) follows Jesus' sermon on the plain in Luke's Gospel. The source for the account is Q (cf. Matthew 8:5-13); however, the author uses the story to highlight his own unique theological perspective.

The centurion owns a valuable slave, who is about to die.
He sends "elders of the Jews" (7:3) to Jesus. The elders declare
that the centurion is worthy of having his slave healed because
he loves the Jewish nation and helped build the local synagogue.
Because of his deeds, he is declared worthy by the Jewish elders,
believers.

However, the centurion himself declares himself to be unworthy. He is a pagan, an unbeliever, a Gentile, living among
believers. He does not consider his deeds to be important or to
represent his worthiness before Jesus.

Once the centurion tells Jesus, "Just say a word and my servant will be healed" (7:7), he explains his trust in Jesus' word: "I

too am a person subject to authority, with soldiers subject to me" (7:8). The centurion submits himself to the higher authority of the word of God. His response echoes that of Mary, Luke's first believer, who responds to the angel by saying, "May it be done to me according to your word" (1:38).

Jesus declares, "I tell you, not even in Israel have I found such faith" (7:9). In other words, Luke emphasizes that faith is not primarily demonstrated by deeds (as the Jewish elders thought) but by obedience to the word of God (as the pagan centurion thought). In effect, Luke declares the centurion an authentic believer and the Jewish elders non-believers. Obedience to the word of God is one of Luke's primary themes.

This narrative is echoed in Luke's second volume — the Acts of the Apostles — in the story of the conversion of Cornelius, a Roman centurion, by Peter (Acts 10:1-49). He is generous to the Jewish nation, and, like the centurion in this Gospel story, demonstrates Luke's understanding of the way that Christians are to use their wealth.

The Lucan frame for the Gospel story is healing. However, the picture in the frame is about faith. For Luke, faith is recognition of one's unworthiness before God but a willingness to obey the word of God.

Meditation: In which ways do you obey the word of God?

Prayer: Eternal God, in times past you spoke your word in various ways to the patriarchs, the judges and the prophets, the kings and the warriors. In our own day you have spoken your word through Jesus, your Servant and your Son. We recognize our unworthiness for such a gift, but we place out trust in you. Make us obedient to the Gospel of Jesus, who lives and reigns with you and the Holy Spirit, one God for ever and ever. Amen.

A GREAT PROPHET

Luke 7:11-17

Scripture: Fear seized them all, and they glorified God, exclaiming, "A great prophet has arisen in our midst," and "God has visited his people" (Luke 7:16).

Reflection: The narrative of Jesus' raising of a widow's son (Luke 7:11-17) follows the healing of a centurion's slave. It is a story which is unique to Luke's Gospel, although it is modeled on the account of the resuscitation of the widow of Zarephath's son by the prophet Elijah (cf. 1 Kings 17:8-24). In its location in the Gospel, it serves to prepare for the next scene — the messengers sent from John the Baptist to Jesus — which is omitted from the weekday lectionary cycle.

Jesus tells John's disciple, "Go and tell John what you have seen and heard: the blind can see again, the lame walk, lepers are cleansed, the deaf hear, the dead are raised, the poor have the good news proclaimed to them" (7:22). This declaration serves as a summary of Jesus' ministry up to this point in the Gospel.

Luke is not interested in narrating a resuscitation story for the sake of telling the story. He has other motivations. At first glance the main character of the account is the dead, only son of his widowed mother. After careful observation, however, the main character is revealed to be the widow.

Without a husband, the widow became helpless and hopeless. Her husband was her life-support system. She was totally dependent upon him. Once he was dead, this widow of Nain (a town that remains unidentified) has some hope in her son. He could assume his father's duty and provide a livelihood for his mother. Once he was dead, his mother was also dead.

By restoring life to the son, Jesus bestows more life to the widow. "Jesus gave him to his mother" (7:15). She is now able to live again. In this way, Luke gets ahead of his own story by giving the reader a glimpse of the new life that Jesus will bestow through his suffering, death, and resurrection. Salvation, life, takes place in the present for Luke.

The reaction of the "large crowd" (7:11) is also important to note. First, the crowd responds with fear, an echo of the response of all Luke's characters to a manifestation of the divine (cf. 1:12, 30; 2:9). Second, the crowd declares that "a great prophet" has arisen. For Luke, Jesus is the greatest of the prophets, who begins his public ministry by declaring that the words of Isaiah — the former greatest of the prophets — are fulfilled in him (cf. 4:16-21).

Finally, the crowd proclaims, "God has visited his people" (7:16). Zechariah had declared the same, after the birth of John the Baptist: "Blessed be the Lord, the God of Israel, for he has visited and brought redemption to his people" (1:68).

For Luke, the narrative concerning the raising of the widow's son points backward to events already related by Luke and it points forward to events which will take place throughout the Gospel.

Meditation: In which ways has Jesus restored life to you? Or, how has God visited you?

Prayer: God of the living and the dead, you never forget your people. When we wander away from you in sin, you restore us to life through your unlimited forgiveness. When we fall asleep in death, you awaken us to the life of the resurrection. Continue to be with us on our journey. Continue to visit us when we are lost. Instill in us the hope of Jesus, your Son, who lives and reigns with you and the Holy Spirit, one God, for ever and ever. Amen.

VINDICATED BY WISDOM

Luke 7:31-35

Scripture: "John the Baptist came neither eating food nor drinking wine, and you said, 'He is possessed by a demon.' The Son of Man came eating and drinking and you said, 'Look at him, a glutton and a drunkard, a friend of tax collectors and sinners'" (Luke 7:33-34).

Reflection: Only a part (7:31-35) of Luke's account of the messengers from John the Baptist (7:18-23) and Jesus' testimony to John (7:24-35) is found in the weekday cycle of the lectionary. This section (7:31-35) is from Q (cf. Matthew 11:16-19).

In this passage, Jesus compares the "people of this generation" (7:31) to children, who cannot agree on two possible types of play. If some play the flute, others will not dance. If some sing a dirge, others will not weep. There is no unity in the play of the children; they merely "sit in the marketplace" (7:32) and taunt each other.

For Luke, the "people of this generation" represents the members of his church. He is dealing with middle-class people who are religiously insincere. They act like children. They make no commitments. All they do is taunt each other. They criticize John the Baptist for his austerity. John's penitential practices lead some people to believe that he was "possessed by a demon" (7:33).

They criticize the Son of Man, Jesus, for his lack of austerity and his association with outcasts — "tax collectors and sinners" (7:34). Jesus' joyful, accepting attitude toward all people got him a reputation as a "glutton and a drunkard" (7:34).

Luke is warning those who have rejected John and Jesus that they are acting like children. For Luke, John and Jesus are the children of wisdom. John prepared the way for Jesus, who preached the kingdom of God. "Wisdom is vindicated by all her children" (7:35). All who are children of wisdom, in contrast to those who are like children sitting in the marketplace taunting each other, know and believe in John and Jesus.

Meditation: In which ways do you sometimes act like a child instead of a wise believer?

Prayer: God of wisdom, you sent John the Baptist to prepare a people for the coming of your Son, Jesus. He preached your good news to your people and baptized them in the waters of repentance. Give us a discerning heart. Make us wise in your ways as we follow Jesus, who lives and reigns with you and the Holy Spirit, one God, for ever and ever. Amen.

GOD MOVES FIRST
Luke 7:36-50

Scripture: Jesus said... , "Simon, I have something to say to you. Two people were in debt to a certain creditor; one owed five hundred days' wages and the other owed fifty. Since they were unable to repay the debt he forgave it for both. Which of them will love him more?" (Luke 7:40-42).

Reflection: The pardon of the sinful woman (Luke 7:36-50) is like stories found in the other Gospels (cf. Mark 14:3-9; Matthew 26:6-13; and John 12:1-8), but Luke uses the account to uncover some of his own unique themes and concerns.

The narrative is set in the home of a Pharisee, one "who rejected the plan of God" (7:30). Jesus reclines at table with the Pharisee, which means that he is united to the Pharisee. However, the Pharisee shows him none of the customary signs of welcome — a kiss, washing his feet, anointing his head.

However, a sinful woman, that is, a prostitute, from the town enters the Pharisee's home (a rather bold move). "Bringing an alabaster flask of ointment, she stood behind [Jesus] at his feet weeping and began to bathe his feet with her tears. Then she wiped them with her hair, kissed them, and anointed them with the ointment" (7:37-38).

The woman demonstrates that she has repented of her sinful ways and has accepted the always-offered forgiveness of God. Her action does not earn forgiveness for her; her action demonstrates that she has accepted the forgiveness that God offers to her.

The Pharisee is a righteous man. He has kept the law. He is no sinner. So, he logically thinks, "If this man were a prophet, he would know who and what sort of woman this is who is touching him, that she is a sinner" (7:39). For Simon the Pharisee, Jesus is a prophet if he can recognize sinners.

The parable that Jesus tells concerns two people who owed money. One person owed $5,000 and another owed $500. In a never-before-heard-of act, the banker canceled both debts. Which debtor was more grateful? Of course, the answer is the one who owed more. The woman is the one who owed more. Simon is the one who owed a small amount. The woman is more grateful than Simon.

Both are forgiven, however. Jesus wants to dine with both Simon and the woman. Simon is making divisions between the righteous and the sinner. Jesus is making a union of both. This is what makes Jesus a prophet for Luke.

Furthermore, Jesus reminds Simon that the woman knows how to love. Simon has not loved as deeply as the woman has. "Her many sins have been forgiven; hence, she has shown great love. But the one to whom little is forgiven, loves little," states Jesus (7:47).

Luke shows Jesus' interest in bringing all people into the kingdom of God. Some people are greater sinners than others, but that does not exclude them from the kingdom. God makes the first move in people's lives; he offers the gift of faith. Then, people respond to this gift by acknowledging their sinfulness and accepting God's forgiveness and sitting down at table with Jesus in the kingdom.

Meditation: In which ways are you like Simon the Pharisee? In which ways are you like the woman?

Prayer: Forgiving God, you never cease to offer the gifts of faith and forgiveness to your people. Time and time again they turn away from you, but you never cease to seek out the lost. Through the working of the Holy Spirit, move us to a deep-felt repentance of sin. Make us grateful for your forgiveness. Give us the peace of Jesus, who lives and reigns with you and the Holy Spirit, one God, for ever and ever. Amen.

FEMALE DISCIPLES

Luke 8:1-3

Scripture: The Twelve were with him (Jesus) as well as some women who had been cured of evil spirits and diseases — Mary, called the Magdalen, from whom seven demons had gone out, Joanna, the wife of Herod's steward Chuza, Susanna, and many others who provided for them out of their resources (Luke 8:1-3).

Reflection: The first three verses which introduce chapter eight of Luke's Gospel illustrate the author's concern with women throughout the work. More than any other evangelist, Luke portrays women as co-guarantors with the Twelve of the Christ-event.

In the opening chapters of the Gospel, Elizabeth, Mary, and Anna are presented. Later, Jesus raises the son of the widow of Nain. He visits the home of Martha and Mary and tells a parable about a woman who lost a coin. These are but a few of Luke's many references to the ministry of women throughout the Gospel. In the Acts of the Apostles there are more references.

Two of the women mentioned in this section (8:1-3) are mentioned again in the resurrection narrative: Mary Magdalen and Joanna (24:10). These women and others accompany Jesus to Jerusalem, where they witness his death. They become sharers of the good news.

This elevation of women to such a role is unique to Luke. The general first-century attitude to women was that they were to be avoided; they were considered inferior to men. However, Luke shows how Jesus raised women to a place of dignity and gave them a share in the ministry of the Twelve. They have an important role to play in the history of salvation.

Meditation: Today, what is the role of women in the history of salvation?

Prayer: God of man and woman, in the marvels of creation, you fashioned men and women in your image and likeness and breathed into them the breath of your own Spirit. Increase the ministry of women in the Church. Continue to make them witnesses of the good news of Jesus, your Son, who lives and reigns with you and the Holy Spirit, one God, for ever and ever. Amen.

FRUIT BORN OF PERSEVERANCE

Luke 8:4-15

Scripture: "A sower went out to sow his seed. And as he sowed, some seed fell along the footpath and was trampled underfoot, and the birds of the sky ate it up. Some seed fell on rocky ground, and when it grew, it withered for lack of moisture. Some seed fell among thorns, and the thorns grew with it and choked it. And some seed fell on good soil, and when it grew, it produced fruit a hundredfold." After saying this, [Jesus] called out, "Whoever has ears to hear let them hear" (Luke 8:5-8).

Reflection: Luke's version of the parable of the sower (8:5-8), the purpose of the parable (8:9-10), and the explanation of the parable (8:11-15) have been borrowed from Mark's Gospel (cf. Mark 4:1-20) and reworked by this particular author to reflect his theme of hearing the word of God and doing it. This theme characterizes the followers of Jesus throughout Luke's Gospel and the Acts of the Apostles, his second volume.

In his explanation of the parable, Luke makes it clear that "the seed is the word of God" (8:11). The hearer is identified with the soil: the footpath doesn't allow the seed to take root and so "the devil comes and takes away the word (the seed)" (8:12); the rocky ground allows no depth of root either and so the seed sprouts but "only for a time" — like persons who "fall away in time of trial" (8:13), the seed shrivels and dies; the thorny ground represents those who "are choked by the anxieties and riches and pleasures of life" (8:14) and don't bear fruit either; the good earth represents those who "have heard the word, embrace it with a generous and good heart, and bear fruit through perseverance" (8:15).

Luke's allegorical interpretation of the parable reflects the various responses to the word that were taking place in his community. Evangelistic efforts were reaping various results in the first century. Luke's interest and focus is on the fruit that is borne by those who hear the word of God and do it. These form the authentic family of Jesus (cf. 8:21).

Not as in Mark, where the disciples ask Jesus to explain a number of parables, the Lucan disciples request that Jesus explain only the parable of the sower. Luke maintains part of Mark's emphasis on "knowledge of the mysteries of the kingdom" that is granted to Jesus' authentic disciples, "those who look and see, those who hear and understand" (cf. 8:10).

Some people believe they look and see and hear and understand, but they do not. The test of authenticity is hearing the word, embracing it with a good and generous heart, and bearing fruit through perseverance. Those who really look and see and hear and understand also act on the word of God.

Meditation: How have you heard the word of God and acted on it? Are you a path, rocky ground, thorns, or good soil?

Prayer: God our sower, you scatter your word throughout the world through your apostles, evangelists, prophets and teachers. Through Jesus, your word became incarnate. Open our eyes that we might see him. Open our ears that we might hear him. Lead us to the kingdom, where you live and reign with him and the Holy Spirit, one God, for ever and ever. Amen.

WHOMEVER AND WHENEVER

Matthew 20:1-16

Scripture: "The kingdom of heaven is like a landowner who went out early in the morning to hire workers for his vineyard.... When evening came, the owner of the vineyard said to his foreman, 'Call the workers and pay them their wages, beginning with the last and ending with the first.' When those who had started about five o'clock came, each received the usual wage. So when the first came, they thought that they would receive more, but each of them also got the usual wage" (Matthew 20:1, 8-10).

Reflection: The parable of the workers in the vineyard is unique to Matthew's Gospel. It deals with the extravagant actions of a vineyard owner, who hires laborers at dawn, about nine o'clock, around noon, around three o'clock, and about five o'clock during a six a.m. to six p.m. workday and pays all of them the same wage.

The vineyard motif echoes the Old Testament metaphor of Israel being the vineyard, which was planted by God. According to this Matthean parable, then, God invites to his kingdom whomever he pleases and whenever he pleases. No one has any advantage over anyone else when it comes to God's kingdom.

The laborers who worked for twelve hours or less presumed that they would receive more than those who worked only one hour. After all, the last hired were the first paid. They received a full day's wage. It only made sense that those who worked longer would receive more.

But this is exactly the point: no person can presume that he or she will inherit the kingdom of heaven. The vineyard owner, God, is "free to do" (20:15) as he wishes. This is no violation of justice, since all agreed to "the usual daily wage" (20:1). God is generous; no one can be envious, unless he or she wants to risk being excluded from the kingdom. In God's kingdom everyone is equal, no matter how long he or she has labored.

The kingdom of God is a gift to people. It cannot be earned; neither can one bargain for it. Matthew makes this clear to those first followers of Jesus who thought that they deserved more because they had worked longer. No matter when a person responds to the call of Jesus, God invites that individual into the kingdom of heaven.

Meditation: How long have you labored in the vineyard? What problems does this parable present to a culture that is always debating the question, "What is fair?"

Prayer: God of the vineyard, once you planted a vine that now extends around the world. You created people to tend your vineyard and, through Jesus, you promised them a share in your kingdom. Preserve us from the sin of presumption. Awaken us to the awareness of your gracious gift. Bring us at last to share in the fullness of that kingdom, where you live and reign with Jesus, your Son, and the Holy Spirit, one God, for ever and ever. Amen.

FIRST IS LAST

Mark 9:30-37

Scripture: On the way [Jesus' disciples] had been arguing among themselves about who was the greatest. He sat down, called the Twelve, and said to them, "If anyone wishes to be first, he must be the last of all and the servant of all" (Mark 9:34-35).

Reflection: Following the transfiguration narrative (9:2-13) and the account of the healing of a boy with a demon (9:14- 29), Mark presents the second prediction of Jesus' passion (9:30-32), which is immediately followed by the discussion about who is the greatest in the kingdom (9:33-37). The later organization of the passion prediction followed by the discussion of greatness is not an accident.

Once Peter has made his confession about Jesus (8:27-30) and Jesus delivers the first prediction of the passion and rebukes Peter (8:31-33), Mark begins his second major Gospel theme of powerlessness. Jesus is the rejected, suffering, and dying Son of Man. He is on his way to Jerusalem to accomplish this mission.

Authentic followers of Jesus are those who are willing to participate in his rejection, suffering, and death, which are not usually thought to be the locus of power. For Mark, power is found in powerlessness.

Throughout Mark's Gospel, the disciples never seem to get this message. This is why they are portrayed as arguing about who is the greatest. Members of Mark's community, who understood power as greatness and not as powerlessness, would see themselves in this description of the disciples. The disciples (historical) and Marcan (contemporary) have it all wrong.

Jesus points this out in this passage by teaching that the person who wants to be first must be "the last of all and the servant of all" (9:35). A child appears on the scene to illustrate this message.

In the ancient world, a child was a powerless person. A child had no rights. A child was totally dependent on his or her parents. A child was the best example of powerlessness.

Therefore, "Whoever receives one child such as this in my name, receives me; and whoever receives me, receives not me but the One who sent me" (9:37), declares Jesus.

Authentic discipleship has nothing to do with greatness or power. Authentic discipleship involves rejection, suffering, and death; it consists of being a servant and being as dependent upon God as a child is upon his or her parents.

Meditation: How does your understanding of discipleship include rejection, suffering, death, servanthood, dependency, and powerlessness?

Prayer: God of Jesus, through the rejection, suffering, and death of your Son you have taught your people the meaning of authentic discipleship. When we seek greatness, make us faithful servants. When we seek importance, make us dependent like a child. Grant us participation in the powerlessness of Jesus, who lives and reigns with you and the Holy Spirit, one God, for ever and ever. Amen.

ACTING PRUDENTLY

Luke 16:1-13

Scripture: "There was a rich man who had a steward who was reported to him for squandering his possessions. He summoned him and said, 'What is this I hear about you? Prepare a full account of your stewardship, because you can no longer be my steward.' [...] And the lord commended the dishonest steward because he had acted wisely" (Luke 16:1-2, 8).

Reflection: The parable of the dishonest steward (Luke 16:1- 8) is followed by three Lucan conclusions (16:8-13). It follows the three parables of the lost sheep, the lost coin, and the lost son (15:1-32) and precedes three sayings against the Pharisees, about the law, and about divorce (16:14-18) and the parable of the rich man and Lazarus (16:19-31). Its location in the Gospel indicates that Luke understood the parable to deal with loss in some sense.

The steward is about to lose his job. He begins to think that he has no one to count on, so he must prepare for his dismissal. He carefully evaluates his current position: "I'm not strong enough to dig and I'm ashamed to beg" (16:3).

However, after thinking a moment, he whispers to himself, "I know what I can do so that, when I am removed from the stewardship, they will welcome me into their homes" (16:5). His decision is to call in his master's debtors and reduce their debts. Then they will feel some responsibility to repay such a favor by taking in the steward when he is dismissed.

Clearly, the steward is dishonest. He is cheating his master. But he is preparing a future for himself. He is so good at being a steward that "the master commended that dishonest steward because he acted wisely" (16:8). Why? Because the steward finally began to function as a steward. In the face of crisis, the steward responds wisely and with prudence.

Luke's first conclusion to or interpretation of the parable recommends to the members of his community the prudent use of wealth, just as non-Christians, "the children of this world" (16:8), do, and as the steward did. This is in light of the coming of the end of the world.

The second conclusion urges members of the community to be faithful to those who are in positions of responsibility. Luke is particularly interested in the wise use of wealth; his position is that prudent use of the goods of the world entails using these goods for the benefit of others. The parable of the rich man and Lazarus will underline this point.

The third interpretation of the parable of the dishonest steward declares that a person cannot "serve two masters" (16:13). In other words, a person cannot be a slave to both God and riches. According to Luke, dependence upon wealth is incompatible with the teaching of Jesus. An authentic follower of Jesus is completely dependent on God alone.

Luke's three conclusions to the parable were originally independent literary units, which have been grouped together in order to form his understanding of the parable and to provide an understanding of it for his middle class, wealthy community.

Meditation: How do you use your wealth prudently? How do you use you wealth responsibly? How are you totally detached from your wealth and dependent on God?

Prayer: God of all creation, you made people the stewards of the earth and handed over to them everything that came from your hands. In the course of time, selfishness entered the world and people began to cling to instead of to share your gifts. Give us the spirit of prudence, that we might use wisely the riches you have given to us. Make us mindful of those in need, that we might be reliable stewards. We ask this through our Lord Jesus Christ, your Son, who lives and reigns with you and the Holy Spirit, one God, for ever and ever. Amen.

REVEALED SECRETS
Luke 8:16-18

Scripture: "Nothing is hidden that will not be revealed, nor secret that will not be made known and brought out into the open. Therefore, watch how you listen" (Luke 8:17-18).

Reflection: The Lucan version of the parable of the lamp (8:16-18) follows the parable of the sower (8:4-8) and its explanation (8:11-15). Luke intends the parable to emphasize his theme of responding to the word of God.

The picture is that of a Roman-style house with a vestibule in which there is a lamp on a stand. The light from the lamp illumines the way into the house for those who wish to enter. In Luke's understanding, those who "have heard the word, embraced it with a generous and good heart, and have borne fruit through perseverance" (cf. 8:15) are to be light for others in God's household.

In this way the "mysteries of the kingdom of God" (8:10) will become visible and known. Therefore, with this responsibility, those who hear the word of God must watch carefully how they listen to the word (8:18). What they have acquired in faith will be multiplied. However, those who have not listened carefully will lose even that which they think is theirs.

In Luke's community, every member is responsible for hearing and doing the word of God. Every member is responsible for being light — showing the way to a more perfect response to the word — to every other member.

Meditation: In which ways are you like a lamp to others in your community of faith?

Prayer: God of light, you illumine the minds and hearts of men and women through your word. Long ago you spoke the word of creation, and the earth was formed. Man and woman were molded with your hands and filled with your breath at your command. Through your prophets you led your people into a solemn covenant. Now, you have made your word incarnate in the person of Jesus, your Son. Give us the grace to listen attentively to him and make us shining examples of his love. We ask this through Christ our Lord. Amen.

HEAR AND ACT

Luke 8:19-21

Scripture: "My mother and my brothers are those who hear the word of God and act on it" (Luke 8:21).

Reflection: Luke's source for the short three-verse section concerning Jesus and his family (8:19-21) is Mark's Gospel (3:31-35). However, Luke has reworked the section and considerably softened the Marcan portrait of Jesus' natural family.

In Marks' Gospel, Jesus' family thinks, "He is out of his mind" (Mark 3:21), so they "set out to seize him." Luke omits this perspective as he has already portrayed Mary as God's obedient servant, one who has heard the word and acted on it.

In this section about Jesus and his family, the family is held up by Luke as an example of what it means to "hear the word of God and act on it" (8:21). People who want to belong to Jesus' family must hear and obey the word of God.

Luke's community is not formed of those who have any physical relationship to Jesus; it is made up of those who hear the word (as presented in the parable of the sower, its explanation, and the parable of the lamp) and, then, act on what has been heard. Being able to trace a blood-line to Jesus is not important to Luke; what is important is hearing and acting on the word of God. The person who hears and acts on the word is an authentic member of the family of Jesus.

Meditation: In which ways are you a member of Jesus' family?

Prayer: God of all people, you never cease to call your people to become one family of faith, one household of love. Continue to call us into the circle of your Son, Jesus. Make us attentive to his word and, through the prompting of the Holy Spirit, give us the grace to act on what we have heard. We ask this through Christ, our Lord. Amen.

FROM VILLAGE TO VILLAGE

Luke 9:1-6

Scripture: He (Jesus) called the Twelve together and gave them power and authority over all demons and to cure all diseases, and he sent them to proclaim the kingdom of God and to heal [the sick] (Luke 9:1-2).

Reflection: The weekday cycle of selections from Luke's Gospel omits the calming of the storm at sea (8:22-25), the healing of the Gerasene demoniac (8:26-39) and the healing of Jairus' daughter and the woman with a hemorrhage (8:40-56). The narrative concerning the mission of the Twelve (9:1-6), today's selection from Luke, is similar to that found in Mark's Gospel (6:7-13), although it contains some unique Lucan features.

According to the context for this section, the reader must remember that Jesus has already called a number of men to follow him, established a new Israel of Twelve, and attempted to form them into a community of believers. Now, they are sent on mission to proclaim the good news. Of course, the historical apostles are not Luke's principal concern here, but his community at the time that this Gospel was written.

Luke is demonstrating that the Church has been endowed by Jesus with the same gifts that Jesus possessed. Four miracles precede the missioning scene. This "power and authority" of Jesus is given to the Church. The Twelve (representative of the whole Church) are sent out to continue the work that Jesus has been

69

performing — proclaiming the kingdom of God, exorcising demons, and healing the sick.

Those who accept and undertake this mission are instructed to "take nothing for the journey" (9:3). Throughout the Gospel, Luke is insistent on absolute material detachment; authentic followers of Jesus rely on God, who will provide for the needs of the missionaries through those who receive them.

If they are not welcomed, then the missionaries are to detach themselves from those who do not provide a welcome. The symbolic gesture is that of shaking the dust from one's feet. It indicates that nothing — not even the dust — of those not providing a welcome will be carried away with the missioner.

The responsibility of setting out and going from "village to village proclaiming the good news and curing diseases everywhere" (9:6) is a theme that Luke will continue to develop through the rest of the Gospel and especially in his Acts of the Apostles.

Meditation: In which ways do you proclaim the good news?

Prayer: Missionary God, you called Moses from the sheepfold and sent him to your Hebrew people with your word of freedom. You called many prophets from their daily toil and sent them to Israel with your word of repentance. Jesus, your Son, called men and women to hear your word and then sent them into the world to proclaim the good news of your kingdom. Keep us faithful to the mission which you have entrusted to us. May we rely only on you, who live and reign with Jesus and the Holy Spirit, one God, for ever and ever. Amen.

WHO IS JESUS?
Luke 9:7-9

Scripture: Herod said, "John I beheaded. Who is this, then, about whom I hear such things?" And he kept trying to see him (Luke 9:9).

Reflection: The short section concerning Herod's opinion of Jesus (Luke 9:7-9), which follows the mission of the Twelve (9:1-6) and precedes the return of the Twelve and the feeding of the five thousand (9:10-17) — which is omitted from the weekday Lucan cycle — is borrowed from Mark's Gospel (6:14-16). Luke, however, has reworked Mark's perspective considerably.

The section serves two purposes in Luke's Gospel. First, it functions to raise the question of Jesus' identity. In Mark's Gospel, Herod believes that Jesus is John, who "has been raised up" (Mark 6:16). Luke, however, places this opinion on the lips of others. "John I beheaded," Herod declares (9:9). The question of Jesus' identity remains. For Luke, Jesus' mission hangs on his identity, which is further explored throughout chapter nine of this Gospel.

Second, the section about Herod's perplexity functions to prepare the reader for two parts of the Gospel which follow. In Luke 13:31-33, Jesus is warned that Herod wants to kill him. He calls Herod a fox and declares that not even the fear of death can impede his mission — rejection, suffering, death, and resurrection — in Jerusalem.

In Luke 23:8-12, Pilate sends Jesus to Herod, a section unique to Luke's Gospel. "Herod was extremely pleased when he saw Jesus; he had been wanting to see him for a long time because he had heard about him and was hoping to see him perform some sign" (23:8). After questioning Jesus, Herod's curiosity remains unsatisfied. Herod never learns the true identity of Jesus.

By this portrayal of Herod, the author of this Gospel raises this question for the reader: Who is Jesus? In the episode about the feeding of the five thousand, which follows this section, Luke declares that Jesus is the one in whom God's power is present and the one through whom God provides for the needs of his people. Throughout the rest of this chapter, Luke will provide the reader with other answers to the question.

Meditation: Who is Jesus? Make a list of your answers.

Prayer: God of Jesus, through your incarnate Word you have revealed the vastness of your love for the whole of your creation. May we, who have been baptized in the suffering, death, and resurrection of Jesus, come to the fullest knowledge of him, who lives and reigns with you and the Holy Spirit, one God, for ever and ever. Amen.

IN SOLITUDE

Luke 9:18-22

Scripture: Once when Jesus was praying in solitude and the disciples were with him, he asked them... , "Who do *you* say that I am?" And in answer Peter said, "The Messiah of God." He said to them, "The Son of Man must suffer greatly and be rejected by the elders, the chief priests, and the scribes, and be put to death and rise on the third day" (Luke 9:18, 20, 22).

Reflection: This section of Luke's Gospel (9:18-22) is borrowed from Mark's Gospel (8:27-33). Luke, however, has removed Jesus' rebuke of Peter as well as changed a few other details to fit his own theological position and characterization of Jesus.

First, it is important to note that Jesus "was praying in solitude" (9:18). For Luke, any major revelation of the identity of Jesus is made only after a period of prayer. Before his baptism (3:21), before the choice of the Twelve (6:12), before Peter's confession (9:18), before the transfiguration (9:28), before teaching the Our Father (11:1), before the Last Supper (22:32), before his betrayal and arrest (22:41), and before his death on the cross (23:46) Jesus in Luke's Gospel is always found in prayer. For Luke, prayer and the disclosure of Jesus' identity are always related.

Second, the disclosure of Jesus' identity is the point of chapter nine and particularly this section (9:18-22) of the chapter. The opening question, "Who do the crowds say that I am?" (9:18) echoes Herod's question of a few verses earlier: "Who is this, then, about whom I hear such things?" (9:9).

Peter's response, "The Messiah of God" (9:20), is equivalent to saying, "The Anointed One of God." For Luke, the Anointed One of God is the bringer of salvation to all God's people now. Since the angels delivered this information to the shepherds (2:11), Luke has been revealing the identity of Jesus to the reader.

However, while in prayer, Jesus also reveals that being the Messiah, the Son of Man, involves suffering, rejection, death, and resurrection. As portrayed by Luke, the statement concerning the death and resurrection of Jesus comes as a direct response to Peter's declaration.

For Luke, the implications of professing faith in Jesus as the Messiah involve suffering, rejection, death, and resurrection. An authentic follower of Jesus will possess the same commitment to his or her mission as Jesus did to his. Knowing Jesus' identity means following him to death.

Meditation: Who is Jesus? How does your answer reflect your commitment to his mission?

Prayer: God of the Messiah, you did not save your only-begotten Son, Jesus, from suffering, rejection and death, but you permitted him to experience the fullness of humanity. Then, you raised him to the heights of new life. Make of us faithful disciples of Jesus; immerse us in the streams of humanity that we may come to share in the divinity of the Son of Man, who lives and reigns with you and the Holy Spirit, one God, for ever and ever. Amen.

CONQUERED EVIL

Luke 9:43-45

Scripture: [Jesus] said to his disciples, "Listen closely to what I'm going to tell you. The Son of Man is to be handed over to men." But they did not understand this saying; its meaning was hidden from them so that they wouldn't ask about it (Luke 9:44-45).

Reflection: The weekday cycle of selections from Luke omits the conditions of discipleship (9:23-27), the transfiguration account (9:28-36), and the healing of a boy with a demon (9:37-43). The second prediction of the passion (9:43-45) functions as the conclusion of the healing account and as a theological statement by this author.

In the account of the healing of the boy with a demon, Luke, following Mark, explains that the disciples were not able to cast out the demon. He omits the disciples' question about why they were not able to cast it out and Jesus' answer about faith and prayer.

By attaching the second prediction of the passion to the healing narrative, Luke is asking the reader to make a connection between the passion of Jesus (no mention is made of the resurrection) and the healing. Power over evil is a result of the passion of Jesus, according to Luke.

Since at this point in the Gospel, there has not yet been the passion, the disciples do not understand what Jesus is talking about. The meaning of Jesus' passion is hidden from them, but it is not hidden from the reader. Jesus' overall mission — preaching, healing, suffering, death, resurrection — is crystallized in the healing of the boy. Through his suffering, death, and resurrection, Jesus has conquered the power of evil.

Meditation: In which ways has Jesus conquered the evil in your life?

Prayer: Healing God, when your people were suffering in the desert, you sent them a cure through Moses, your servant. When your people were suffering in sin, you sent them Jesus, your Son, who, through his passion, has restored all people to health. Continue to reveal to us the meaning of Jesus' passion and give us the healing we need. We ask this through Christ our Lord. Amen.

THE FATHER'S WILL

Matthew 21:28-32

Scripture: "A man had two sons. He came to the first one and said, 'Son, go work in the vineyard today.' He said in reply, 'I will not,' but later he changed his mind and went. The man went up to the other son and gave the same order. He said in reply, 'Yes, sir,' but did not go. Which of the two did his father's will?" (Matthew 21:28-31).

Reflection: The parable of the two sons (Matthew 21:28-32) is unique to Matthew's Gospel. It follows the questioning of Jesus' authority by the chief priests and the elders of the people (21:23-27), and it precedes the parable of the tenants (21:33-46) and the parable of the wedding feast (22:1-14).

As the first of three parables concerning the author's judgment on Israel, it also serves to interrupt a series of controversies, which are introduced by the cleaning of the Temple and resume with the paying of taxes to the emperor after the third parable.

The parable illustrates a favorite Matthean theme — the difference between saying and doing. Matthew is interested in the son who did his father's will. The only answer possible to the question, "Which of the two did his father's will?" (21:31) is the son who first said "No" but later changed his mind.

However, the author makes an application of the parable and turns it into an allegory. The vineyard represents Israel, God's chosen people. The religious leaders, represented by the second son, are those who say "Yes" but never go to work. The outcasts (tax collectors and prostitutes), represented by the first son, are those who say "No" but later change their minds and repent. These outcasts, who do the father's will, were considered to be outside the vineyard!

Matthew's application of the parable reverses this generally considered status. At the preaching of John the Baptizer sinners and prostitutes repented, while the religious leaders did not. Therefore, the sinners and the prostitutes "are entering the kingdom of God" ahead of them (21:31).

The author indicts the religious leaders of Israel on one more point. He tells them that they witnessed the repentance of sinners and prostitutes and this event should have moved them to reform and believe John, a man who did God's will. "Yet even when you saw that, you did not change your minds and believe him" (21:32).

It is important to note that the parable opens with a questions, "What is your opinion?" (21:28), which is addressed to the religious leaders of Israel. When they give their answer about which son did the will of the father, they condemn themselves. And thus, as Matthew views the scenario, there continues the sad story of an unfaithful Israel, who continues to reject those whom God sends to call her to repentance.

Meditation: Who has motivated you to repent and to do God's will?

Prayer: God of Israel, once you chose a people and made them your own. You entered into a covenant with them, and, even when they strayed, you renewed your dedication and your love for them. Never have you abandoned them, but often through your prophets you have called them to repentance and a change of heart. Jesus, your Son, preached conversion and taught us how to do your will. Through your Holy Spirit, turn our hearts to you and guide us through repentance to the joy of your kingdom, where you live and reign with Jesus and the Holy Spirit, one God, for ever and ever. Amen.

A WIDE CIRCLE

Mark 9:38-43, 45, 47-48

Scripture: "If your hand causes you to sin, cut it off. It is better for you to enter into life maimed than with two hands to go into Gehenna.... And if your foot causes you to sin, cut it off. It is better for you to enter into life crippled than with two feet to be thrown into Gehenna. And if your eye causes you to sin, pluck it out. Better for you to enter into the kingdom of God with one eye than with two eyes to be thrown into Gehenna" (Mark 9:43, 45, 47).

Reflection: The narrative describing an exorcist not of Jesus' company (9:38-41) and the discourse about the temptations to sin (9:42-43, 45, 47-48) follow the discussion concerning the greatest in the kingdom (9:33-37) and precede the simile of salt (9:49-50). Mark deals with two issues in these two sections.

The first issue centers on those outside the official circle of Jesus, that is, outside the community. Mark portrays Jesus as an exorcist, and Mark's community must have had exorcists; but there were other persons, outside the community, who were exorcising demons in Jesus' name. Anyone who does God's will is to be tolerated, according to this author. "For whoever is not against us is for us" (9:40). Such a simple act as giving another a cup of water to drink in the name of Christ will be noticed by God.

As is usual in Mark's Gospel, the disciples always want to

narrow the circle, as in the preceding discussion about who is the greatest in the kingdom of God. Mark, who is not fond of the disciples, sets them up against Jesus, who continuously attempts to widen the circle of his followers and make the requirements for discipleship less strenuous than the disciples wish they would be.

In the second section, Mark emphasizes the powerlessness of authentic followers of Jesus. Jesus calls them "little ones who believe [in me]" (9:42). This reference completes the frame begun with the child used as an example for the disciples who want greatness. Those who are in the inner circle with Jesus are not to be let outside of it.

"It would be better… if a great millstone were put around" the neck of a person who attempts to do this, and that person be "thrown into the sea" (9:42).

Whatever gets in the way of discipleship has to be eliminated — no matter if it is a hand, a foot, or an eye. This, of course, is Marcan hyperbole and is not meant to be taken literally. The point is that the kingdom of God is more important than anything else in life or any aspect of life. It is to be the disciple's only cause.

By not eliminating that which gets in the way of authentic discipleship, the person is risking Gehenna, the Jerusalem garbage dump. Again, hyperbole is used to emphasize the seriousness of discipleship. The non-serious disciple is garbage. The non-serious disciple is not even good garbage!

Meditation: In your life, what is it that keeps you from authentically following Jesus?

Prayer: Almighty God, you are with those who perform great deeds in the name of your Son, Jesus. Remove all jealousy from our lives. Enable us to see and to remove whatever leads us away from you. Draw all men and women into the circle of your kingdom, where you live and reign with Jesus and the Holy Spirit, one God, for ever and ever. Amen.

RICHES AND POVERTY DO NOT SEPARATE

Luke 16:19-31

Scripture: "There was a rich man who used to dress in purple garments and fine linen and dined sumptuously each day. Now lying at his door was a poor man named Lazarus, covered with sores, who would gladly have eaten his fill of the scraps that fell from the rich man's table. Dogs even used to come and lick his sores. When the poor man died, he was carried away by angels to the bosom of Abraham. The rich man also died and was buried, and from the netherworld, where he was in torment, he raised his eyes, and saw Abraham far off and Lazarus at his side" (Luke 16:19-23).

Reflection: The parable of the rich man and Lazarus (16:19-31) is unique to Luke's Gospel and illustrates some of Luke's favorite themes. It follows a series of sayings against the Pharisees, (16:14-15), about the law (16:16-17), and about divorce (16:18). The parable is followed by instructions about temptations to sin and forgiveness (17:1-4).

As it is addressed to the Pharisees, "who loved money" (16:14) and who believed that the one who possessed riches was loved by God, whereas the one who was poor was cursed by God, the parable fosters not only the undoing of these popular notions, but it emphasizes that wealth is to be used for those who have no riches. One of Luke's favorite themes throughout the Gospel is that riches are given to a person to be given away to others.

In the parable the rich man separates himself from the poor man, Lazarus, with a door or a gate. After both die, the division

81

established by the rich man continues. Abraham tells him, "Between us and you a great chasm is established to prevent anyone from crossing who might wish to go from our side to yours or from your side to ours" (16:26).

In the parable the popular conceptions about the rich and the poor are reversed. The rich man, who should have ended up with Abraham, finds himself in torment. The poor man, who should have ended up in torment, finds himself in the bosom of Abraham.

It is important to note that Abraham was a rich man. However, Abraham used his wealth wisely. Abraham is remembered for his hospitality. The rich man's sin is his failure to take care of the poor man, who died on his doorstep. The rich man violated the law relating to the poor (cf. Deuteronomy 15:4).

The rich man's desire that Abraham send a messenger to the rich man's house to warn the rest of his family cannot be accomplished. Moses and the prophets have already explained the duty that a person has towards the poor; this is enough. "Let them listen to them" (16:29).

The word of God has spoken. A person who will not listen to Moses and the prophets, would certainly not "be persuaded if someone should rise from the dead" (16:31). Luke knows that even after Jesus' resurrection, there were members of his community who failed to repent and use their wealth for the good of others.

Luke issues a stern warning to his church through this parable. People cannot be separated from each other, he declares. Riches and property are not sufficient grounds to determine who will enter the kingdom and who will not. In fact, those who think that they are out may suddenly discover that they are in. All is reversed in God's kingdom.

Meditation: In which ways do you share your wealth with the poor?

Prayer: God of the poor, you defend those who have nothing in this world and you give them the fullness of your kingdom. Teach us to use wisely the goods of this world. Make us aware of our brothers and sisters in need. Guide us in treating all men and women with equal human dignity. We ask this through our Lord Jesus Christ, your Son, who lives and reigns with you and the Holy Spirit, one God, for ever and ever. Amen.

LEAST IS GREATEST

Luke 9:46-50

Scripture: "The one who is least among all of you is the one who is the greatest.... Whoever is not against you is with you" (Luke 9:48, 50).

Reflection: Following the second prediction of the passion (9:43-45) Luke places the narrative about the greatest in the kingdom (9:46-48) and the mention of an exorcist who was using Jesus' name but was not part of his company (9:49-50). Both of these sections are shorter versions of Marcan stories (Mark 9:33-41).

As Luke weaves the story, the disciples fail to understand the second prediction of the passion and begin to argue about who among them is the greatest. Bringing forward a child, Jesus declares, "The one who is least among all of you is the one who is the greatest" (9:48). Thus, a child becomes a model for discipleship.

This is paradoxical. In the culture of the time, a child possessed no rights. At birth, the father had to claim the child as his own. Until the child grew up, he or she was guaranteed no legal rights. Such an image of dependence and powerlessness is used for Christian discipleship. Anyone who claims to be a follower of Jesus cannot be concerned about rivalry — who is the greatest — but should be preoccupied with being like a child — the least among disciples!

Another issue facing Luke's community was that of other

exorcists who cast out demons in Jesus' name but were not members of the church. The principle which Jesus gives is simple: "Whoever is not against you is with you" (9:50). In other words, people who do not belong to the official community can accomplish good too.

One of the central issues in this chapter (9) of Luke's Gospel is Jesus' victory over evil. Once the boy with a demon has been healed, the second prediction of the passion illustrates that healing is a direct result of Jesus' victory over suffering and death. In the Christian community there can be no rivalry or intolerance of outsiders. All must work together to further the effects of Christ's victory over evil.

Meditation: How do you further the effects of Christ's victory over evil?

Prayer: God of victory, you conquered the power of evil through the suffering and death of your only Son, Jesus. When we become preoccupied with greatness, remind us that it is the least among us who is greatest. When we are intolerant of others, remind us that whoever is not against us is with us. Through the power of your Holy Spirit, bring all followers of Jesus into unity in the kingdom where you live and reign, one God, for ever and ever. Amen.

TOWARD JERUSALEM

Luke 9:51-56

Scripture: Now it happened that as the days were drawing near for Jesus to be taken up, he resolutely determined to go to Jerusalem, and he sent messengers ahead of him (Luke 9:51-52).

Reflection: Verse 51 of chapter nine of Luke's Gospel begins a new section of the narrative. The Galilean ministry of Jesus is finished. He now sets out for Jerusalem, where he will be taken up — a reference to his suffering, death, resurrection, and ascension. During his last days in Jerusalem, all these things will be accomplished.

The first event in this uniquely Lucan section (9:51-56), commonly referred to as the journey to Jerusalem, is the unwelcome reception in a Samaritan village. Here, Luke reflects the ethnic and religious opposition of Jews and Samaritans and prepares the reader for the tables-turning parable of the good Samaritan a few verses later (10:29-37).

The rejection by the Samaritans also parallels the rejection that Jesus received in Nazareth at the beginning of his Galilean ministry. Just as he was not accepted in Nazareth, so he is not accepted in Samaria, and, likewise, he will not be accepted in Jerusalem. Thus, Luke is preparing the reader for the rest of this first volume of his work.

In this section of Luke's Gospel, Jesus disassociates himself from those who would punish those who do not accept him. James and John, after witnessing Jesus' rejection by the Samaritans, ask Jesus, "Lord, do you want us to call down fire from heaven to consume them?" (9:54)

The disciples' question alludes to an incident in the second book of Kings (ch. 1) where Elijah calls down fire from heaven to consume King Ahaziah's captain and his fifty men as punishment for consulting a pagan god. By rebuking the disciples, Jesus does not advocate punishment of those who reject him.

The role of the disciples, that is, the Church at the time of Luke's writing, is to prepare for Jesus' suffering, death, resurrection, and ascension. They are to preach the word of God. The only fire that will be called down upon anyone is the fire of the Holy Spirit who, in volume two of Luke's work, the Acts of the Apostles, will transform all people.

Meditation: In which ways do you prepare for the suffering, death, and resurrection of Jesus in your life?

Prayer: God of the journey, you are always with your people as they make their pilgrimage to you. In the desert, you did not abandon your chosen people. Throughout the past two thousand years, you have been with your Church. May your Spirit guide our footsteps through the suffering, death and resurrection of Jesus, your Son, who lives and reigns with you and the Holy Spirit, one God, for ever and ever. Amen.

DON'T LOOK BACK

Luke 9:57-62

Scripture: "No one who sets a hand to the plow and looks to what was left behind is fit for the kingdom of God" (Luke 9:62).

Reflection: Following his departure for Jerusalem and the unwelcomed response he received from some Samaritans, Jesus encounters three would-be followers (9:57-62).

To each of the would-be followers he makes a statement concerning the nature of Christian discipleship. For Luke, these three anonymous people represent the types of people who might consider following Jesus in his community.

The first narrative about a would-be disciple is from Q (cf. Matthew 8:19-20). "I will follow you wherever you go" (9:57), someone says to Jesus. "Jesus answered him, 'Foxes have dens and birds of the sky have nests, but the Son of Man has nowhere to lay his head'" (9:58).

Followers of Jesus must separate themselves from their earthly homes, according to the Lucan understanding of discipleship. Following Jesus is a rootless, lifetime journey. Authentic disciples cannot be like the foxes and the birds, who have homes, but must imitate the Son of Man, who calls no place home.

The second narrative about a would-be disciple is also from Q (cf. Matthew 8:21-22). In this encounter Jesus takes the initiative and says to a person, "Follow me" (9:59).

"Let me first go and bury my father" (9:59), is the reply Jesus receives. Jesus responds, "Let the dead bury their dead. But you, go and proclaim the kingdom of God" (9:60-61).

Discipleship involves complete detachment from family, according to Luke. Both the Jewish and the Hellenistic world considered burying the dead, especially a parent, to be of supreme importance. However, when the issue is discipleship, all filial obligations must take the second place. No person or thing can get in the way of the disciple's principal duty — to proclaim the kingdom. There is an urgency to the mission; it cannot be delayed.

The third narrative that involves a would-be disciple is unique to Luke. A person declares, "I will follow you, Lord, but first let me take leave of those at home" (9:61). Jesus tells him, "No one who puts his hand to the plow and looks behind is fit for the kingdom of God" (9:62).

According to Jesus, past relationships must be abandoned in favor of discipleship. Just as a person who begins to plow a field and turn over the soil cannot look behind and still plow a straight row ahead, so an authentic disciple must not look back but keep going forward, as Jesus did, making the heralding of the kingdom of God his or her most important task. On this journey, there can be no looking back.

These three types of possible disciples were found in Luke's world. By portraying them as referring to Jesus as "Lord," Luke demonstrates what types of Christian attitudes are necessary if such would-be followers wish to join the Church. From this author's perspective, there is a severity and an unconditional nature to the dimension of Christian discipleship.

Meditation: What type of disciple are you? What demands does authentic discipleship place on you?

Prayer: God of the journey, for almost two thousand years you have called men and women to walk in the steps of Jesus, your Son. Make us authentic followers: when we get comfortable, rouse us from our security; when we get attached, remind us of our primary relationship with you; when we get scared, help us to proclaim the good news of the kingdom, where you live and reign with Jesus and the Holy Spirit, one God, for ever and ever. Amen.

LABORERS NEEDED
Luke 10:1-12

Scripture: Now after this, the Lord appointed seventy-two others and sent them ahead of him in pairs to every town and place he intended to visit. He said to them, "The harvest is great but the laborers are few; so implore the lord of the harvest to send out laborers to his harvest" (Luke 10:1-2).

Reflection: Chapter ten (vs. 1-12) of Luke's Gospel begins with the narrative about the mission of the seventy-two. It is set in the wider context of Jesus' journey to Jerusalem and in the narrower context of the continuing discussion about discipleship and its mission. For this latter reason, then, it follows the section about the would-be followers of Jesus (9:57-62), and it precedes the reproaches to unrepentant towns (10:13-16), the return of the seventy-two (10:17-20), and the privileges of discipleship (10:23-24).

This section (10:1-12) is from Q (cf. Matthew 9:37-38; 10:7-14, 16).

Only Luke's Gospel contains two separate incidents of Jesus sending out disciples on a mission. The first one (9:1-6) is based on Mark's Gospel (6:6-13); it is concerned with the mission of the Twelve. This incident is about the mission of the seventy-two, who represent the Gentile mission of the Church in the author's time.

There is little difference between the mission of the Twelve and the mission of the seventy-two, as Luke presents them. By portraying their similarity, this author demonstrates that the mission of Jesus continues in the evangelist's own day through those who succeed the Twelve. This mission will be fully developed in his second volume, the Acts of the Apostles.

Here Jesus instructs the seventy-two to pray for more laborers for the harvest. By the time that Luke is writing this Gospel, the mission of the post-Ascension Church is greatly expanded. More missioners are required to meet the needs of the various Christian communities.

Certain guidelines must be observed by these new missioners. They are to be totally dependent on God for their protection; they are to be "like lambs among wolves" (10:3).

They are also to depend on God for their sustenance: "Carry no money bag, no sack, no sandals" (10:4).

The greeting of "Peace to this household" (10:5), which the missioners are to give to "whatever house" they enter, echoes the greeting of the risen Jesus to his disciples after his resurrection. For Luke, the missioner represents the risen Christ to others.

Missioners are to rely upon the hospitality of others by staying in the same house and eating and drinking what is offered to them (cf. 10:7). They are not to worry about dietary laws as they are told to eat what is set before them (cf. 10:8).

Their mission is simple: "The kingdom of God is at hand" (10:9, 11). And there is an urgency to the mission of proclaiming this message. But deeds must also accompany this word. By following these guidelines, by shaking the dust from their feet in protest when they are not received, missioners demonstrate that the kingdom of God is at hand.

By naming seventy-two, who are sent out in pairs, Luke echoes the book of Numbers' account of Moses' gathering of seventy elders of Israel, who received a share of Moses' spirit and would assist him in leading the people. The variant reading of seventy-two alludes to the two men, Eldad and Medad, who were outside the camp when the seventy received the spirit but got a portion nevertheless.

Luke's seventy-two missioners are the leaders of the Church who have received the Spirit of God at Pentecost (cf. Acts 2:1-4) and are commissioned and sent out to proclaim the kingdom of God. They are sent out in pairs, a point which will reappear after the resurrection, where two disciples on the road to Emmaus encounter the Risen One in the breaking of bread (cf. Luke 24:13-35).

More instructions for missionaries are contained in the sections of Luke's Gospel which follow.

Meditation: In which of the following ways are you an active missioner: dependence upon God for protection and sustenance; offering peace to every household; accepting whatever is given to you by others; proclamation by word and deed that the kingdom of God is at hand?

Prayer: God of missionaries, you instructed Moses, your servant, to choose seventy elders of Israel to help him in governing your people. He chose the seventy, but you chose seventy-two and poured out your Spirit on them. You continue to choose men and women to proclaim that your kingdom is at hand by word and deed. Make us worthy missioners. Protect us on our way. Give us the sustenance we need. Guide us with your Holy Spirit, who lives and reigns with you and your Son, Jesus, one God, for ever and ever. Amen.

UNREPENTED WOES

Luke 10:13-16

Scripture: "Woe to you, Chorazin! Woe to you Bethsaida! because if the mighty works that took place in you had taken place in Tyre and Sidon, they would have repented long ago and sat in sackcloth and ashes" (Luke 10:13).

Reflection: Following the Lord's instruction to the seventy-two, who are sent on mission (Luke 10:1-12), Luke inserts a section (10:13-16) which expands the judgment theme concerning unrepentant towns, a theme introduced in verses 10-12 of the guidelines for missioners. The source of this material is Q (cf. Matthew 11:20-24; 10:40).

In this section, Luke is interested in demonstrating that the proclamation of the kingdom of God involves a call to repentance. Those who hear the call and repent listen to the missioners and to Jesus (cf. 10:16). Those who hear the call and reject the missioner also reject Jesus and the One who sent him (cf. 10:16). In other words, there is a severe judgment involved in rejection of the message, "The kingdom of God is at hand" (10:11).

Two Jewish towns, Chorazin and Bethsaida, are contrasted to two Gentile towns, Tyre and Sidon, by the author. The two Jewish towns have witnessed "mighty works" (10:13), a reference to the ministry of Jesus, but they have not repented. The two Gentile towns, pagan cities denounced by the prophet Joel (4:4-7) for their wickedness, would have repented if they had the opportunity to hear and witness what the Jewish towns have heard and seen. Therefore, "it will be more tolerable to Tyre and Sidon at the judgment" (10:14).

Here, Luke is anticipating the rejection of Jesus by the Jews and the acceptance of him by the Gentiles. Because of his interest in the Gentile mission — the sending of the seventy-two — these reproaches to these towns fit with Luke's theme in this section of his Gospel.

Capernaum, another Jewish town, receives the most severe condemnation, for there Jesus had saved a demoniac, cured Simon's mother-in-law, and healed many other people (cf. Luke 4:31-41). When Jesus did these "mighty deeds" in Capernaum, "the crowds went looking for him, and when they came to him, they tried to prevent him from leaving them" (4:42).

It is because of Capernaum's pride, its delusions of grandeur, that it is condemned. Luke has maintained the faint echo of Isaiah's taunt of Babylon (cf. Isaiah 14:13-15), the great city which falls into the pit, the netherworld. For Luke, no town can escape judgment unless it listens and repents. Simply witnessing "mighty deeds" is not enough.

Meditation: In which ways does your town (city) need to listen and to repent?

Prayer: God of repentance, through your prophets you called men and women to conversion of life. Through the preaching and mighty deeds of Jesus, your Son, your have called us to listen and to repent. May the deeds that you continue to work among us and the word that you continue to speak to us lead us to repentance and a share in the kingdom where you live and reign with Jesus and the Holy Spirit, one God, for ever and ever. Amen.

THE PRIVILEGE OF DISCIPLESHIP

Luke 10:17-24

Scripture: The seventy-two returned rejoicing and said, "Lord, even the demons are subject to us in your name." And Jesus said to them, "I saw Satan fall like lightning from the sky" (Luke 10:17-18).

Reflection: Three short narratives make up this section of Luke's Gospel (10:17-24). These include the narrative concerning the return of the seventy-two (10:17-20), who had been sent on mission earlier (cf. 10:1-12); Jesus' prayer of praise of the Father (10:21-22); and the declaration concerning the privilege of discipleship (10:23-24).

The narrative concerning the return of the seventy-two is unique to Luke. In this section he revives one of his favorite themes — Jesus' resurrection has broken the power of evil in the world. Therefore, the post-resurrectional disciples explain how evil is subject to them, just as it had been subject to Jesus. Jesus responds by reminding them that this power comes from him. Evil is defeated as the kingdom of God is established.

A warning immediately follows the rejoicing over Satan's fall. "Do not rejoice because the spirits are subject to you," Jesus states, "but rejoice because your names are written in heaven" (10:20). The primary concern of followers of Jesus is not miraculous power but salvation.

The second narrative, Jesus' prayer of praise to the Father, is from Q (cf. Matthew 11:25-27) with the Lucan editorial addition of the introduction, which states that Jesus "rejoiced [in] the

Holy Spirit" (10:21). Thus, the reader is reminded of the tremendous role of the Holy Spirit in this Gospel.

The prayer declares that through Jesus God's revelation has come to the "childlike" (10:21), those who understand the mysteries of the kingdom (cf. 8:10), the disciples and authentic followers of Jesus. These are the people who continue Jesus' mission, one which he received from the Father.

The power and authority of the disciples comes from God through Jesus. "All things have been handed over to me by my Father" (10:22), declares Jesus. Because "no one knows who the Son is except the Father, and who the Father is except the Son and anyone to whom the Son wishes to reveal him" (10:22), Jesus makes the will of God known to the disciples.

The third narrative, Jesus' explanation of the privileges of discipleship, comes from Q (cf. Matthew 13:16-17). Because the seventy-two have seen and heard, they are like Chorazin, Bethsaida, and Capernaum, the three unrepentant towns mentioned earlier in chapter 10. They have seen what "many prophets and kings longed to see... but did not see... and to hear what [they] heard, but did not hear it" (10:24).

The seventy-two are blessed because they detached themselves from family and property for a single mission — to continue the preaching and work of Jesus. They have heard Jesus' words and witnessed his works; they have repented; they have been given the power of Jesus; they have made a commitment to the end.

Meditation: In which ways do you share in the privileges of being a disciple of Jesus?

Prayer: Father, Lord of heaven and earth, you hide the mysteries of the kingdom from the learned and the clever and you reveal them to the childlike. Through Jesus, your Son, you have disclosed your gracious will. Share with us the mission of Jesus; make us eager to preach his word and to do the will you have made known through him. One day may we be called blessed in the kingdom, where you live and reign with Jesus and the Holy Spirit, one God, for ever and ever. Amen.

WHAT WILL THE OWNER DO?

Matthew 21:33-43

Scripture: "When vintage time drew near, [a landowner] sent his servants to the vinedressers to obtain his produce. But the vinedressers took hold of the servants and beat one, killed another, and stoned yet another.... He sent his son to them, thinking, 'They will respect my son.' But... the vinedressers... seized him, threw him out of the vineyard, and killed him. What will the owner of the vineyard do to those tenants when he comes?" (Matthew 21:34-35, 37-40)

Reflection: The source of the parable of the tenants (Matthew 21:33-43) is Mark 12:1-12, although, as is characteristic of Matthew's Gospel, the evangelist has allegorized it further than the author of Mark's Gospel did. The parable may have some authentic parabolic roots in Jesus, but, due to tradition which reworked it to form an allegory of the history of salvation, it is impossible to recover the original.

The Matthean allegory, then, becomes a summary of the history of salvation up to the time that the author was writing his Gospel. The landowner is God, who "planted a vineyard, put a hedge around it, dug a wine press in it, and built a tower" (21:33). As is typical of Matthew, the allusion to the prophet Isaiah is obvious: "Let me now sing of my friend, my friend's song concerning his vineyard. My friend had a vineyard on a fertile hillside; he spaded it, cleared it of stones, and planted the choicest vines; within it he built a watchtower, and hewed out a wine press" (Isaiah 5:1-2). A few verses later Isaiah identifies the vineyard: "The vineyard of the Lord of hosts is the house of Israel and the men of Judah are his cherished plant" (Isaiah 5:7).

The vinedressers or tenants, those who have the lease on the vineyard, represent the religious leaders of Israel. For Matthew these are the "chief priests and the elders of the people" (21:23), the groups to whom this parable is addressed. In an editorial comment at the end of the parable, Matthew also informs the reader that the parable is addressed to the Pharisees, who represented Judaism at the time that Matthew was writing. "When the chief priests and the Pharisees heard his (Jesus') parables, they knew he was speaking about them" (21:45).

In the course of time, God "sent his servants to the vinedressers to obtain his produce" (21:34). The first group of servants are the pre-exilic prophets, who suffered beatings, killings, and stonings. The second group of servants are the post-exilic prophets who suffered the same fate.

The landowner, God, sent his prophets "to obtain his produce" (21:34), the good works, the righteousness, the doing of the will of God, which God demands. Matthew has radically altered the Marcan version of the story; in Mark, the owner wants "some of the produce of the vineyard" (Mark 12:2), but Matthew records that he wants it all. For Matthew, God demands righteousness, justice, of his people, and his claim is total.

The son represents Jesus, who was sent by God to his people. He is the heir. If a Jewish proselyte died without an heir, then the tenants, who worked his land, would have the final claim to it. By killing the heir, the tenants would "acquire his inheritance" (21:38). By killing Jesus, the Jewish leaders would retain their supposed right to the vineyard.

Matthew reflects Jesus' passion in his narrative of the vineyard owner's son's death: "They seized him, threw him out of the vineyard, and killed him" (21:39). Later in the Gospel, Matthew will narrate how Jesus is seized "by a large crowd... who had come from the chief priests and elders of the people" (26:47). He is taken outside of Jerusalem and crucified.

The question at the end of the parable is posed to the chief priests and the elders of the people: "What will the owner of the vineyard do to those tenants when he comes?" (21:40). The answer they give indicts them: "He will put those evil men to a miserable death and lease his vineyard to other vinedressers who will give him the produce at the proper times" (21:41).

Who are these new vinedressers? For Matthew they are the members of the Church who are responsible for doing deeds of righteousness. God has come in Jesus, and Israel has indicted itself by not producing righteous works. Now the Church is entrusted with this responsibility.

The quotation from Psalm 118:22-23 about "The stone that the builders rejected has become the cornerstone" serves to vindicate Jesus. Jesus, God's chosen stone, who was rejected by the religious leaders of Israel, has, through his death and resurrection, become the cornerstone of the Church, the new people of God.

The final line — uniquely Matthean — of the allegory summarizes the point that Matthew has been making throughout the narrative: "Therefore, I say to you, the kingdom of God will be taken away from you and given to a people that will produce its fruit" (21:43). Those Jewish persons who accept Jesus as the Messiah of God and those Gentile persons who believe that Jesus is the Messiah of God are included in the kingdom, which is now signified by the vineyard.

Meditation: What produce has God obtained from you, a tenant of his vineyard?

Prayer: God of the vineyard, once you planted a vineyard, put a hedge around it, dug a wine press in it, and built a tower. Then you leased it to tenants, your people Israel. Because you were

not able to obtain righteousness from them, you sent your prophets to renew your covenant. In the fullness of time, you sent your
own Son, who announced that your kingdom would be given to
a people who would produce according to your will. Make us
faithful tenants of your kingdom. Through the guidance of your
Holy Spirit lead us to do your will. We ask this through our Lord
Jesus Christ, your Son, who lives and reigns with you and the Holy
Spirit, one God, for ever and ever. Amen.

GOD'S INTENTION OF PERMANENCE

Mark 10:2-16

Scripture: "From the beginning of creation, 'God made them male and female. For this reason a man shall leave his father and mother and be united to his wife, and the two shall become one flesh.' So they are no longer two but one flesh. Therefore what God has joined together, let no one separate" (Mark 10:6-9).

Reflection: The question about marriage and divorce (10:2-16) in Mark's Gospel takes place after Jesus leaves Capernaum and goes to the district of Judea across the Jordan. Geographically, Jesus is on his way to Jerusalem, where he will confront his enemies for the last time. In this section he is confronted by the Pharisees, who represent Jesus' opposition in Mark's Gospel. The question which they pose to him deals with divorce alone: "Is it lawful for a husband to divorce his wife?" (10:2). This is a religious, legal question. It is a test, as the author of the Gospel indicates (cf. 10:21).

The legal answer to the question is found in the book of Deuteronomy (24:1), which permitted divorce. Instead of answering the legal question himself, Jesus asks the legal experts to give the answer: "What did Moses command you?" (10:3). Their reply, "Moses permitted a bill of divorce to be written and to dismiss her" (10:4), is quite correct.

But Jesus moves the questions beyond the legal sphere to the divine sphere, that is, to the intention of God in instituting marriage: "He wrote that commandment for you because of the hardness of your hearts" (10:5), Jesus states. To accuse people of being "hard of heart" is to accuse them of one of the greatest sins. This means that they are not teachable and that they fail to obey the higher law of God contained in the very Torah which they quote. Because of their failure to keep the higher law, Moses dispensed them from it and gave them permission to divorce.

The greater law, the intent of the Creator, is permanence. God did not initiate divorce; God initiated marriage. "God made them male and female. For this reason a man shall leave his father and mother and be united to his wife, and the two shall become one flesh" (10:7-8). Jesus' declaration, "What God has joined together, let no one separate" (10:9), reinstates the permanency of marriage for the Marcan community.

After this pronouncement, the scene changes. Jesus and his disciples move "in the house" (10:10), which indicates that Mark is updating Jesus' teaching and applying it to the members of his community.

Jesus tells the disciples, "Whoever divorces his wife and marries another commits adultery against her; and if she divorces her husband and marries another, she commits adultery" (10:11-12). The question is no longer divorce; now the question is one of sin. First, on the part of the man: "Whoever divorces his wife and marries another commits adultery against her" (10:11). Then Mark applies this teaching to Gentile Christian women, who were living under Greco-Roman law, which permitted a woman to divorce her husband. Jesus states, "And if she divorces her husband and marries another, *she* commits adultery" (10:12). Men and women are equal in human dignity. Divorce shames both of them.

Meditation: In which ways do you treat all people with equal human dignity?

Prayer: God, Creator of male and female, you not only join man and woman together in an inseparable bond, but you also instill in them an equal human dignity. Teach us to honor every human being with the dignity born of your image and likeness. We ask this through our Lord Jesus Christ, your Son, who lives and reigns with you and the Holy Spirit, one God, for ever and ever. Amen.

FAITH TO DO THE IMPOSSIBLE

Luke 17:5-10

Scripture: "Would any of you who had a servant who was plowing or tending sheep say to him when he came in from the fields, 'Go sit down at table at once'? Would you not rather say to him, 'Prepare something for me to eat. Put on your apron and wait on me while I eat and drink. You can eat and drink when I am finished'? Is he grateful to that servant because he did what was commanded?" (Luke 17:7-9)

Reflection: The section of Luke's Gospel about faith (17:5-6) and the story which illustrates the proper attitude of a servant (17:7-10) is intimately connected to the verses about forgiveness (17:1-4), which precede it. Here Jesus urges unlimited forgiveness on the part of those who follow him. Because of their influence, Christians are called to a responsible use of their influence in the world; this involves an unlimited forgiveness of those who sin against them and repent.

Because of this requirement of Jesus, the apostles ask him, "Increase our faith" (17:5). In order to practice unlimited forgiveness, they need an increase of faith. Unlimited forgiveness seems impossible.

Jesus' response, most likely a combination of two sayings — one from Mark (11:23) and one from Q (cf. Matthew 17:20, 21:21) — is that the apostles have enough faith to do the impossible: "If you have faith the size of a mustard seed, you could say to [this] mulberry tree, 'Be uprooted and planted in the sea,' and it would obey you" (17:6). With even the minutest amount of faith, the impossible — unlimited forgiveness — is possible.

For Luke, faith is not a type of magic whereby a person can control God. Faith is a personal response to God's initiative. God makes the first move; God offers the gift of faith. In faith then, people respond to God's offer of a relationship. Luke will demonstrate this in the story about the cleansing of ten lepers (10:11-19), one of whom returns in faith to glorify God. The author of this Gospel believes that people who respond to God's offer of faith, that is, live in faith, are able to do whatever God asks of them.

He quickly makes this point with a unique story that shows how limited we are to do anything meritorious. The man or woman who has received the gift of faith and responded to it as a servant does no more than what is required. The examples of slaves who do double duty — a farm hand plowing and tending sheep, and the domestic servant preparing and serving the evening meal — who receive no word of gratitude, illustrates the attitude that Christians are to possess.

Christians have no claim on God's graciousness. When they have forgiven unlimitedly, they have done no more than what God has commanded and given them the faith to accomplish. No Christian achievement can go beyond what is expected. There can be no superiority among Christians. "When you have done all you have been commanded, say, 'We are unprofitable servants; we have done what we were obliged to do'" (17:10).

Meditation: What recent experience reminds you that God gave you sufficient faith to do what is asked of you?

Prayer: Gracious God, faith is your gift to your people. With faith the size of a mustard seed, we are able to accomplish whatever it is you ask of us. We realize that we may never make a claim on this gift, but we are simply unprofitable servants who strive to do your will. Only you can make the impossible possible through the power of your Holy Spirit, who lives and reigns with you and your Son, our Lord Jesus Christ, one God, for ever and ever. Amen.

IMITATE THE SAMARITAN!
Luke 10:25-37

Scripture: A certain lawyer stood up to test him (Jesus) and said, "Teacher, what must I do to gain eternal life?" Jesus said to him, "What is written in the law? How do *you* read it?" He said in reply, "You shall love the Lord, your God, with all your heart, with all your being, with your strength, and with all your mind, and your neighbor as yourself." Then Jesus said to him, "You have answered correctly; do this and you will live" (Luke 10:25-28).

Reflection: The question from the scholar of the law about eternal life and the greatest commandment (10:25-28) serves to introduce the parable of the Good Samaritan (10:29-37) in Luke's Gospel, as well as the story of Martha and Mary (10:38-42), which follows the parable.

The question, which is asked by the scholar of the Mosaic law, deals with inheriting eternal life. The lawyer wants to know what he, as an individual, must do to guarantee a place for himself among the people of God (Jews), who would inherit eternal life. The question might be more clearly phrased: What must I do to insure my place among God's people? Since the man asking the question is a scholar, Jesus answers with a counter-question, which forces the lawyer to answer his own question. The answer he gives consists of the greatest commandment — love of God and neighbor. The parable of the Good Samaritan serves to illustrate how a person is to love one's neighbor. The story about Martha and Mary illustrates how a person is to love God.

The "man who fell victim to robbers as he went down from Jerusalem to Jericho" (10:30) is a Jew. The scholar who asked the original question is also a Jew. Jesus is a Jew. The Jews interpreted "neighbor" in terms of members of the same people or religious community, that is, fellow Jews. All other people were excluded.

The stripped and beaten man is left half-dead along the road. A priest, a fellow Jew and therefore a neighbor, "happened to be going down that road, but when he saw him, he passed by on the opposite side. Likewise, a Levite came to the place, and when he saw him, he passed by on the opposite side" (10:31-32). The Levite is another fellow Jew and, consequently, a neighbor.

Both the priest and the Levite behave correctly, according to the law. The laws concerning ritual cleanness and ritual uncleanness included one which rendered one unclean by touching a dead body. The priest and the Levite, then, did as the law instructed them to do and did not risk uncleanness (the possibility that the man along the road was dead) by touching the half-dead man.

Samaritans were not considered to be neighbors by Jews. In fact Jews despised Samaritans, who were descendants of a mixed population and possessed a mixed religion and a rival temple on Mount Gerazim.

In this parable, "a certain Samaritan who was on a journey came upon him (the half-dead man), and when he saw him was moved with compassion. He came up to him, poured oil and wine over his wounds and bandaged them. Then he set him on his own mount, brought him to an inn and took care of him. The next day when he left, he took out two silver coins and gave them to the innkeeper with the instruction, 'Take care of him and if you spend more than what I have given you, I will repay you on my way back'" (10:33-35).

The hero of the parable is obvious; it is the Samaritan, who was not considered to be a neighbor to the Jews. The priest and Levite end up as villains. They, who followed the law, did not love their neighbor — one of their own. The question, which is asked by Jesus, is hard to answer: "Which of these three, in your opinion, was neighbor to the man who ran into the robbers?" (10:36).

In order to answer this question, the scholar of the law must forget everything that he knows about the law and about who belongs to God's people and who does not. He has to reverse his previous presupposition of good priest and Levite and bad Samaritan to bad priest and Levite and good Samaritan. His stereotypes are challenged; he is called to conversion.

His response to Jesus' question, "The one who treated him with mercy" (10:37), indicates that he cannot even pronounce the name "Samaritan." He did not realize that when he asked, "Who is my neighbor?" (10:29), that he would have to declare that a Samaritan is his neighbor!

And there is more. "Jesus said to him, 'Go and do likewise'" (10:37). The scholar is told to go and behave like the Samaritan. He is instructed to imitate the Samaritan! Why? Because the Samaritan was neighbor to the half-dead man. Loving one's neighbor means meeting human needs wherever they are found. This is a sure sign, according to Jesus, that one is numbered among the people of God, which includes a much wider group than the lawyer ever envisioned. This is a sure sign that one has heard the word of God and is doing it.

Meditation: In which ways do you function as a neighbor? Who has been neighbor to you?

Prayer: God of all people, you instruct us to love all men and women as we love ourselves. When we tend to exclude others, remind us that we are all equal. When we tend to despise others, remind us that we are all brothers and sisters. Give us the gift of compassion that we might reach out to those who are in need. We ask this through our Lord Jesus Christ, your Son, who lives and reigns with you and the Holy Spirit, one God, for ever and ever. Amen.

HOW TO LOVE GOD

Luke 10:38-42

Scripture: [Jesus] entered a certain village where a woman whose name was Martha welcomed him. She had a sister Mary who seated herself at the Lord's feet and listened to him speak. Martha was distracted by all the serving, so she came up to him and said, "Lord, doesn't it matter to you that my sister has left me all by myself to do the serving? Tell her to help me" (Luke 10:38-40).

Reflection: The narrative about Martha and Mary (Luke 10:38-42) follows the parable of the Good Samaritan (10:29-37) and serves to illustrate the first part of the greatest commandment — love of God — recited by the lawyer in response to Jesus' counter-question to him regarding what the law says about inheriting eternal life. The parable of the Good Samaritan answers the lawyer's question about loving one's neighbor — the second part of the greatest commandment.

Hearing the word of God and doing it is a crucial theme throughout Luke's Gospel. The doing of the word of God has been illustrated in the most unlikely character — a Samaritan. Now, Luke must balance this doing with hearing, which illustrates one's love of God.

Mary represents the person who hears the word of God.

Luke portrays her as taking up the position of a disciple — sitting at the Lord's feet and listening to him speak. This is rather astonishing and cannot reflect first-century Palestinian Judaism, but it reveals another Lucan concern — Jesus' positive attitude toward women.

Mary is contrasted with Martha, who is "distracted by all the serving" (10:40). She is doing, but it is the wrong time for doing! Jesus says to her, "Martha, Martha, you are anxious and upset over many things. One thing only is necessary" (10:41-42). And what is this one thing? It is hearing the word of God.

Mary has recognized that Jesus is the host. He has come to serve her, to share with her the word of God. The position she has assumed — that of disciple, listener — illustrates that she is sharing in the main course before Martha can even get out of the kitchen! This is why "Mary has chosen the better part and it will not be taken from her" (10:42).

For Luke, loving God means submission to Jesus and receiving from him. Mary is focused on Jesus. Martha is distracted with doing. In attempting to meet all the dictates of hospitality and be the perfect host, she misses the true host in her midst. She functions as the Good Samaritan, but this is not the time for doing; this is the time for hearing. The way to become a good Martha is by being a good Mary.

As Luke presents this story, then, Mary becomes the example of hearing the word of God; she is the embodiment of what it means to love God with all one's heart, being, strength, and mind. The good Samaritan is the example of doing the word of God; he is the embodiment of what it means to love one's neighbor as one loves one's self.

Meditation: In which ways are you like Mary? In which ways are you like Martha?

Prayer: God of Mary and Martha, you teach us to love you with all our heart, with all our being, with all our strength, and with all our mind by sitting quietly at the feet of Jesus and listening to his word. You also teach us to love our neighbor as we love ourselves by doing the word that Jesus has given us. Through your Holy Spirit instill in us a greater love of you and our neighbor. We ask this through our Lord Jesus Christ, your Son, who lives and reigns with you and the Holy Spirit, one God, for ever and ever. Amen.

TEACH US TO PRAY

Luke 11:1-4

Scripture: He (Jesus) was praying in a certain spot, and when he was done, one of his disciples said to him, "Lord, teach us to pray just as John taught his disciples" (Luke 11:1).

Reflection: The first thirteen verses of chapter eleven of Luke's Gospel are concerned with prayer. Luke divides up the material into three sections — the Lord's Prayer (11:1-4), the need for persistence in prayer (11:5-8), and the effectiveness of prayer (11:9-13). This section of the Gospel (11:1-4) deals only with the Lord's Prayer.

Typical of any important event in Luke's Gospel, Jesus is found to be praying before he teaches the disciples how to pray. For Luke, this serves as a model for the Church. If Jesus prayed throughout his life, then Christians must also pray throughout their lives.

Luke's version of the Lord's Prayer is not the traditional Matthean form, which circulated among Jewish-Christians. It is the version which was used by Gentile-Christians near the end of the first century. Since Luke is writing primarily for Gentiles, he records the version of the prayer which they were already using at the time he was composing his Gospel.

The prayer addresses God as "Father." There is no Matthean "our." "Father" is the translation of the Hebrew "Abba," which means "Daddy." This is the traditional way that a Jewish child referred to his or her dad. Christians, according to Jesus, call upon God as their "Daddy."

This makes all Christians children of God and brothers and sisters. Communally, all the brothers and sisters declare that their Daddy's name is hallowed, holy, deserving of great respect. In other words, all that children can do is offer their Daddy the praise that is due him alone.

"Your kingdom come" (11:2), Christians pray. For Luke, the followers of Jesus already stand within the kingdom of God; it is already present. This petition asks God to bring the kingdom to its completion. When the fullness of the kingdom is made present, then God's rule will be fully acknowledged and his name fully reverenced by all his children.

God's children are dependent upon God for their daily sustenance. They pray, "Give us each day our daily bread" (11:3). However, this petition also points towards the fullness of the kingdom. Bread reminds the children of God of the manna in the desert and the multiplication of the loaves by Jesus, signs of the messianic banquet, a metaphor for the kingdom of God.

"Forgive us our sins for we ourselves forgive everyone in debt to us" (11:4), is the next petition. The children ask their Daddy to forgive them just as they are willing to forgive everyone who sins against them. Forgiveness is an important theme throughout Luke's Gospel. The forgiving, reconciling community is the kingdom of God being-made-present.

The last petition, "Do not subject us to the final test" (11:4), is a request by the members of the Christian community to be preserved from temptation and its source, the Evil One. In the final encounter between God and the Devil, Christians ask that they be spared any period of severe trial before the coming of the fullness of God's kingdom.

The communal nature of the prayer cannot be over emphasized. Luke's perspective is that it is the community, made up of brothers and sisters, that petitions God to "give us... our daily bread and forgive us… for we forgive everyone in debt to us, and do not subject us to the final test" (11:3-4). The prayer is the prayer of a community.

Meditation: In which ways have you experienced God supplying your community's daily needs, forgiving your community's sins, and bringing the kingdom closer to its fullness?

Prayer: "Father, hallowed be your name, your kingdom come. Give us each day our daily bread and forgive us our sins for we ourselves forgive everyone in debt to us, and do not subject us to the final test" (Luke 11:2-4). Amen.

ASK, SEEK, KNOCK

Luke 11:5-13

Scripture: "If any of you had a friend and you went to him at midnight and said to him, 'Friend, lend me three loaves of bread — a friend of mine has arrived from a journey and I have nothing to offer him.' I tell you, even if he doesn't get up and give you something because he is your friend, he will get up and give you whatever you need out of a sense of shame.... Ask and you will receive; seek and you will find; knock and the door will be opened to you" (Luke 11:5-6, 8-9).

Reflection: After preaching the Lord's Prayer that was used by Gentile-Christians, Luke presents a narrative about the importance of persistence in prayer (11:5-8) and a narrative about the effectiveness of prayer (11:9-13). In the Lord's Prayer, Luke teaches his Christian community how to pray. In these two sections which follow it, he teaches the community why it should pray.

The first reason why the community should pray is the example of Jesus, who "was praying" (11:1) before he taught his disciples how to pray.

The second reason is found in the unique Lucan parable about a man who, faced with the unexpected arrival of a friend at midnight, has no bread to offer him. So, he goes to a neighbor's house, knocks on the door, and hears from within a voice which says, "Go away and leave me alone." However, the man at the door continues to knock until the friend within gets up and gives him the three loaves of bread which he needed.

The motivation for getting up and giving the man the bread

115

is probably not friendship but, rather, how to get rid of the man without creating an embarrassing scene. In other words, knowing this the man on the outside persists until he gets what he wants. This type of unrelenting insistence will move God to respond to the requests of Christians, according to Luke. God is eager to answer prayers. Christians should pray because God wants to answer their prayers.

The third reason Luke gives for Christian prayer is that it is effective. God does answer prayer, Jesus declares. "The one who asks, receives; and the one who seeks, finds; and to the one who knocks, the door will be opened" (11:10). Christians pray because God answers them.

The fourth reason given for prayer centers on the good gifts that God gives to his children. Christians should pray because God gives only good gifts. Just as a father would not "hand his son a snake when he asks for a fish, or a scorpion when he asks for an egg" (11:11-12), so "how much more will the Father in heaven give the Holy Spirit to those who ask him?" (11:13).

Sinful people give only good gifts to their children. God, who is not sinful, will give greater gifts to his children. The greatest of these gifts is himself — the Holy Spirit. Christians should pray because he gives himself — his Holy Spirit — to his children.

The gift of the Holy Spirit is, of course, one of Luke's primary themes, and it brings the author back full circle to the beginning of this whole section on prayer. In the gift of the Spirit, who has been given to the Church, the kingdom of God has come. It is the Father's desire to give the kingdom to his children and, through them, to bring it to its fullness.

Meditation: In which single instance in your life of prayer have you persisted until God gave you what you wanted? In which way was the Holy Spirit involved in your persistent request?

Prayer: Father, through the teaching and example of Jesus, your Son, you have revealed to us your eagerness to answer our prayers. Through the works of the Holy Spirit in our lives, guide us in prayer. Give us confidence that when we ask, we will receive; when we seek, we will find; and when we knock, the door will be opened to the kingdom, where you live and reign for ever and ever. Amen.

BY THE FINGER OF GOD

Luke 11:15-26

Scripture: "Every kingdom divided against itself will be laid waste, and house divided against house will fall.... If I drive out demons by the finger of God, then the kingdom of God has come upon you.... Whoever is not with me is against me, and whoever does not gather with me scatters" (Luke 11:17, 20, 23).

Reflection: This section of Luke's Gospel (11:14-36) deals with the author's perspective of Jesus as an exorcist and the questions this raised for his community. The weekday lectionary cycle includes only a portion of this material (11:15-32) and divides it between three separate days. Much of the entire section has parallels in Matthew and Mark (Matthew 12:23-30; 9:34, 12:38, 16:1, 12:43-45; Mark 3:20-27; 8:11; 9:40), but in these Gospels there is no systematic treatment or unifying pattern to match what Luke has done.

Luke characteristically organizes his material around an action of Jesus, which is followed by an accusation and a question from the crowd and two replies by Jesus. The smaller section for today (11:15-26) omits Jesus' action, the "driving out" of "a demon that was mute" (11:14), a uniquely Lucan verse. Furthermore, the section only includes Jesus' reply to the accusation; that is, "by the power of Beelzebul, the prince of demons, he drives out demons" (11:15).

117

Jesus' reply to the question, that is a request "for a sign from heaven" (11:16), is partially omitted; only 11:29-32 are used and 11:33-36 are entirely omitted from the weekday cycle of readings.

To declare that Jesus drives out demons by Beelzebul, the prince of demons, is to call him a magician. Jesus, accused of using demonic power to achieve his end, gives two responses to this accusation.

First, Jesus declares the accusation to be illogical. "Every kingdom divided against itself will be laid waste, and house divided against house will fall. Now if Satan is divided against himself, how will his kingdom stand?" (11:17-18). In other words, division leads to destruction. Satan would not cast himself out! To do so would be to destroy himself.

Second, the accusation is inconsistent. "If I drive out demons by Beelzebul, by whom do your own people drive them out? Therefore, they will be your judges" (11:19-20).

There were other Jewish exorcists, who were active at the same time as Jesus. These performed exorcisms without being identified with Beelzebul. Therefore, to identify Jesus with him and not the other exorcists is inconsistent logic.

Jesus' miraculous exorcism does not mean that Jesus is a magician; it does mean that his power is different from that of other Jewish exorcists. For Luke, what the exorcism does mean is that "the kingdom of God has come" (11:20). Jesus is the stronger man, who has attacked the fully armed Satan and taken away his armor, upon which he relied, and distributed the spoils (cf. 11:21-22). By the "finger of God" (11:20) Jesus declares the kingdom of God to be present and Satan defeated.

It is easy to determine which side people are on. Whoever is not with Jesus is against him, and whoever does not gather with him scatters (cf. 11:23). Those who accused Jesus of acting by the power of Beelzebul must look upon what side of the line they stand.

For those who do not believe that the kingdom of God has

come, exorcism is useless. The unclean spirit may be cast out of someone, but it will return with "seven other spirits more wicked than itself" (11:26). Then, "the last condition of that person is worse than the first" (11:26). It is only the acceptance of God's rule, God's kingdom, in a person's life that prevents the return of the demon.

Meditation: In which ways have you experienced the finger of God establishing his kingdom in your life?

Prayer: God of healing, Jesus, your Servant and your Son, freed those who were possessed by disease. He made the lame walk, the dumb speak, and the deaf hear, and in so doing he demonstrated that your kingdom had come, your rule had already begun. Heal us of everything that keeps us from following Jesus with a lively faith, and bring to fruition the kingdom you share with him and the Holy Spirit, one God, for ever and ever. Amen.

HEAR AND OBSERVE

Luke 11:27-28

Scripture: A woman in the crowd raised her voice and said to him (Jesus), "Blessed is the womb that bore you and the breasts at which you nursed." He replied, "Rather, blessed are those who hear the word of God and keep it" (Luke 11:27-28).

Reflection: The two verses (11:27-28) about true blessedness are included in the section of Luke's Gospel which consists of Jesus' response to the crowd's charge that he was a magician, that is, that he cast out demons "by the power of Beelzebul, the prince of demons." In fact, these two verses (27-28) form the conclusion of Jesus' two-pronged response and commentary.

Within this context, then, the woman from the crowd who calls out, "Blessed is the womb that bore you and the breasts at which you nursed" (11:27), is declaring the human source of Jesus' life — his mother — to be blessed, that is, favored by God. Jesus, however, corrects her.

"Blessed are those who hear the word of God and observe it" (11:28), he declares in a beatitude. Those who are favored by God listen to the word of God and recognize that God's kingdom has come. This is a re-emphasis of a favorite theme for Luke — hearing and doing the word of God.

Jesus is one who has heard the word of God, and, through the exorcism that he performed, he has observed the word of God.

It is only the rule of God over human life that can prevent the return of the demonic into a person's life. Therefore, a person must respond properly to God's kingdom. The one making the proper response, the blessed person, is the one who hears and observes the word of God.

Meditation: In which ways are you blessed because you hear and observe the word of God?

Prayer: God of the spoken word, at the beginning of creation you pronounced "earth," "light," and "darkness," and these came to be. On the last day you uttered "man" and "woman," and you declared people to be made in your image and likeness. When they sinned, you did not abandon them, but through Moses you delivered the word of your law. When man and woman wandered away from your covenant, you invited them through your word spoken by your prophets to repent. In the fullness of time you spoke through your incarnate word, Jesus the Christ, who proclaimed your kingdom. He declared those blessed who heard his word and observed it. Open our ears and hearts that we might receive your word with joy, and then make us obedient to that which we have heard. We ask this through our Lord Jesus Christ, your Son, who lives and reigns with you and the Holy Spirit, one God, for ever and ever. Amen.

BAD AND GOOD ALIKE
Matthew 22:1-14

Scripture: "[The king] said to his servants, 'The wedding feast is ready, but those who were invited were not worthy to come. Go out, therefore, into the main roads and invite to the wedding feast whomever you find.' The servants went out into the streets and gathered everyone they found, bad and good alike, and the hall was filled with guests" (Matthew 22:8-10).

Reflection: The parable of the wedding feast (Matthew 22:1-14), is addressed to the chief priests, the Pharisees (cf. 21:45), and possibly, the elders of the people (cf. 21:23). The source of the parable is Q (cf. Luke 14:15-24); Luke has retained more of the original parable in comparison to Matthew's allegorized version, which is typical of this author.

According to Matthew, the king — God — gives a wedding feast (the image of final salvation as found in Isaiah 25:6) for his son — Jesus. The invited guests — the people of Israel — "refused to come" (22:3), when summoned two different times by the king's servants, the prophets.

The second time the servants are sent to the invited guests, they are told to tell them, "'Behold, I have prepared my banquet, my oxen and fattened calves have been killed, and everything is ready; come to the feast.' Some ignored the invitation and went off, one to his farm, another to his business. The rest laid hold of his servants, treated them shamefully, and killed them" (22:4-6).

The parable-allegory emphasizes the strong desire of the king to have the invited guests attend his banquet, to enter into final salvation. The prophet Isaiah is loudly echoed: "The Lord of hosts will provide for all peoples a feast of rich food and choice wines, juicy, rich food and pure, choice wines" (Isaiah 25:6). Because the invited guests refused the double invitation the "king was enraged and sent his troops, destroyed those murderers, and burned their city" (22:7).

This action of the king is unique to Matthew; it reflects the destruction of Jerusalem by the Romans in 70 A.D. The author is declaring that Jerusalem was destroyed because Israel refused the invitation to the kingdom of heaven. The reader must remember that the destruction of Jerusalem by the Romans was a trauma for both Jews and Jewish-Christians. It was an event that should never have happened but did. The city was considered to be God's dwelling place on earth; therefore, it was thought to be indestructible.

Like Mark and Luke, Matthew attempts to give meaning to this event and to issue a warning to the Church about God's judgment. Matthew had alerted the reader to this event earlier in the Gospel when he narrated the visit of the magi (2:1-12). The magi followed a star until they got to Jerusalem, where they lost it. Jerusalem, the city of light, was no longer the city of light. The magi discovered that they had to leave Jerusalem and travel to Bethlehem, where they would find the true light, Jesus. As they left the city, the star reappeared! After Jerusalem was destroyed and Matthew had declared what he believed to be God's judgment on Israel, he indicates that now a new group of people has been invited to the wedding feast. This new group consists of Gentiles (magi in 2:1-12) and those from the main roads and the streets. These are the supposed outcasts, with whom Jesus has associated throughout the Gospel.

"Bad and good alike" (22:10) enter the hall. Again, a typical Matthean theme enters the parable. Matthew's view is that no one, except God, can judge who is in the kingdom and who is not. This was illustrated in the parable of the weeds among the wheat (13:24-30) and its explanation (13:36-43) and the parable of the fishnet (13:47-50). According to Matthew, good and bad co-exist until God's day of judgment.

The day of judgment comes as a unique Matthean addition to the parable of the wedding feast: "When the king came in to meet the guests he saw a man there not dressed in a wedding garment. He said to him 'My friend, how is it that you came in here without a wedding garment?' But the man was reduced to silence" (22:11-12). The wedding garment represents the repentance and change of heart, which ought to be characteristic of Christians who want to enter the kingdom of heaven. There may also be an allusion here to Christians who entered the Christian community and then, because of their failure to repent of their sins, were expelled (cf. 18:15-20).

The fate of such Christians will parallel that of the Jews who have rejected Jesus; that is, they will be cast "into the darkness outside, where there will be wailing and gnashing of teeth" (22:13), Matthew's favorite way of describing final condemnation.

The final verse of the parable, "Many are invited, but few are chosen" (22:14), is also Matthew's final warning to the members of the Church to take their invitation seriously. Otherwise, some of them may find themselves not numbered among the smaller group of those chosen for the kingdom of heaven. Matthew's parabolic allegory spans the whole of salvation history. It involves God's constant invitation and the free response of people. If God's invitation is not taken seriously, then the invitation is offered to those who will respond. Even among these, however, there may be some who are excluded from the kingdom of heaven. The final judgment is left to God (cf. 25:31-46).

Meditation: In your life what characterizes you as a person who has accepted God's invitation to the wedding banquet? Or, what does your wedding garment look like?

Prayer: God of the wedding feast, on the mountain of your salvation you promise a banquet of rich foods and choice wines. We thank you for the invitation to be your guests at the feast. Guide us in our response; open our ears and our hearts to hear your servants, the prophets, and your Son, our Lord Jesus Christ. Clothe us in the wedding garment of repentance that we might be counted among the chosen in the kingdom, where you live and reign with Jesus and the Holy Spirit, one God, for ever and ever. Amen.

GO, SELL, GIVE, FOLLOW

Mark 10:17-30

Scripture: As he (Jesus) was setting out on the road, a man ran up, knelt down before him, and asked him, "Good teacher, what must I do to gain eternal life?" Jesus answered him. "You know the commandments...." He replied and said to him, "Teacher, I have observed all of these from my youth." Jesus, looking at him, loved him and said to him, "One thing is left for you to do. Go, sell what you have, and give to the poor and you will have treasure in heaven; then come, follow me." At that statement his face fell, and he went away sad, for he had many possessions (Mark 10:17-22).

Reflection: Mark's story of the rich man (10:17-22) and the teaching of Jesus about the difficulty of entering the kingdom of God (10:23-27) and the reward offered to those who have left everything to follow Jesus (10:28-31) occur in the second half of the Gospel, which is concerned with the true understanding of discipleship. In the section preceding this one (10:13-16), Jesus has specified that discipleship involves accepting "the kingdom of God like a child" (10:15), that is, in total dependence upon obedience to the Gospel.

This theme is developed further in this section (10:17-31), although the Sunday cycle omits the last verse — "But many who are first will be last, and the last will be first" (10:31), a reference to the reversal of roles that usually accompanies any of Jesus' stories.

The narrative about the rich man begins with the man in a position of worshiping Jesus — kneeling down before him (cf. 10:17). Already, Mark has revealed that this is not a historical account, but it is meant for the members of his community who already worship Jesus as the Messiah.

"Good teacher, what must I do to gain eternal life?" (10:17) the rich man asks Jesus. To gain eternal life is the same as to enter the kingdom of God. The emphasis of the question is on what the rich man must *do*, as if the kingdom of God can be earned.

Immediately, Jesus rebukes the man by asking, "Why do you call me good? No one is good but God alone" (10:18). God is the source of all goodness. God alone grants the gift of eternal life. "For human beings it is impossible, but not for God. All things are possible for God" (10:27).

Salvation cannot be earned or inherited, Mark is telling his community.

The rich man has tried to earn salvation. After Jesus reminds him of the commandments, all of which deal with relationships with his neighbor — killing, adultery, stealing, bearing false witness, defrauding, honoring father and mother — the rich man declares, "Teacher, I have observed all of these from my youth" (10:20). Because the rich man has observed all of these, he should be an heir of the kingdom.

But according to Jesus, this is not enough. Keeping the commandments is not enough. "One thing is left for you to do. Go, sell what you have, and give to the poor and you will have treasure in heaven; then come, follow me" (10:21), Jesus tells him as he looks at him and loves him.

Mark is making two important points about discipleship.

First, discipleship involves more than the keeping of the commandments. If this were not the case, then the rich man would have already inherited eternal life.

Second, discipleship involves the renunciation of riches, a sign of security, power, social status, and God's favor. Treasure in heaven can be had only by stripping oneself of treasure on earth and using one's wealth to serve others. By giving his riches to the poor, the man would pile up treasure in heaven.

Underlying this understanding is a concept in the ancient world that there were only so many goods and riches to be had. Those who had them also had an obligation to share with those who did not have any; otherwise, there was no way for those who were poor to get any. In Mark's Gospel, Jesus defines discipleship as total identity with the poor, the powerless.

Discipleship involves the relinquishing of all possessions and the distribution of these to those who have no wealth. This goes beyond the keeping of the commandments concerning one's neighbor. It is not sufficient not to have killed, not to have committed adultery, not to have stolen, not to have borne false witness, not to have defrauded, to have honored father and mother. More is demanded of authentic followers of Jesus — namely, a sharing of one's wealth with one's neighbors.

The rich man in the story "went away sad, for he had many possessions" (10:22); he was not able to reduce himself to the level of poverty. Mark rejects the popular notion concerning riches and declares wealth to be a false security when it comes to entering the kingdom of God. The fact is that there can be no security to entering the kingdom of God. Eternal life is God's gift, which cannot be earned.

The story gives the author of this Gospel an opportunity to elaborate on the message. Now Jesus looks around at his disciples, Mark's community, and says, "How hard it will be for those with wealth to enter the kingdom of God!" (10:23).

The disciples are amazed because Jesus has just reversed the popular notion concerning riches — that is, that wealth was a sign of favor from God. Riches become a wall between God and people.

In a second address to the disciples, Jesus declares, "Children, how hard it is to enter the kingdom of God!" (10:24). By calling the disciples "children," Mark makes a reference back to the preceding section of the Gospel where Jesus states, "Whoever does not accept the kingdom of God like a child will not enter it" (10:15).

Marcan hyperbole now enters the dialogue: "It is easier for a camel to pass through the eye of a needle than for one who is rich to enter the kingdom of God" (10:25). In other words, it is impossible for a rich man to enter the kingdom of God, if he attempts to earn it through wealth. The way to the kingdom of God is not a human achievement, but God's gift. Riches have nothing to do with it.

Riches are given to some people to be shared with others because these others are one's neighbors. When it comes to entrance to the kingdom of God, all people are equal; all are dependent on God for salvation. It makes no difference whether one is rich or not.

Those who have riches, however, have an obligation to care for those who do not. Failure to do this will bar them from eternal life.

Those who, like Peter, "have given up everything and followed" (10:28) Jesus will inherit "eternal life in the age to come" (10:30). Discipleship is the door to eternal life. Discipleship involves the renunciation of riches; but it also includes the gracious gift of God — his kingdom — for those who are willing to follow his Son. When put in the Marcan scale, the side marked discipleship outweighs that marked riches.

Meditation: In which ways have you renounced your riches and cared for your neighbor's needs in order to be a disciple of Jesus?

Prayer: Good and gracious God, you have given us riches that we might share our wealth with our neighbor. Guide our use of the goods of this world, and do not permit them to become a hindrance to our inheriting eternal life. Teach us to rely on you alone for our salvation, for you make possible the impossible. Make us genuine disciples of Jesus, your Son, who lives and reigns with you and the Holy Spirit, one God, for ever and ever. Amen.

HAVE PITY ON US!

Luke 17:11-19

Scripture: As he (Jesus) was entering a village he was met by ten lepers who stood at a distance from him and raised their voice, saying, "Jesus, Master! Have mercy on us!" When he saw them, he said, "Go show yourselves to the priests." And it happened that as they were on their way they were cleansed. Now one of them, realizing he had been healed, returned, glorifying God in a loud voice; and he fell at the feet of Jesus and thanked him. He was a Samaritan (Luke 17:12-16).

Reflection: The account of the cleansing of ten lepers (Luke 17:11-19) is unique to Luke's Gospel. In the story Luke deals with the relationship between salvation and healing, an issue for his community. It is difficult not to miss the obvious source for Luke's story — the healing of Naaman the Syrian at the command of Elisha in 2 Kings 5:1-19.

After washing in the Jordan seven times, Naaman was cured of his leprosy. Then, he returned to Elisha who had told him that he would be cured by plunging into the river, and he confesses his faith in the God of Israel. "Now I know that there is no God in all the earth, except in Israel" (2 Kings 5:15), he declares. Thus, a miracle-story becomes the occasion for the conversion of a foreigner.

The cleansing of ten lepers is a similar two-part story, which consists of a miracle and the conversion of a foreigner. Like the story about Naaman, the emphasis in the account is not on the miracle but on the faith of one of the characters in the story.

Luke sets the stage by portraying Jesus as traveling "through Samaria and Galilee" (17:11) in order to make some geographical sense with the presentation of a Samaritan later and to remind the reader that Jesus is making his way to Jerusalem.

As he narrates the action of the ten lepers, Luke accurately portrays the distancing and the avoidance of physical contacts which was required of lepers by those not infected with the contagious disease. In the ancient world leprosy was defined as any type of skin disease and not necessarily Hansen's disease, as it is known today.

The ten lepers address Jesus as Master and call out, "Have mercy on us!" (17:13). The Greek word for "mercy" can also be translated as "compassion" or "pity." It means to have a feeling for another person which comes from one's guts. In this sense, Luke echoes his other story about a Samaritan, who treated a half-dead man with mercy (cf. 10:29-37).

Jesus tells the lepers, "Go show yourselves to the priests" (17:14). Here, Luke echoes his other story about the cleansing of a leper (cf. 5:12-14) and the detailed instructions in the book of Leviticus (13:1-46; 14:2-9) concerning the re-admittance of a person who has had leprosy into the mainstream of society. The Old Testament priests functioned like a primitive health department.

Luke narrates nothing about a cure. All he writes is, "They were made clean while they were on the way" (17:14). In effect, the reader concludes that Jesus has acted like a good Samaritan and had pity on the lepers. All ten are healed (cf. 17:17). But "one of them, realizing he had been healed, returned, glorifying God in a loud voice; and he fell at the feet of Jesus and thanked him" (17:16). Jesus said to him, "Stand up and go; your faith has saved you" (17:19).

For Luke, the inauguration of the kingdom by Jesus brings healing. Therefore, all ten lepers are cured. Luke's concern is with salvation. Only one leper acknowledges what God has done in Jesus. Only this one leper professes a faith that saves him. Salvation is professing faith in God's gift of Jesus, who delivers people from sin and alienation.

The irony is that the leper who was cured "was a Samaritan" (17:16). The author is always presenting the most unlikely of people who recognize God's activity and respond with praise and thanks. The faith of this foreigner is contrasted to that of the other nine Jews, who did not return to give thanks to God. Thus, Luke gives the reader a hint of how the Gospel will be rejected by the Jews and enthusiastically accepted by foreigners, Gentiles, in the Acts of the Apostles.

Luke carefully makes his point that it is faith that saves. God's gracious gift of salvation is offered to all people through Jesus. All people need to do is to imitate the healed Samaritan leper by responding in faith and gratitude to God's gift. The kingdom of God has already begun; with faith anyone can share it.

Meditation: Today, who do you think are the foreigners who respond in faith to God's gracious gift of salvation through Jesus?

Prayer: Saving God, once you rescued your people from Egyptian slavery and led them to a promised land flowing with milk and honey. Time and time again your people broke your covenant, but you called them back to the waters of your grace. In these last days you have revealed your saving gift through Jesus, your Son, who announced the presence of your kingdom. Give us faith to respond to your gift that we might glorify and praise you, your Son, and the Holy Spirit, one God, for ever and ever. Amen.

SIGN OF JONAH
Luke 11:29-32

Scripture: "Just as Jonah became a sign to the Ninevites, so will the Son of Man be to this generation.... The men of Nineveh will stand up at the judgment against this generation and condemn it, because at the preaching of Jonah they repented, and, behold, one greater than Jonah is here" (Luke 11:30, 32).

Reflection: This section (11:29-32) of Luke's Gospel is part of the unified treatment of material concerning Jesus as an exorcist. It functions as the first and second parts of a three-part answer to the request "for a sign from heaven" (11:16), which occurred earlier in the narrative.

In the first part of the answer that confirms that Jesus' action as exorcist is by God's authority is the "sign of Jonah" (11:29). Luke understands the sign of Jonah to be Jonah's call to repentance. At the preaching of Jonah the men of Nineveh repented (cf. 11:32). The sign of Jesus' authority, then, is his prophetic call to repentance; he is the "one greater than Jonah" (11:32).

The second part of the answer involves mention of "the Queen of the South," who "will rise up at the judgment against the men of this generation and will condemn them, because she came from the ends of the earth to hear the wisdom of Solomon" (11:31). The Queen of the South, along with the men of Nineveh, represents the Gentiles, who will condemn Israel.

135

She is held up as an example of one who made the correct response to the wisdom of Solomon. The Ninevites are held up as an example of those who made the correct response to the preaching of Jonah. Israel continues to fail to make the proper response, "and, behold, there is one greater than Solomon" (11:31) and Jonah here — Jesus whose ministry is filled with the Father's gift of the Holy Spirit.

The idea of Gentiles witnessing against Jews at the judgment was contrary to Jewish belief. As typical of Jesus in Luke's Gospel, the usual is reversed. Jesus' second-part answer to the demand for a sign of his authority is to declare that Gentiles respond to the call to repentance better than do the Jews.

The third part of Jesus' response (11:33-36) is omitted from the weekday cycle of readings.

The person who wants to know whether or not Jesus acts on God's authority in his exorcisms must first hear his call to repentance. Repentance, then, enables a person to recognize in Jesus, the Son of Man, the presence of God's kingdom which conquers the demonic. This is the sign "to this generation" (11:30).

Meditation: What functions as a sign of your need for repentance?

Prayer: God of signs, you sent Jonah to preach repentance to the Ninevites, who responded in sackcloth and ashes. You gave your servant, Solomon, great wisdom so that the Queen of the South came to sit at his feet. You have given us Jesus, your Son, the sign of your kingdom's presence. Enable us to respond with repentance. Move us to listen to Jesus' wisdom. Help us to recognize the kingdom, where you live and reign with Jesus and the Holy Spirit, one God, for ever and ever. Amen.

WASH UP!
Luke 11:37-41

Scripture: "Oh, you Pharisees! Although you cleanse the outside of the cup and the dish, inside you are filled with greed and evil. You fools! Did not the maker of the outside make the inside as well?" (Luke 11:39-40).

Reflection: This sub-section (11:37-41) begins a three-day selection from the section on the denunciation of the Pharisees and the scholars of the law (11:37-54) of Luke's Gospel. The author ties this Q material (cf. Matthew 23:25-26) into that which preceded it by demonstrating what it means to keep, or observe, the word of God (cf. 11:28).

The setting is the house of a Pharisee who "invited [Jesus] to dine at his home" (11:37). The reader should automatically recall an earlier and similar situation where another Pharisee invited Jesus to dine with him (7:36-50); in that narrative Luke dealt with Jesus' relationship with sinners. Now, he will deal with Jesus' own behavior at table. "He entered and reclined at table to eat. The Pharisee was amazed to see that he did not observe the prescribed washing before the meal" (11:37-38). While eating was supposed to be a sign of a unitive relationship between people, any meal with the Pharisees in Luke's Gospel becomes an occasion for Jesus to point out the division that exists.

Jesus immediately dismisses the issue of his own behavior and concentrates on the social actions of the Pharisees, who are careful about external practices but pay no attention to their inner attitudes, without which the external practices lose their authenticity.

The Pharisees are compared to cups and dishes, which are washed on the outside but remain dirty on the inside. From the outside the cups and dishes look clean, but upon closer examination a person can see that they are not fit for food or drink. Such pretension leads Jesus to declare the Pharisees to be fools. "Did not the maker of the outside make the inside as well?" (11:40). In other words, the Pharisees, who supposedly heard the word of God and observed it scrupulously, were only pretending to observe it. Their inner attitude did not harmonize with their external expression.

Jesus tells them, "But give what's within as alms and then everything will be clean for you" (11:41). Almsgiving was considered one of the greatest expressions of the true unity of all people, for those who had more than others shared what they had with those who had less. True almsgiving expressed the gift of oneself to another and fulfilled the intention of God, who shared his gift of creation with his people.

By giving alms the Pharisees have the opportunity to achieve a harmony between their inner attitude and their external display. They cannot give alms and at the same time be "filled with greed and evil" (11:39). Then, "everything will be clean" (11:41).

Jesus can dismiss with ritual washing before meals because he demonstrates in his ministry the harmony between an inner attitude of hearing God's word and an external practice of observing it. Of course for Luke the social issue is wider than that of ritual washing before meals; it involves "greed and evil" (11:39). A follower of Jesus cannot be like the Pharisees, who look good on the outside but are a complete contradiction on the inside.

Meditation: In which ways do your internal attitudes harmonize with your external actions? In which ways do they not?

Prayer: Creator God, you formed man and woman from the clay of the earth and breathed into them your own life. You gave them dominion over all that you made. When they sinned, you promised to send your Son, who would teach them how to observe your word. Remove our blindness that we may see our evil. Make known our pretenses that we may be clean. Enable our almsgiving to be authentic. We ask this through our Lord Jesus Christ, your Son, who lives and reigns with you and the Holy Spirit, one God, for ever and ever. Amen.

LEAVE A GOOD
IMPRESSION

Luke 11:42-46

Scripture: "Woe to you Pharisees! You pay tithes on mint and rue and every garden herb, but you neglect justice and the love of God. You love the seats of honor in the synagogues and greetings in the marketplaces. You are like unmarked graves over which people unknowingly walk" (Luke 11:42-44).

Reflection: This sub-section (11:42-46) of Luke's Gospel is part of a larger section (11:37-54) whose setting is the home of a Pharisee who invited Jesus to dine with him. Here, Luke presents three "woes" against the Pharisees and the first of three "woes" against the scholars of the law. Luke's sources are Q and possibly Mark.

The first woe against the Pharisees pronounced by Jesus concerns tithing. Luke continues to contrast the Pharisees to those who hear the word of God and observe it. The Pharisees "pay tithes on mint and rue and every garden herb" (11:42), but this is a minor manner when compared to "justice and the love of God" (11:42), which they neglect. "Justice and the love of God... should have been practiced without overlooking the others" (11:42). Therefore, while they seem to be observing the word of God, the Pharisees have in fact missed the point of God's word — justice.

The second woe against the Pharisees concerns their love of "seats of honor in the synagogues and greetings in the market-places" (11:43). Here, Luke points out that public recognition does not necessarily mean that someone is observing the word of God. In fact it may be all outward display meant to impress others; there is no inward attitude that corresponds to one's actions.

The third woe declares that the Pharisees are "like unmarked graves over which people unknowingly walk" (11:44). Any type of contact with the dead, graves, or bones meant ritual impurity. Here Jesus accuses the Pharisees of contaminating others who have no idea that they are being infected. From all appearances, it looks like they are leading others down the correct road; however, they are really leading other people astray.

The first of three woes against the scholars of the law, experts in the Mosaic law, is the result of a statement by one of the scholars to Jesus: "Teacher, by saying this you are insulting us too" (11:45). The woe accuses them of imposing "on people burdens hard to carry," but they "do not lift one finger to touch them" (11:46). In other words, the scholars of the law impose the law on others, but they themselves do not observe it; they are hypocrites.

The woes are aimed at religious leaders who give the impression that they are hearing and observing the word of God but they possess no inner attitude which motivates their observation. Such hypocrisy cannot be a part of the life of a follower of Jesus, according to Luke.

Meditation: In which way do you get caught up in leaving a good impression instead of hearing and observing the word of God?

Prayer: God of justice, you always call your people to integrity through your law and your covenant. When we neglect justice, remind us of the good Samaritan. When we seek recognition, teach us again about Martha and Mary. When we lead others the wrong way, turn us around. Send your Holy Spirit to open our ears and hearts to hear your word and to guide our observance of it. We ask this through our Lord Jesus Christ, your Son, who lives and reigns with you and the Holy Spirit, one God, for ever and ever. Amen.

MEMORIALS TO MURDERS

Luke 11:47-54

Scripture: "Woe to you! You build the monuments of the prophets whom your ancestors killed.... You have taken away the key of knowledge. You yourselves would not enter and you hindered those who were trying to go in" (Luke 11:47, 52).

Reflection: This sub-section (11:47-54) of Luke's Gospel is part of a larger section of denunciations of the Pharisees and the scholars of the law (11:37-54). Luke's source is Q and, possibly, Mark. In this sub-section Luke presents the second and third woes against the scholars of the Torah, experts in Mosaic law, and concludes the narrative with an editorial comment about how "the scribes and Pharisees began to act with hostility toward [Jesus] and to question him about many things, for they were plotting to catch him at something he might say" (11:54).

The second woe against the scholars of the law concerns "the monuments of the prophets whom [their] ancestors killed" (11:47). Jesus argues that they "bear witness and approve of their ancestors' deeds" (11:48) for, while their ancestors killed the prophets, the scholars of the law build their monuments. Therefore, "this generation will be responsible for their blood!" (11:51), Jesus declares.

"This generation will be responsible for the blood of all the prophets shed since the foundation of the world, from the blood

141

of Abel to the blood of Zechariah who died between the altar and the sanctuary of the Temple" (11:5-51). Abel represents the first murder recorded in the Old Testament (cf. Genesis 4:8), and Zechariah represents the last murder presented in the Hebrew canon of the Old Testament (cf. 2 Chronicles 24:20-22).

Luke stretches the guilt for the murders of the prophets to the time of his writing by including the "apostles" (11:49). The mission of the Church, identified with the apostles in this journey-to-Jerusalem section of Luke's Gospel, is connected with the mission of Israel, identified with the prophets. Just as the prophets were killed and persecuted by their contemporaries, so were the apostles.

The third woe against the scholars of the law accused them of taking away "the key of knowledge" (11:52), that is, the word of God as delivered by prophets and apostles. The scholars of the law did not enter, that is, they did not observe the word of God, and by killing the prophets and the apostles, they "hindered those who were trying to enter" (11:52).

These last two woes against the scholars of the law set the stage for the next part of Luke's Gospel, which focuses on the appropriate response to persecution.

Meditation: Which modern prophets do you "kill" by not listening to them?

Prayer: God of prophets and apostles, you sent your prophets to awaken your people to your word and to call them back to you. You sent your apostles to preach the kingdom of Jesus, your Son, and to awaken your people to your presence in the world. When we sin, call us back through the prophets. When we forget your kingdom, remind us through the apostles. We ask this through our Lord Jesus Christ, who lives and reigns with you and the Holy Spirit, one God, for ever and ever. Amen.

GOD CARES

Luke 12:1-7

Scripture: "I say to you, my friends, Fear not those who kill the body and after that can do no more" (Luke 12:4).

Reflection: The last third of Luke's Gospel's chapter eleven, which contains the denunciation of the Pharisees and the scholars of the law (11:37-54), prepares for the beginning of chapter twelve and Jesus' exhortation to his disciples, "Beware of the leaven — that is, the hypocrisy — of the Pharisees" (12:1).

This sub-section (12:1-7) of the Gospel is part of a larger section (12:1-12), which deals with the appropriate response to persecution. Furthermore, 12:1-12 is the first of three areas of life that the Lucan Jesus addresses in this larger unit of the Gospel, namely 12:1-48. The addresses on three different areas of life are climaxed with a section on the divisive effects of Jesus' ministry (12:49-53), after which Jesus addresses the crowds (12:54-13:21) and issues a call for conversion.

Luke's source for the first sub-section (12:1-7) of this larger unit of his Gospel is Mark (8:15) and Q (cf. Matthew 10:26-33). The material is ordered in such a way as to reflect the appropriate response that Christians should make after the resurrection of Jesus.

The scene opens with a description of the crowd: "Meanwhile, so many people were crowding together that they were trampling on each other" (12:1). Luke has mentioned the crowd before. As the journey continues and gets closer to Jerusalem the size of the crowds increases. In this way the author is able to characterize the popularity of Jesus and his disciples, as well as the scope of the missionary challenge of the early Church.

The warning against hypocrisy, that is, not being inside what one appears to be externally, is issued by Jesus to the crowd. Sooner or later, either during a time of persecution or at the last judgment, there is "nothing concealed that will not be revealed, nor hidden that will not be made known. Therefore whatever you have said in the darkness will be heard in the light, and what you have whispered behind closed doors will be proclaimed from the housetops" (12:2-3).

What leads to hypocrisy is fear, especially during a time of persecution. Jesus exhorts the crowd (early Church), "Fear not those who kill the body and after that can do no more" (12:4). Followers of Jesus should have no fear of being persecuted and killed.

However, they should "be afraid of the one who after killing has the power to cast into Gehenna" (12:5). This is the route of hypocrisy. A hypocrite, according to Luke, will end up in the Jerusalem garbage dump, Gehenna. During a time of persecution, anyone who reneges on his or her faith is considered to be worthless garbage.

But fear of God should not be the motivation for steadfastness during persecution, according to Jesus. Authentic motivation should be the disciple's trust in God's benevolent care. "Are not five sparrows sold for a few cents? Yet not one of them has escaped the notice of God. You are worth far more than many sparrows" (12:6-7). If God is concerned about the sparrows, then how much more is God concerned about people.

Using hyperbolic language, Luke emphasizes God's care for people: "Even the hairs of your head have all been counted" (12:7). There is no limit to God's care for those who refuse hypocrisy during times of persecution. They have nothing to fear.

Meditation: When your discipleship is questioned (attacked) by others, in which ways do you witness to your trust in God's care for you?

Prayer: God of care, you have never abandoned the people whom you have chosen to be your own. During times of persecution, you fill them with the strength of the Holy Spirit so that they can bear witness to their faith in your Son, our Lord Jesus Christ. Touch our lives with your caring hand, remove our fears, teach us to trust in your benevolent care, and count us among those worthy to enter the kingdom, where you live and reign with Jesus and the Holy Spirit, one God, for ever and ever. Amen.

TAUGHT BY THE SPIRIT

Luke 12:8-12

Scripture: "When they bring you before synagogues and rulers and officials, don't worry about how to state your case or about what you are to say. The Holy Spirit will teach you what you should say at that moment" (Luke 12:11-12).

Reflection: This sub-section (12:8-12) of Luke's Gospel is part of the larger section (12:1-12), which deals with the appropriate Christian response during persecution. It is followed by sections which are concerned with possessions (12:13-34) and preparation for the Second Coming of Jesus (12:35-48). Luke's source for this material is Mark (8:38; 3:29; 13:11) and Q (cf. Matthew 12:31-32), although the author has considerably reworked this material and set it in the context of the fearlessness which should be the mark of a follower of Jesus in the face of persecution. This paves the way for his presentation of the Holy Spirit as the guiding force of the Church in his second volume, the Acts of the Apostles.

Christians can give one of two responses to persecution: witness or denial. Each response carries with it a corresponding acknowledgment or denial by the Son of Man on the day of judgment. "Everyone who acknowledge me before others the Son of Man will acknowledge before the angels of God. But whoever denies me before others will be denied before the angels of God" (12:8-9).

However, "everyone who speaks a word against the Son of Man will be forgiven, but the one who blasphemes against the Holy Spirit will not be forgiven" (11:10). In the first case, those who speak against the Son of Man can be forgiven because they do so out of ignorance; in Luke's schema, the Holy Spirit has not yet been given to the Church. After the resurrection and once the Spirit is poured out on the Church at Pentecost, ignorance will be removed, and those who speak against Jesus will be blaspheming the Holy Spirit who "will teach [them] what [they] should say at that moment" (12:12).

Therefore, when Christians are subjected to persecution, that is, when taken "before synagogues and before rulers and officials," they need "not worry about how [they should] state their case or about what [they] are to say" (12:11). As long as they have not blasphemed against the Holy Spirit, they will be given the wisdom and strength to witness to their faith in Jesus. As he had already told his followers, all they have to do is ask and the Father in heaven will give them the Holy Spirit (cf. 11:13).

Meditation: In which ways have you experienced the Holy Spirit giving you enlightenment and courage when your faith seems weak?

Prayer: Father in heaven, through wind and fire you have given the gift of your Holy Spirit to your people to strengthen them in bearing witness to your Son, Jesus. Pour out on us the same Spirit that we might know what we are to say about you, your Son, and your Holy Spirit, who live and reign as one God, for ever and ever. Amen.

WHO IS EMPEROR?

Matthew 22:15-21

Scripture: They (the Pharisees)... sent their disciples to him (Jesus), with the Herodians, saying... "Is it lawful to pay the census tax to Caesar or not?" Jesus... said, "Show me the coin for the tax." So they handed him the Roman coin. He said to them, "Whose image is this and whose inscription?" They replied. "Caesar's." At that he said to them, "Render, therefore, to Caesar the things that are Caesar's and to God the things that are God's" (Matthew 22:16-17, 19-21).

Reflection: Matthew's source for the debate concerning the paying of taxes to the emperor (Matthew 22:15-21) is Mark (12:13-17), although he places more emphasis on the Pharisees as instigators of the plot to entrap Jesus in speech (cf. 22:15). Matthew also mentions Herodians, but since these have disappeared by the time of his writing, he gives them only a passing nod. However, the reference to the disciples of the Pharisees reflects the author's own time, when the Pharisaic rabbis became the undisputed teachers of Judaism.

This debate is located in the Temple after Jesus' triumphant entry into Jerusalem and his cleansing of the Temple. The debate was a historical one between the Pharisees, who did not favor the payment of the tax, and the Herodians, who did favor paying it. Both parties address Jesus as "Teacher" (22:16),

Matthew's favorite way of portraying unbelievers who speak the truth without knowing it.

"Is it lawful to pay the census tax to Caesar or not?" (22:17) concerns the law of God. However, this is a loaded question. If Jesus says yes, he will fall on the side of the Herodians, accept taxation from Rome, and lose the support of those to whom he has ministered throughout the Gospel. If Jesus says no, he will fall on the side of the Pharisees, risk arrest for subversion of the state, and be counted among the rebels of the time.

But the real question and concern of the author is not about paying taxes to the emperor but what is owed to God. Underlying basic Judaism was the concept from Genesis that everything belonged to God; people were given dominion as stewards of God's creation. The only person to whom one owed duty (taxes) is God.

With this in mind, Jesus reduces both Pharisees and Herodians. When he tells them to show him the coin used to pay the tax, they readily produce it. This means that they use it, and, therefore, accept the Roman taxation of Palestine. This also means that they break the law by carrying a pagan coin whose inscription claimed divinity for the person whose image was on the coin.

Jesus' response raises their legal question to a new level. Those who possess and use Caesar's coin should render to Caesar what belongs to him. In other words, they should pay the tax because they enjoy the economic benefits of Rome. But God must also be brought into the picture. What belongs to God — the praise, honor and glory of the whole of creation — should also be rendered to him.

In relationship to God, the question of paying the tax is minute! Caesar might be the earthly ruler, but God is the ruler of the world. We are merely the stewards of his creation. To God belongs the "fruits in their seasons" (21:41). Here, the author reminds the reader of the parable of the tenants and their failure to give the landowner his share of the produce from his vineyard.

The lawfulness of the tax is never decided. The payment or non-payment of it depends on whom one acknowledges as emperor — Caesar or God. Since the Pharisees and the Herodians possess the coin used for the tax, they have already indicated who their emperor is; for this reason they are "hypocrites" (22:18).

But they are hypocrites for another reason. They know the Scriptures and the law concerning God's dominion of the universe. Yet, they have not given God what is due him. They are more concerned about the emperor's tax than about the real Emperor, whose kingdom is being "taken away from [them] and given to a people that will produce its fruit" (21:43).

Meditation: In which ways do you acknowledge the supremacy of God? In which ways do you acknowledge the supremacy of the state?

Prayer: God of all creation, to you every man, woman, and child owes the breath of their existence. Earthly rulers have no splendor in comparison to your glory. Teach us to honor those who rule over us. Make us faithful and loyal citizens. Guide us to worship only you, who live and reign with Jesus, your Son, and the Holy Spirit, one God, for ever and ever. Amen.

CUP AND BAPTISM

Mark 10:35-45

Scripture: Jesus summoned them (the disciples) and said to them, "You know that those who are recognized as rulers among the Gentiles lord it over them, and their great ones make their authority felt. But it shall not be like that among you. Instead, whoever wishes to be great among you will be your servant; whoever wishes to be first among you will be the slave of all" (Mark 10:42-44).

Reflection: Mark's account of James' and John's request for positions on the right and the left of Jesus in his glory (Mark 10:35-45) immediately follows the third prediction of the passion (10:32-34) on the way to Jerusalem and precedes the story of blind Bartimaeus (11:46-52), which serves as the end-frame of this section (8:22-11:52) of the Gospel. James' and John's request and Jesus' teaching serves to indicate that the disciples have still not understood what, according to Mark, it means to follow Jesus.

The reader must remember that since Peter's confession of Jesus at Caesarea Philippi (8:27-33), Mark has been following a new plot line. Before Peter's confession, Jesus is portrayed as a miracle worker, an exorcist, a healer — a man of power. After Peter's confession, Jesus is portrayed as the suffering, rejected, condemned, crucified Son of Man — a person utterly devoid of any power.

Discipleship for Mark is powerlessness.

153

In this context the account of the ambition of James and John serves to highlight the ignorance of the disciples — possibly the historical ones, and certainly those of Mark's time and community. They are still seeking power and position, while Jesus has predicted his powerless rejection, suffering, and death for the third time. In other words, they haven't gotten it yet!

In response to their request, Jesus asks them, "Can you drink the cup that I drink or be baptized with the baptism with which I am baptized?" (10:38). To drink from the cup is an Old Testament metaphor for accepting one's destiny as assigned by God. Addition of the reference to baptism forms a metaphor for the rejection, suffering, and death of Jesus. Thus, the question that Jesus is asking concerns discipleship. The authentic disciple is willing to accept God's destiny for him or her, even if such destiny includes rejection, suffering, and death. The example to follow is the Son of Man who gave "his life as a ransom for many" (10:45). Anyone who wants to be counted among the followers of Jesus accepts this cup and this baptism.

James and John answer Jesus' question in the affirmative to which he replies, "The cup that I drink, you will drink, and with the baptism with which I am baptized, you will be baptized" (10:39). In other words, the fate of every follower of Jesus is like that of Jesus. Discipleship is not to be taken lightly; it involves the willingness to give one's whole life.

Once Mark has made this point he returns to the original question about the positions on the right and the left of Jesus in glory. Jesus tells James and John, "To sit at my right or at my left is not mine to give but it is for those for whom it has been prepared" (10:40). In other words, God will assign places in his kingdom.

Discipleship is not to be modeled after the "rulers among the Gentiles" (10:42) because "their great ones make their authority over them felt" (10:42). Discipleship, according to Jesus, is exactly the opposite: "It shall not be that way with you... Whoever wishes to be great among you will be your servant;

whoever wishes to be great among you will be the slave of all"
(10:43-44).

This understanding of discipleship reverses all earthly conceptions. Greatness does not equal servanthood; greatness equals
a position of power. Being first does not equal being a slave; being
first equals a position of power. Discipleship is having no power,
no position, no rank. The authentic follower of Jesus is like the
Son of Man, who "did not come to be served but to serve" (10:45).

Meditation: In which ways do you serve and illustrate authentic
discipleship?

Prayer: God of James and John, you taught the disciples of your
Son that he must drink the cup that you gave to him and that they
must drink from the same cup. In your kingdom, real power is
powerlessness; the great are servants, and the first are slaves of
all. We have been baptized with the baptism of Jesus; make us
faithful disciples. Bring us to the fullness of the kingdom, where
you live and reign with the Son of Man and the Holy Spirit, one
God, for ever and ever. Amen.

SPEEDY JUSTICE

Luke 18:1-8

Scripture: "Won't God, then, vindicate the rights of his chosen ones when they cry out to him day and night? Will he be slow to answer them? I tell you, he will see to it that justice is done for them with all speed" (Luke 18:7-8).

Reflection: The parable of the persistent widow (Luke 18:1-8), the first of two parables on prayer in the continuing journey-to-Jerusalem section of Luke's Gospel, is unique to this author. It is set within the context of "the necessity… to pray always without becoming discouraged" (18:1). It follows Jesus' declaration that "the kingdom of God is among you" (17:21) and his discourse about "the day the Son of Man is revealed" (17:30). It is followed by the parable of the Pharisee and the tax collector (18:9-14).

There are two characters in the parable: the judge and the widow. The judge is described as one "who neither feared God nor felt shame before any human being" (18:2). Such a description in a shame-honor culture places the judge outside of any group. His honor would have come from the group for whom he functioned as judge. Since this judge neither fears God nor respects any human being, he is without honor, shameless.

The judge is contrasted to "a widow in that town [who] kept coming to him and saying, 'Do me justice against my adversary'" (18:3). The widow is a woman, one who can only be shamed, one who has no means of financial support and must rely on the

157

judge to render justice for her. She appeals to and threatens his supposed honor by pleading that he defend her honor — which she doesn't have!

"For a while the judge was unwilling, but eventually he thought, 'While it is true that I neither fear God nor feel shame before any human being, because this widow keeps bothering me I'll do her justice so she won't keep coming and end by doing me violence'" (18:4-5).

The judge finally decides to render justice to the widow, but his decision is not based on any good reason — such as the desire to protect helpless widows or to defend his own honor. The judge decides in favor of the widow out of his own convenience, and, thus, he remains without honor, shameless. The judge, who neither fears God nor feels shame before any human being, is worn down by the helpless widow!

The judge should function as a metaphor for God in the parable. Just as God takes care of widows, so should the judge function as a protector of widows. But this judge fails because he does not act out of justice but out of convenience.

The widow is the bearer of the kingdom of God! The woman exposes her own shame by pestering the shameless judge until she gets what she wants. Thus, in this passage from Luke, Jesus declares that the kingdom of God comes because of persistence and not necessarily justice or honor.

Luke situates this parable within the context of persistent prayer. He uses a "how much more" argument. If the judge acts out of convenience, how much more will God, the just judge, "vindicate the rights of his chosen ones who cry out to him day and night? Will he be slow to answer them?" (18:7). The implied answer is, of course, "No." "He will see to it that justice is done for them with all speed" (18:8).

In context, Luke employs the parable as an example for and an exhortation to Christians to keep praying for the coming of the day of the Son of Man. The last sentence asks, "When the Son of Man comes, will he find faith on earth?" (18:8). Earlier in the Gospel, Jesus taught his followers to pray for the coming of the kingdom (11:2). By the time of Luke's writing, however, the kingdom had still not come.

Faith is maintained, according to this author, by prayer. Faith depends on persistent prayer, like the widow's persistent pestering of the judge. God is the just judge, who will "vindicate the rights of his chosen ones" (18:7) as long as they do not lose heart and give up hope for "the day [that] the Son of Man is [to be] revealed" (17:30).

Meditation: When were you most recently so persistent in prayer that you pestered God until you got what was just?

Prayer: God of justice, you teach us to not lose heart but to persistently pray to you for all our needs. Give us the courage to keep bothering you until our desires for your kingdom are met. Do not be slow in answering, but secure our rights as your chosen sons and daughters. Help us to keep faith until the coming in glory of your Son, our Lord Jesus Christ, who lives and reigns with you and the Holy Spirit, one God, for ever and ever. Amen.

GUARD AGAINST GREED

Luke 12:13-21

Scripture: "Take care to guard against all greed, because your life does not consist in the abundance of your possessions" (Luke 12:15).

Reflection: The Lucan saying against greed (12:13-15), which serves as an introduction to the parable of the rich fool (12:16-21), forms the first of a two-part sub-section wherein Jesus specifies what the Christian response should be to possessions. The second sub-section (12:22-34) is omitted from the daily cycle of readings.

The concern with the issue of greed is peculiar to Luke's Gospel. Most likely, greed, or covetousness, was a problem before Luke's time; it shows up again in the Acts of the Apostles and in some of the Pauline letters.

Luke begins this section by portraying "someone in the crowd" addressing Jesus, "Teacher, tell my brother to share the inheritance with me" (12:13). The plea echoes Martha's request of Jesus (cf. 10:38-42), and the one who makes it expects Jesus to render a decision.

Typical of Luke, however, Jesus responds with the question, "Friend, who appointed me as your judge and arbitrator?" (12:14). Jesus will not judge such matters; he will raise the issue to a higher plane — the greed which gives rise to the request. Jesus cautions, "Take care to guard against all greed, because your life does not

161

consist in the abundance of your possessions" (12:15). In other words, what a person is cannot be summed up or even confused with what a person has. An individual is not defined by his or her riches.

This statement prepares for the parable. "There was a rich man whose land produced a bountiful harvest" (12:16).

From the outset the reader is informed that the man is rich and, because of a miraculous harvest, he has grown even richer.

According to Luke's underlying theme through the Gospel and the Acts of the Apostles, riches are given to a person by God in order that they be shared with others. Riches are for the good of the community. Because there is only a limited supply of riches, the only way that others can have some riches is if the rich man shares what he has with them.

The question that the rich man in the parable asks himself is not in keeping with this Lucan understanding: "What shall I do, for I do not have room to store my harvest?" (12:17). The rich man immediately exposes the avaricious side of his nature. He is greedy.

He already has enough for himself (he is rich), but now he wants to hoard his abundance. His decision is a simple one: "This is what I shall do: I'll pull down my barns and build larger ones. Then I'll store all my grain and other goods there and I shall say to myself, 'Now you have many good things laid up for many years. Relax, eat, drink, be merry!'" (12:18-19).

The rich man believes that his possessions are his security. Thus, he has committed idolatry; he is storing "up treasure for himself but is not rich in what matters to God" (12:21) — love of God and neighbor. The rich man has confused who he is with what he possesses.

Therefore, God says to him, "You fool, this night your life will be demanded of you; and these things you have prepared, to whom will they belong?" (12:20). The rich man, who was considered to be blessed by God because he was rich, is now called a fool because he trusted in the wrong riches and violated the principle that wealth is given to be shared. He has misman-aged God's gifts.

After the rich man dies and his body is carried away, his stored-up riches will go to those for whom they were given — people who have no riches. The poor are always taken care of by God — either through those to whom he gives riches to be shared, or, when these fail, directly by himself. At death a per-son cannot take what he or she owns with him or her. "Your life does not consist in the abundance of your possessions" (12:15); it consists of love of God and neighbor as one loves one's self. A person becomes "rich in what matters to God" (12:21) by shar-ing with others what God has given.

Meditation: In which ways are you rich in what matters to God?

Prayer: God of love, through Jesus, your Son, you have taught us to take care to guard against all greed, for wealth is your gift which is given to be shared with others. Continually remind us of our dependence on you that we may be kept from hoarding your miraculous benefits. Help us to recognize that our lives are not measured by the abundance of our possessions, but that our real treasure consists in our growing rich in what matters to you. We ask this through our Lord Jesus Christ, who lives and reigns with you and the Holy Spirit, one God, for ever and ever. Amen.

WAITING FOR THE MASTER

Luke 12:35-38

Scripture: "Let your loins be girt and your lamps be bright like servants awaiting their master's return from a wedding, ready to open immediately when he comes and knocks" (Luke 12:35).

Reflection: The daily cycle of readings divides up the third unit of this section of Luke's Gospel into two sub-sections.

The entire unit deals with being prepared for the Second Coming of Jesus. Luke's source for this sub-section (12:35-38) is Q (cf. Matthew 24:45-51), although the evangelist has collected and reworked the material to reflect his understanding of being faithful to the teaching of Jesus until he comes again. Thus, these sayings are from a post-Easter perspective.

The followers of Jesus, disciples, are "awaiting their master's return from a wedding" (12:36). The master is Jesus; the wedding is a metaphor for the Second Coming, the fullness of the kingdom of God. They are to be "ready to open immediately when he comes and knocks" (12:36).

Their preparedness is described as "girt loins," that is, the outer garments are to be gathered at the waist so that they will not interfere with strenuous activity. This is to be a constant state of readiness to make the journey with Jesus.

Their preparedness is also described as "lighted lamps," that is, vigilance, wakefulness, watchfulness for the Lord's coming.

"Blessed are those servants whom the master finds vigilant on his arrival" (12:37). "And should he come in the second or third watch and find them prepared in this way, blessed are those servants" (12:39).

Being ready and watchful is characteristic of the type of servants whom the master will regard, when he comes. In fact, those Christians who are ready and watchful discover that they are no longer servants but served. "Amen, I say to you, he will gird himself, have them recline at table, and proceed to wait on them" (12:37). This sudden reversal of roles is what awaits all Christians who are ready and watchful for the Second Coming of Jesus.

Meditation: In which ways are you ready and how do you wait for the Second Coming of Jesus?

Prayer: Servant God, you raised your only Son, our Lord Jesus Christ, from the death of the cross to the glory of the resurrection and you promised that one day he would return in glory. Keep us ready and watchful for his coming. Prepare us to recline at the table of the heavenly wedding banquet, which you share with all your faithful servants. We ask this through Christ our Lord. Amen.

WHO IS WAITING?

Luke 12:39-48

Scripture: "Who, then, is the faithful and prudent steward whom the master will put in charge of his servants to distribute their food allowance at the allotted time?" (Luke 12:42).

Reflection: This section of Luke's Gospel (12:39-48) is the second and last part of the large unit concerned with being prepared for the Second Coming of Jesus (12:35-48). Luke's source is Q (cf. Matthew 24:45-51), but the evangelist has reworked the material to reflect his community's expectation of the Second Coming of Jesus.

The sub-section begins with an exhortation concerning perpetual preparedness: "If the master of the house had known the hour when the thief was coming, he would not have let his house be broken into" (12:39). Luke calls for a constant alertness: "You must also be prepared, for at an hour you do not expect, the Son of Man will come" (12:40).

Luke then portrays Peter as asking, "Lord, is this parable meant for us or for everyone?" (12:41). Peter represents those who have leadership roles in the Church. Jesus exhorts those in such roles to be "faithful and prudent stewards whom the master will put in charge of his servants to distribute their food allowance at the allotted time" (12:42). In fact, "Blessed is that servant whom his master on arrival finds doing so. Truly, I say to you, he will put him in charge of all his property" (12:43-44).

Luke also addresses himself to those leaders who act irresponsibly during the delay of the Second Coming of Jesus. He

167

warns them that if they "beat the servants and maids, eating and drinking and getting drunk," that the master will punish them severely and assign them "a place with the unbelievers" (12:45-46).

The irresponsible leader will be punished by the master in proportion to the degree of his irresponsibility. The servant who abandons all imminent expectation of the return of Jesus will be punished severely, that is, "cut in two" — death — and he will be assigned "a place with the unbelievers" (12:46).

The "servant who knew his master's will but did not make preparations nor act in accord with his will shall be beaten severely" (12:47). In other words, the neglectful leader will be severely punished.

"The servant who was ignorant of his master's will but acted in a way deserving of a severe beating shall be beaten only lightly" (12:48). This is the category of unintentional neglect, and the punishment is lighter.

Jesus summarizes the exhortation to faithfulness for leaders in the Church by reminding them, "Much will be required of the person entrusted with much, and still more will be demanded of the person entrusted with more" (12:48). The leaders of Luke's community are exhorted to be more prepared for the Second Coming of Jesus than other Christians. Their preparedness is their faithfulness in fulfilling the mission given them by the master, Jesus.

Meditation: In which ways do you find that you function as a faithful, prepared leader in and of the Church today?

Prayer: Master God, you exhort your people to be prepared for your Son's coming in glory as they would be for a thief in the night. You commission the leaders of your people to be prepared for his Second Coming by being faithful to the position that you have entrusted to them. Guide our leaders; give them the gift of prudence. Fill them with the Holy Spirit that they might be prepared for that unexpected hour of the coming of the Son of Man, who is Lord for ever and ever. Amen.

DIVISIVE MINISTRY

Luke 12:49-53

Scripture: "Do you think that I have come to establish peace on the earth? No, I tell you, but rather division" (Luke 12:51).

Reflection: The conclusion (12:49-53) of the larger section of Luke's Gospel (12:1-53), which is addressed to Luke's disciples (cf. 12:1), consists of three originally independent sayings which deal with the divisive effects of Jesus' ministry.

The first of the three sayings reminds the reader of the initial proclamation of John the Baptizer: "He (Jesus) will baptize you with the Holy Spirit and fire" (3:16). Here, Jesus declares, "I have come to set the earth on fire, and how I wish it were already ablaze!" (12:49). The union of fire and Spirit will be accomplished at Pentecost, when the disciples are driven forth on their mission of spreading the good news.

The second of the three sayings echoes the Marcan account of the request by James and John for the places on the right and left of Jesus (cf. Mark 10:38-39). There, Jesus refers to his rejection, suffering, and death as a baptism. Here in Luke, Jesus declares, "There is a baptism with which I must be baptized, and how great is my anguish until it is accomplished!" (12:50). After Jesus' death the fire (Holy Spirit) will come. Pentecost follows Jesus' suffering and death.

The third of the three sayings explains the result of the fire which will come after Jesus' suffering and death — division. "Do you think that I have come to establish peace on the earth? No, I tell you, but rather division. From now on a household of five will be divided, three against two and two against three; a father will be divided against his son and a son against his father, a mother against her daughter and a daughter against her mother, a mother-in-law against her daughter-in-law and a daughter-in-law against her mother-in-law" (12:51-53).

The third saying, which comes from Q (cf. Matthew 10:34-35), portrays Jesus as the great divider of families. The proclamation of the Gospel will result in division. From Luke's point of view, the Spirit produces division before the Spirit brings unity in families and in the Church.

Meditation: In which ways have you experienced division in your family because of matters of faith?

Prayer: God of fire, once you poured out the gift of your Spirit on the disciples who were chosen by your Son, and you sent them to proclaim the good news of your kingdom. We have been baptized into the suffering, death, and resurrection of Jesus, and you have filled us with the Holy Spirit. Keep us faithful. When division in our families and our Church seems imminent, remind us that Jesus was a cause of division. We ask this through our Lord Jesus Christ, who lives and reigns with you and the Holy Spirit, one God, for ever and ever. Amen.

INTERPRETING THE PRESENT

Luke 12:54-59

Scripture: "When you see [a] cloud rising in the west you say immediately that it is going to rain — and so it does; and when you notice that the wind is blowing from the south you say that it is going to be hot — and so it is. You hypocrites! You know how to interpret the appearance of the earth and the sky; why do you not know how to interpret the present time?" (Luke 12:54-56)

Reflection: This section (12:54-59) of Luke's Gospel begins an address of Jesus to the crowds and forms the first of a two-part call to conversion. Luke's source for this material is Q (cf. Matthew 16:2-3; 5:25-26); however, the evangelist has reworked the material and placed it into a different context.

The first part of 12:54-59, 12:54-56, consists of an exhortation by Jesus to interpret correctly the "present time" (12:56), that is, the meaning of Jesus' mission. People look at the clouds in the sky and take careful notice of the direction that the wind is blowing and correctly determine the weather. Likewise, they should be able to look at the ministry of Jesus and determine that the kingdom of God is in their midst. If they cannot do this, then they are hypocrites (cf. 12:56).

The second part of 12:54-59, 12:57-59, is an exhortation to respond correctly to the challenge of the moment. Jesus says,

"Why do you not judge for yourselves what is right?" (12:57). While people have the chance, they should be as concerned about the reality of God's judgment as they are about settling a matter with an opponent on the way to the magistrate (cf. 12:58).

If they wait until the last possible minute, then they will become liable to the decision of the judge, who will hand them over to the constable, who in turn will throw them into prison (cf. 12:58). In other words, Jesus warns the crowds that it is wise to be reconciled with God before the day of judgment. Otherwise, they "will not be released until [they] have paid the last penny" (12:59), the tiniest amount.

Meditation: At the present time, what does Jesus' ministry and mission mean to you?

Prayer: God of judgment, you instill in your people an innate knowledge that enables them to predict the weather from the signs in the sky and the direction of the wind. Give us a deeper understanding of the meaning of the ministry and mission of Jesus, your Son. Enable us to hear his call of repentance that we might meet the challenge of the moment and be reconciled to you, who live and reign with him and the Holy Spirit, one God, for ever and ever. Amen.

STILL TIME TO REPENT

Luke 13:1-9

Scripture: "A man had a fig tree planted in his vineyard, and when he came in search of fruit on it but found none, he said to the vinedresser, 'For three years now I have come in search of fruit on this fig tree but have found none. Cut it down. Why should it exhaust the soil?' The vinedresser said to him in reply, 'Sir, leave it for one more year. I'll cultivate the ground around it and fertilize it; it may bear fruit in the future. If not it can be cut down'" (Luke 13:6-9).

Reflection: The second part of Jesus' address to the crowds in Luke is found in 13:1-9, which contains a call to repentance (13:1-5) and the parable of the barren fig tree (13:6-9). The call to repentance echoes the previous section which dealt with reading the signs of the present time and taking the opportunity to be reconciled with God before the day of judgment (cf. 12:54-59).

Two unique Lucan signs are given by Jesus in the call to repentance along with their interpretation. The first is that of "the Galileans whose blood Pilate had mingled with the blood of their sacrifices" (13:1). The issue raised by this sign is the meaning of the absence of tragedy in a person's life.

According to the culture of the time, the absence of any tragedy meant that a person had not sinned; tragedy was God's way of punishing a person for his or her sin. If there was no tragedy, then there had been no sin and, consequently, the person must be blessed by God. Therefore, there is no need to repent.

Jesus quickly declares that this is not the proper interpretation of the Galilean slaughter. "Do you think that because these Galileans suffered in this way they were greater sinners than all other Galileans? By no means!" (13:2-3). In other words, human tragedy is not God's way of punishing sin. Likewise, the absence of tragedy does not imply the lack of sin in a person's life. In this case, tragedy was due to a human cause — Pilate, who is known throughout history for his ruthlessness.

According to Jesus, everyone needs to repent. "I tell you, if you do not repent, you will all perish as they did!" (13:3) The lack of repentance will bring about the greatest tragedy of all — lack of admittance to the kingdom of God.

The second sign given by Jesus consists of "eighteen people who were killed when the tower of Siloam fell on them" (13:4). The falling of the tower represents a natural cause of tragedy. The same question as that posed in the first sign is asked by Jesus here, "Do you think they were more guilty than everyone else who lived in Jerusalem?" (13:4).

The answer, of course, is "By no means!" (13:5). This natural tragedy did not happen to those who were greater sinners than anyone else. God does not use natural tragedies to punish people for sin. Natural tragedies are simply that — natural tragedies. They do not measure sinfulness.

All people need to repent. "I tell you, if you do not repent, you will all perish as they did" (13:5). All people are sinners and need to repent. The greatest tragedy of all will be brought about by a lack of repentance — no admittance to the kingdom of God.

The parable of the fig tree, unique to Luke but probably garnered from Q (cf. Matthew 21:19) and Mark (cf. 11:13), illustrates God's patience in waiting for all people to repent. Since a fig tree reached maturity in three years, when no fruit was found on it, the owner of the vineyard (God) has every right to cut it down because it exhausts the soil and takes up valuable space where something else could grow.

The gardener (Jesus), however, asks for one more year. With some cultivation and fertilizing (hearing the word and keeping it) "the tree may bear fruit in the future" (13:9). If not, then, it can be cut down by the owner. Luke is saying that there is still time for repentance, but this time is not unlimited.

The absence of judgment as tragedy at the present moment should not lead people to conclude that they are righteous. The correct conclusion is that God is merciful, and he is giving people a little additional time to repent, one last chance. From God's point of view, there is always the possibility that people will repent.

Meditation: How has God given you one last chance to repent? In which areas of your life do you need to repent?

Prayer: God of repentance, you do not punish sin with either human or natural tragedy, but you call all people to repent. Your patience is like that of the owner of the vineyard, who gave the tree one last chance to produce fruit before it is cut down and removed from the soil. With the assistance of the Holy Spirit guide us to true repentance that we might produce abundant fruit and come to share in the kingdom, where you live and reign with Jesus, your Son, and the Holy Spirit, one God, for ever and ever. Amen.

BALANCED LOVE

Matthew 22:34-40

Scripture: "You shall love the Lord, your God, with all your heart, with all your soul, and with all your mind. This is the greatest and the first commandment. The second is like it: You shall love your neighbor as yourself" (Matthew 22:37-39).

Reflection: Matthew's presentation of the greatest commandment (22:34-40) follows the question about the resurrection (22:23-33) and is followed by the question about David's son (22:41-46). The setting is the Temple with debates between Jesus and the Pharisees and the Sadducees after Jesus' entry into Jerusalem. The source for this section is Mark (12:28-34), which has been severely condensed by Matthew.

According to Matthew, a scholar of the law, a Pharisee, poses a test question to Jesus: "Teacher, which commandment in the law is the greatest?" (22:36). The address of Jesus as "Teacher" reflects Matthew's favorite description of Jesus by nonbelievers.

This is a test question because there were 613 commandments of the law. All were to be diligently observed. The question of which of these commandments was the greatest was debated among the experts in the law.

Here Jesus answers the question by quoting the shema, the ancient Hebrew prayer found in the book of Deuteronomy: "You shall love the Lord, your God, with all your heart, with all your soul, and with all your mind" (22:37; cf. Deuteronomy 6:4-5). Put simply, the greatest commandment means that a person is to love God with all that one is: with one's heart, the source of willing and feeling; with one's soul, the source of one's life; and with one's mind, the source of one's knowing and energy. "This is the greatest and the first commandment" (22:38).

Jesus goes beyond the extent of the question asking for the greatest commandment and joins the first to a second. He declares, "The second is like it: You shall love your neighbor as yourself" (22:39). The source of this commandment is also the law (cf. Leviticus 19:18). Thus, Jesus provides a careful balance between love of God, neighbor, and self. By providing two answers to a single question, Jesus passes the test-trap by the Pharisaic scholar of the law.

Matthew is quick to add, "The whole law and the prophets depend on these two commandments" (22:40). In Judaism, a commandment was considered to depend on a particular passage from Scripture. Jesus greatly expands this concept to declare that the entire law and the prophets depend on but these two passages from Scripture. In other words, God's will — love — is summarized in the double commandment of love. If these two commandments are kept, there is no need to worry about the other 611, as they will automatically be kept by observance of the first and the second commandments.

Meditation: In which ways do you love God and your neighbor as you love yourself?

Prayer: God of love, you will that your people love you with all their heart, with all their soul, and with all their mind. You also will that they love their neighbor as they love themselves. Fill us with this love. Enable us to recognize that the whole law and the prophets depend on this love. We ask this through our Lord Jesus Christ, your Son, who lives and reigns with you and the Holy Spirit, one God, for ever and ever. Amen.

THE BLIND SEE
Mark 10:46-52

Scripture: Bartimaeus, a blind man, the son of Timaeus, sat by the roadside begging.... He began to cry out, "Jesus, son of David, have pity on me." Jesus said to him, "What do you want me to do for you?" The blind man replied to him, "Master, I want to see" (Mark 10:46-47, 51).

Reflection: The story of the blind Bartimaeus (Mark 10:46-52) forms the back cover of the book of Jesus' teaching about authentic discipleship involving rejection, suffering, and death — powerlessness — in contrast to the disciples who constantly seek power and position. The front cover is a similar story about the blind man of Bethsaida (Mark 8:22-26). In order to understand the function of the account about blind Bartimaeus, the reader must refer to the blind man of Bethsaida account and carefully consider the material which has been presented in between these two restoration of sight stories.

In both stories Mark is ironically contrasting the blind men, who receive their sight, to the seeing disciples, who are blind when it comes to what Jesus continually teaches them. The blind man of Bethsaida comes to sight in two stages, an indication that the disciples (and the reader) may expect to come to faith gradually. This blind man is sent home by Jesus and told not to go into the village. He does not become a disciple because Jesus has not yet been revealed as the Messiah.

179

The material that Mark presents in between these two blind men accounts deals with the revelation of Jesus' true identity — the rejected, suffering, Son of Man, who will be put to death in Jerusalem. Peter fails to understand this. As Jesus continues to teach them that real power is powerlessness, they keep arguing about who is the greatest or who will have the places on the right and the left of Jesus when he is glorified.

Then comes the story of blind Bartimaeus. This man has no sight, yet he declares that Jesus is the son of David, a refrain that will be echoed in the next few verses as Jesus enters Jerusalem triumphantly to suffer and die. Furthermore, "Son of David" (10:47, 48) denotes Jesus' Messiahship; he is the one whom Israel awaited. Blind Bartimaeus recognizes the Messiah! The seeing disciples still haven't figured out who Jesus really is!

Bartimaeus cries out, "Jesus, son of David, have pity on me" (10:48). In the context of a healing story, the blind man seeks to have his sight restored. Ironically, he already sees better than any of the other characters in the story! He has faith (cf. 10:52) in contrast to the disciples, who are portrayed as not having any faith.

Mark also cleverly brings in the "many" who at first rebuke Bartimaeus for crying out and later urge him to take courage and go to Jesus once Jesus calls him. These "many" represent some of the wishy-washy members of Mark's community. The author is warning them (and the reader) to consider carefully the meaning of authentic discipleship.

Up to this point, Jesus has usually urged secrecy when it comes to any proclamation of his identity. Now, members of the crowd try to silence the blind man. Jesus permits the title, "Son of David," to be heard clearly by all. By now, everyone should understand that the title implies not triumph but rejection, suffering, and death.

Once the blind Bartimaeus receives his sight, a rather anticlimactic action (since he already sees better than any other person — except Jesus — in the story), he follows Jesus "on the way"

(10:52). He becomes a disciple. He is contrasted to those who have been following Jesus and will shortly scatter.

The journey of Jesus with his disciples to Jerusalem was meant to heal the blindness of the disciples, but they still do not see. Two blind men, however, now see! They were aware of their dependence upon God, who gave them the gift of faith, to which they responded. As the Gospel proceeds, many never become aware of their dependence upon God, and, consequently, they never come to authentic discipleship and faith.

Meditation: In which ways do you see? In which ways are you blind?

Prayer: God of the blind and the seeing, you offer your gift of sight to those who need your healing touch, and you leave in confusion and darkness those who refuse to accept your always-offered gift. Give us the gift of faith that we might become authentic disciples of the rejected, suffering, put-to-death, and raised-to-life Son of David, Jesus Christ our Lord, who lives and reigns with you and the Holy Spirit, one God, for ever and ever. Amen.

TWO AT PRAYER

Luke 18:9-14

Scripture: "Two people went up to the Temple to pray; one was a Pharisee and the other was a tax collector.... The latter went home justified, not the former; for everyone who exalts himself will be humbled, and the one who humbles himself will be exalted" (Luke 18:10, 14).

Reflection: The parable of the Pharisee and the tax collector (Luke 18:9-14) is unique to Luke's Gospel. It follows the parable of the persistent widow, and it illustrates both the appropriate and the inappropriate way to pray.

The parable is addressed "to those who were convinced of their own righteousness and despised everyone else" (18:9).

Righteousness has to do with doing God's will, having everything straightened out between people and God. Luke's editorial comment makes it clear that self-assured piety and spiritual condescension have no part in the kingdom of God.

The two characters in the parable are a Pharisee and a tax collector. The Pharisee was a member of one of Judaism's most devoted and pious sects. He "stood up front by himself and offered this prayer, 'O God, I thank you that I am not like other people — greedy, dishonest, adulterous — or even like this tax collector. I fast twice a week, and I pay tithes on my whole income'" (18:11-12).

It is important to note that the Pharisee addresses his prayer to God but he is really talking to himself. He affirms his self-righteousness and avoidance of greed, dishonesty, and adultery. He goes beyond what is required of him; that is, he is more than righteous since he fasts twice a week, and pays tithes on his entire income. His fault is that he compares himself to the tax collector.

The tax collector was one of the most despised persons within Judaism. He was considered greedy, dishonest, and disloyal because he was a traitor, a Jew who worked for the Romans. He made his living by raising the designated tax and pocketing the difference. If he repented and gave up his job he would have to make restitution to his fellow Jews and he would be the object of hostility by the Romans; he would, of course, lose his livelihood.

"The tax collector stood off at a distance and would not even raise his eyes to heaven but beat his breast and prayed, 'O God, be merciful to me a sinner'" (18:13). The tax collector directly addresses his prayer to God. He assumes the position and posture of one who is repentant. He acknowledges his sin and requests that God be merciful to him. There is no streak of self-righteousness in him.

Therefore, Jesus declares, "I tell you, the latter went home justified, not the former; for everyone who exalts himself will be humbled, while whoever humbles himself will be exalted" (18:14). Thus, the presupposed status of the two characters is reversed. The reader is left with a bad Pharisee and a good tax collector! Why?

The Pharisee is characterized as trusting in himself and being proud of what he had done. He assumes the posture of idolatry — that is, he was judging, a prerogative that belongs to God alone. While proper thanks to God is necessary, it can never turn into condescension toward others.

The tax collector did not trust in himself but rather in God. He assumed the posture of worship. He acknowledged his sinful condition and he asked for mercy. Therefore, he humbled himself and God exalted him, whereas the Pharisee exalted himself and God humbled him. In God's kingdom all preconceptions about righteousness are reversed.

Meditation: In which ways are you like the Pharisee? In which ways are you like the tax collector?

Prayer: Righteous God, you humble those who exalt themselves and you exalt those who humble themselves. When we enter your temple to pray, remind us of our sinful status before you. Extend your hand in unlimited mercy toward us as we seek your forgiveness. Bring us one day into the kingdom where you live and reign with Jesus, your Son, and the Holy Spirit, one God, for ever and ever. Amen.

SET FREE

Luke 13:10-17

Scripture: "Hypocrites! Does not each one of you untie his ox or ass from the manger and lead it out for watering on the Sabbath? Wasn't it proper for this daughter of Abraham, whom Satan has bound for eighteen years now, to have been set free from her bondage on the Sabbath day?" (Luke 13:15-16).

Reflection: The cure of the crippled woman on the Sabbath (Luke 13:10-17) is unique to Luke's Gospel. It follows the call to repentance (13:1-5) and the parable of the barren fig tree (13:6-9) and precedes the parables of the mustard seed and the yeast (13:18-21). The account functions to reemphasize the need for the Israelites to repent, as the kingdom of God is manifested by Jesus. This healing story also reveals the parallel style of the author of this Gospel. Luke likes to write accounts that echo each other. In this narrative, a crippled woman is healed on the Sabbath. Later, a man with dropsy will be healed on the Sabbath (14:1-6). A comparison of both stories reveals an identity in structure and purpose and shows the author's concern for women and men in need (cf. Luke 7:11-17 and 8:49-56).

The setting for the healing is a synagogue, a place of study and teaching. "A woman was there who for eighteen years had been crippled by a spirit; she was bent over, and completely incapable of standing erect" (13:11). In the ancient world, any type of affliction was considered to be an indication that a "spirit" or "Satan" had a hold on the person. Therefore, the woman needs to be liberated from the spirit's power.

Jesus, "filled with the Holy Spirit" (4:1), has already defeated Satan in the desert (cf. 4:1-13) and inaugurated the kingdom of God. Therefore, "when Jesus saw her, he called to her and said, 'Woman, you are set free of your infirmity.' He laid his hands on her, and she at once stood up straight and glorified God" (13:12-13). Thus, Jesus demonstrates that God's kingdom is present now and manifest now in the healing of a "daughter of Abraham" (13:16), an heir of the promises of God. Later in this Gospel, Luke will bring up this issue again when he tells the story of Zacchaeus (cf. 19:1-10).

Jesus' ministry began with his rejection from a synagogue (cf. 4:16-30); this section of Luke's Gospel ends with a confrontation in a synagogue. Thus, Luke portrays Jesus and the synagogue as being in sharp contrast; this reflects the stage of the Church at the time of the writing of this Gospel. Most likely, the Church had already broken away from the synagogue and Sabbath service.

The "leader of the synagogue" (13:14) does not confront Jesus directly, although he is "indignant that Jesus had cured on the Sabbath" (13:14). He addresses the crowd: "There are six days when work should be done. Come on those days to be cured, not on the Sabbath day" (13:14). The manifestation of the kingdom of God, however, is not limited. In fact, the law is lenient enough to permit the untying of oxen and asses on the Sabbath for the purpose of leading them to water. If this can be done, Jesus argues, then certainly a woman can be released from her illness (cf. 13:15-16).

Thus, Jesus, declares God's kingdom to be superior to the Sabbath law. Gradually, the kingdom spreads throughout the world (to be demonstrated in the parables of the mustard seed and the yeast; 13:18-21), and it heals all those who accept it.

The ruler of the synagogue is not effective. In fact, all Jesus' "adversaries were humiliated; and the whole crowd rejoiced at all the splendid deeds done by him" (13:17). Jesus' healing ministry is a sign of the gradual in-breaking of the kingdom of God, which supercedes the synagogue and its leaders.

Meditation: In which ways have you experienced the kingdom of God breaking into your life?

Prayer: God of the kingdom, you manifest your power through human weakness. Once you chose people and led them from slavery to freedom. Through Jesus, your Servant and your Son, you proclaimed the freedom of your children. Hear our prayer today: Give us true liberty from sin and a desire to serve you with all our heart. When we are crippled and bent over, straighten us up with your grace that we might glorify you, Father, Son, and Holy Spirit, one God, for ever and ever. Amen.

MUSTARD SEED OR YEAST?

Luke 13:18-21

Scripture: "What is the kingdom of God like and to what shall I compare it? It is like a mustard seed that a person took and planted in the garden, and it grew and became a large bush, and the birds of the sky dwelt in its branches.... It is like yeast that a woman took and mixed into three measures of wheat flour until the whole batch of dough was leavened" (Luke 13:18-19, 21).

Reflection: Within the context of Luke's Gospel, the parables of the mustard seed and the yeast (13:18-21), which follow the account of the cure of the crippled woman on the Sabbath (13:10-17), serve to highlight the fact that the small beginnings of the kingdom of God through the ministry of Jesus will continue to grow. The parable of the mustard seed comes from Mark's Gospel (4:3-23), while the parable of the yeast is from Q (cf. Matthew 13:33).

The smallness of the kingdom of God as revealed through the teaching, healing, and preaching ministry of Jesus in Luke is compared to a mustard seed, a very tiny seed. However, such smallness results in fully grown largeness.

The reference to the mustard seed growing to become large enough for the birds of the sky to dwell in its branches (13:19) is a reference to and parody on the noble cedar, which represents Israel's restoration, in the prophet Ezekiel: "Thus says the Lord

191

God: I, too, will take from the crest of the cedar, from its top-most branches... a tender shoot, and plant it on a high and lofty mountain; on the mountain heights of Israel I will plant it. It shall put forth branches and bear fruit, and become a majestic cedar. Birds of every kind shall dwell beneath it, every winged thing in the shade of its boughs" (Ezekiel 17:22-23).

What is Luke saying? The author is declaring that Israel will be restored, but the metaphor for the kingdom is no longer great-ness (the cedar) but smallness (the mustard seed). The surprising parallel that is drawn between the kingdom of God and the mus-tard seed is a departure from the usual description of its vastness. The parable of the yeast also departs from the usual understand-ing of the kingdom. Yeast, or leaven, was considered to be cor-rupt (evil) in the ancient world. Therefore, unleavened (non-cor-rupted) bread was prescribed for Jewish holy days, especially Passover. One could not use leaven in the presence of God.

In the parable, Jesus compares the kingdom of God to leaven! In other words, the kingdom of God corrupts everything it touches, just as leaven makes the whole batch of dough rise.

There are other surprising moments in the parable. The agent of the kingdom is not a man but a woman. The ancient world had no regard for women, so to declare the agent of the king-dom to be a woman is to reduce its importance. This detail would have been highly regarded by Luke, since he portrays women as having a significant role in the ministry of Jesus and in the early Church.

The amount of wheat flour that is leavened is an unusually large proportion. "Three measures" (13:21) recalls Old Testament epiphanies, manifestations of God, to Abraham (cf. Genesis 18:1-15), Gideon (cf. Judges 6:19-24), and Hannah (cf. 1 Samuel 1:1-28). By using this parable, Luke is declaring that the kingdom of God is appearing now through the most unlikely of people (women, sinners, tax collectors), and it is corrupting everyone with whom it makes contact.

Meditation: In which ways has the kingdom of God grown from a seed to a tree in your life? How has the kingdom of God corrupted you?

Prayer: God of seeds and leaven, you revealed the power of your kingdom in Jesus of Nazareth. He planted the seeds of awareness in the garden of his followers and urged them to watch for its gradual growth in their lives. He spread the kingdom like leaven through a whole batch of dough until the whole community began to recognize your presence. Make us grow from the seed of awareness to the tree of proclamation. Corrupt us with your presence that we might hear your word and keep it. We ask this through our Lord Jesus Christ, your Son, who lives and reigns with you and the Holy Spirit, one God, for ever and ever. Amen.

THE NARROW GATE

Luke 13:22-30

Scripture: "Strive to enter through the narrow gate, for many
I tell you, will try to enter but will be unable.... There will
be wailing and gnashing of teeth when you see Abraham,
Isaac, and Jacob and all the prophets in the kingdom of
God and you yourselves cast out" (Luke 13:24, 28).

Reflection: After telling the parables of the mustard seed and the
yeast (Luke 13:18-21), Jesus proceeds to stress the great effort that
one must make in order to enter the kingdom of God (13:22-30).
Luke has collected a number of sayings from Q and worked them
together into this section of his Gospel (cf. Matthew 7:13-14, 21-
23; 25:10-12; 8:11-12; 19:30).

In the introduction to this section of the Gospel, Luke reminds the reader that Jesus is "making his way to Jerusalem"
(13:22). The journey to Jerusalem motif comprises a major portion of this Gospel (9:51-19:27).

A question is asked by someone in the crowd: "Lord, will
only a few people be saved?" (13:23). Jesus does not answer this
question, because salvation is already (and always) taking place
through the preaching of the Gospel, according to Luke.

Instead, Jesus declares, "Strive to enter through the narrow
gate, for many, I tell you, will attempt to enter but will not be
strong enough" (13:24). Because salvation is present in Jesus,
there is an urgency to accept it (and him) now. The offer is not

unlimited; the Son of Man will come "in a cloud with power and great glory" and people will know that "redemption is at hand" (21:27-28).

A short parable emphasizes preparedness by accepting the offer of salvation in the present: "After the master of the house has arisen and locked the door, then you will stand outside knocking and saying, 'Lord, open the door for us.' He will say to you in reply, 'I do not know where you are from.' And you will say, 'We ate and drank in your company and you taught in our streets.' Then he will say to you, 'I do not know where you are from. Depart from me, all you evildoers!'" (13:25-27).

The story is clearly post-resurrectional, as the "master" has "arisen" and locked the door. According to this author, there is more to salvation than merely eating and drinking with Jesus or being in his company. In other words, mere association with Jesus is not sufficient for salvation. Those who think they are insiders may find themselves locked out! The insiders will be those who have consistently heard the word of God and kept (done) it.

The last part of the story sharpens its focus. Luke is interested in those who consider themselves insiders — Jews — and those they consider outsiders — Gentiles, tax collectors, and sinners. Jesus tells the Jews, "There will be wailing and grinding of teeth when you see Abraham, Isaac, and Jacob and all the prophets in the kingdom of God and you yourselves cast out" (13:28).

The patriarchs and prophets represent those who have heard the word of God and kept (done) it. Some of the Jews think that they are imitating them, but, as Jesus points out, they are not. Luke is not interested in condemning Israel, but he does want to jar his readers (hopefully some of whom are Jews) into a response to God's offer of salvation.

Jesus makes it clear that "people will come from the east and the west and from the north and the south and will recline at table in the kingdom of God" (13:29). Those who do not "enter through the narrow gate" (13:24) of Jesus' way will find their places in the kingdom of God given away to the Gentiles, who will come from the four corners of the world. Gentiles who "are last… will be first, and some (Jews) are first who will be last" (13:30). No one can presume salvation; however, everyone must presume the need to repent.

Meditation: In which ways do you need to heed Jesus' warning: "Strive to enter through the narrow gate, for many, I tell you, will try to enter but be unable"?

Prayer: Master God, you invite all people to repentance that all might recline at the table in your kingdom. Guide us to the narrow gate and make us strong enough to enter through it. Help us to enter before the door is locked that we might share in your feast. We ask this through our Lord Jesus Christ, your Son, who lives and reigns with you and the Holy Spirit, one God, for ever and ever. Amen.

MOTHER HEN

Luke 13:31-35

Scripture: "Jerusalem, Jerusalem, you who kill the prophets and stone those sent to you, how many times I yearned to gather your children together as a hen gathers her brood under her wings, but you were unwilling!" (Luke 13:34).

Reflection: The last two sections of chapter thirteen of Luke's Gospel consist of some Pharisees' announcement to Jesus that Herod desires to kill him (13:31-33) and Jesus' lament over Jerusalem (13:34-35). The Pharisees tell Jesus, "Go away, leave this area because Herod wants to kill you" (13:31). At first this might look like a friendly warning, but in effect the Pharisees are trying to side-track Jesus from his mission — Jerusalem, where he will be rejected, suffer, die, and rise.

Jesus' response to the warning declares that nothing — not even the possibility of death — will stand in his way of establishing the kingdom of God through preaching, healing, and teaching: "Go and tell that fox, 'Behold, I'll drive out demons and perform healings today and tomorrow, and on the third day I will have finished my work'" (13:32).

Jerusalem is Jesus' goal; the journey will lead him there, where his work will be accomplished. So, he declares, "'I must continue on my way today, tomorrow, and the following day, for it is impossible that a prophet should die outside of Jerusalem'" (13:33). Like the prophets before him, Jesus will meet his death in Jerusalem.

But until that time he yearns to gather the children of Jerusalem together "as a hen gathers her brood under her wings" (13:34). Using this Q material (cf. Matthew 23:37-39), Luke demonstrates that Jesus already knows his fate. Jerusalem is "unwilling" (13:34) to accept the salvation that he brings.

"Behold, your house will be abandoned" (13:35). Here, Luke gives the reader a hint of the full blown prediction of the fall of Jerusalem in 19:41-44. Likewise, he deals with the historic destruction of the city in 70 A.D. by the Romans by giving a reason — non-acceptance of salvation — for the city's demolition.

The prediction of the fall of Jerusalem will take place after the triumphant entry into the city. However, the city will not see Jesus until the crowds cry out, "Blessed is he who comes in the name of the Lord" (13:35). Thus, Luke ties together this aspect of the journey narrative with the final destination of the journey — Jerusalem.

Meditation: What fears often cause you to turn back instead of moving forward on your journey? Where is your Jerusalem?

Prayer: God of prophets, throughout history you have sent men and women to your people to call them to repentance and a change of heart. Again and again you have renewed your covenant with your people. Be with us when we are afraid. Accompany us on our pilgrimage of life. Enable us to respond to the words of your prophets. Blessed are you, Lord God — Father, Son, and Holy Spirit, one God, for ever and ever. Amen.

WHO'S AT TABLE?
Luke 14:1-6

Scripture: Jesus spoke to the lawyers and Pharisees and said, "Is it lawful to cure on the Sabbath or not?" (Luke 14:3).

Reflection: The account of the healing of a man with dropsy on the Sabbath (14:1-6) is somewhat like Matthew's account of the healing of a man with a withered hand on the Sabbath (Matthew 12:9-13); therefore, Luke's account could come from Q. He has radically reworked the story to function as a parallel to the cure of a crippled woman on the Sabbath, which he narrated earlier (cf. 13:10-16).

The story is set within a "home of one of the leading Pharisees" where Jesus "went to dine" (14:1). Therefore, the issue will be table fellowship; that is, who can gather around the table and who cannot. This is an issue throughout Luke's Gospel, and this section of his Gospel forms the first of four instructions concerning table fellowship. As in similar situations (cf. 7:36-50, 11:37-44), such meals develop into confrontational situations between Jesus and the Pharisees.

This narrative also reflects the post-Easter community. Those who are considered outcasts are the very ones who are usually invited to sit at the table and dine with Jesus. Those who are considered the righteous are the very ones who are usually asked to give up their places to the more deserving!

This part (14:1-6) of the table fellowship issue serves only as an introduction to four closely related sections, which will be investigated during the next four days. As seen before, Jesus exposes the disparity between the inner attitude of the Pharisees and their outer appearance.

Outwardly, they are persons who keep the law. The question of curing on the Sabbath was a debatable one. The man with dropsy, an abnormal swelling of the body because of the retention and accumulation of fluid, is compared to a "son or ox" falling "into a cistern" on the Sabbath (14:5). Jesus asks the Pharisees if they would not "immediately pull him out on the Sabbath day?" (14:5).

With such a comparison, the Pharisees are uncovered as people who appear to keep the law but underneath are unconcerned about people in need. They keep silent when Jesus asks about the lawfulness of curing on the Sabbath. They do not answer his question about rescuing a son or an ox from a pit on the Sabbath.

The Pharisees would break the law in the case of a son or an ox, presumes Jesus. Then how much more should the law be broken in the case of a man suffering with dropsy. People come first, declares Jesus. The outer appearance of always keeping the law must be harmonized with an inner attachment to the purpose of the law — people. People who join Jesus at table are to possess an inner reality concerning the importance of people that corresponds to their outward actions.

Meditation: In the past, how have you broken the Sabbath law in order to take care of people first?

Prayer: Healing God, you created people in your own image and likeness and taught them to love you and each other as they love themselves. Guide us with your Spirit in keeping this law of love so that we do not turn the law into an idol but always remember its purpose. Direct us to our brothers and sisters in need that through our service to them we might worship you, Father, Son, and Holy Spirit, one God, for ever and ever. Amen.

PLACE OF HONOR
Luke 14:1, 7-11

Scripture: "When you're invited by someone to a wedding banquet, do not recline at the place of honor, lest someone more distinguished than you may have been invited… and the host who invited both of you may approach you and say, 'Give your place to this man,' and then you would proceed with embarrassment to take the lowest place" (Luke 14:8-9).

Reflection: The second (14:7-11) of four sections concerned with table fellowship in Luke's Gospel is unique to this author. The Pharisees have been exposed; their outward appearance does not harmonize with their inner attitude. This disparity is further highlighted when Jesus tells a parable to those who had been invited to a wedding banquet, while "noticing how they were choosing the places of honor" for themselves at table (14:7-8).

The parable functions as a warning to those who are self-seeking and presumptuous. Because the Pharisees considered themselves righteous (that is, behaving as God wills), they presumed that the places of honor at table were reserved for them. According to Jesus, this is not how God acts: "Everyone who exalts himself will be humbled, but the one who humbles himself will be exalted" (14:11), he declares. In other words, in the kingdom of God (wedding banquet), God invites whom God wills to the places of honor. No one can assume that he or she has earned a place of honor at the table.

The self-seeking and presumptuous individual will discover that "someone more distinguished... may have been invited" (14:8). After being requested by the host to relinquish the seat, such a presumptuous person "would proceed with embarrassment to take the lowest place" (14:9).

The way a person demonstrates God's will and an inner harmony between outward expression and inner attitude is by taking "the lowest place so that when the host comes... he may say, 'My friend, move up to a higher position'" (14:10). In God's kingdom all the usual social presumptions and rules concerning table etiquette are reversed. If a person wants to be served first, he or she must take the last place.

This reversal theme was already presented earlier in Luke's Gospel. Mary declared, "He (God) has pulled down the mighty from their thrones and lifted up the lowly" (1:52). Humility means knowing that all people are equally lowly and that God will exalt them.

Meditation: When did you exalt yourself and God humbled you? When did you humble yourself and God exalted you?

Prayer: God our host, you spread the table of the kingdom for your people and invite them to come to your feast. In your eyes, all people are created with equal human dignity. Give us a deep respect for every man, woman, and child. Help us to recognize the lines of your love in all our brothers and sisters. Bring us to the eternal wedding banquet which you share with Jesus, your Son, and the Holy Spirit, one God, for ever and ever. Amen.

PRACTICE WHAT YOU PREACH

Matthew 23:1-12

SUNDAY
of Week

31

Cycle A

Scripture: "The scribes and the Pharisees have taken their seat on the chair of Moses. Therefore, do and observe everything they tell you, but do not follow their example. For they preach but they do not practice" (Matthew 23:2-3).

Reflection: This narrative (Matthew 23:1-12) of the denunciation of the scribes and the Pharisees (Matthew 23:1-39) forms part of the final section of the fifth book of Matthew's Gospel. The author is dependent on Mark (cf. 12:38-39) and Q (cf. Luke 11:37-52; 13:34-35) and his own special source for his material. Jesus' speech denouncing the scribes and the Pharisees reflects more of the situation of Matthew's church than it does any historical conflict during the ministry of Jesus.

Here Jesus addresses "the crowds and... his disciples, saying, 'The scribes and the Pharisees have taken their seat on the chair of Moses'" (23:1-2). "Scribes and Pharisees" is Matthew's favorite way of describing the Jewish teaching authority, although in Jesus' time the scribes were the lawyers and theologians while the Pharisees were laymen who sought to live out a strict observance of the law and tradition. "Scribes and Pharisees" represent the Judaism which Matthew's community was facing at the time he wrote this Gospel.

The "chair of Moses" represents the claim of the rabbis to

have the authority to teach and to interpret the law at the time of Matthew's composition. Using a hyperbolic statement, Matthew makes it clear that this is not the teaching and the interpretation that the members of his community are to follow: "Therefore, do and observe everything they tell you, but do not follow their example" (23:3). While their teaching of the law is considered correct (Matthew never wants to throw out the law completely), their practice of it is sorely lacking. According to Matthew, actions must be in harmony with faith.

The scribes and Pharisees "tie up heavy burdens [hard to carry] and lay them on people's shoulders, but they will not lift a finger to move them" (23:4). In other words, their strict observance of the 613 commandments of the law and tradition is for the sake of keeping the law instead of understanding the purpose of the law. People suffer because of this, but the scribes and Pharisees will not help them.

Jesus accuses the scribes and Pharisees of hypocrisy: "All their works are performed to be seen" (23:5). They are not authentic. Their outer acts do not spring from the proper inner motivation. Three examples are given.

First, "They widen their phylacteries and lengthen their tassels" (23:5). Phylacteries were little boxes which contained parchments, upon which were Exodus 13:1-16 and Deuteronomy 6:4-9; 11:13-21. These were worn on the left forearm and on the forehead during prayer. Four tassels were worn on the cloaks of pious Jews to remind them to keep the law in accordance with Numbers 15:38-39 and Deuteronomy 22:12.

The scribes and Pharisees are accused of widening their phylacteries and lengthening their tassels so that other people would notice their piety. For Matthew the issue is not piety but authenticity. Members of his community are to be authentic; there must be a harmony between their actions and their inner motivation.

Second, the scribes and the Pharisees "love places of honor at banquets [and] seats of honor in synagogues" (23:6). By being seated next to the host during a banquet or in the special place in front of the people in the synagogue, the scribes and the Pharisees are noticed by all. However, it is only an outward display.

Third, they "love… greetings in marketplaces and the salutation 'Rabbi'" (23:7). According to ancient custom, those who were inferior had the responsibility to greet those they considered superior. The scribes and Pharisees consider themselves superior and wish to receive such greetings.

The salutation of "Rabbi," meaning "my great one," was a title of respect for Jewish teachers and leaders. The leaders of the Church, however, are told, "Do not be called 'Rabbi.' You have but one teacher, and you are all brothers [and sisters]" (23:8). Jesus is the one teacher for Christians.

Followers of Jesus are told, "Call no one on earth your father; you have but one Father in heaven" (23:9). From this evidence it appears that a practice may have developed in the early Church of referring to some leaders as "father." Matthew is interested in stopping this because only God is called "Abba" by Christians.

Finally, Christian leaders are told, "Do not be called 'Master'; you have but one master, the Messiah" (23:10). Again, this reference indicates a use in Matthew's community. The author does not think that leaders should be referred to as "Master."

This author's perspective is that there is no hierarchy among the followers of Jesus. "The greatest among you must be your servant" (23:11). Indeed, authentic discipleship springs from being a servant, like Jesus. The One to be imitated is "the Son of Man [who] did not come to be served but to serve" (20:28).

On the day of judgment, when the good and bad are finally separated, God will reveal everyone's true colors. The scribes and Pharisees, who have exalted themselves, will be humbled; but those authentic followers of Jesus, who have humbled themselves, will be exalted (cf. 23:12). In God's kingdom all earthly positions will be reversed.

Meditation: In which ways do you find that you sometimes act like the scribes and the Pharisees?

Prayer: Father in heaven, you have sent the Master, your Son, to be our Messiah and to teach us the way of authentic discipleship. When we seek superiority, remind us of the equality of all people. When we seek recognition, remind us that all persons are called to be servants. When we seek exaltation, humble us. May we always keep in mind the example of Jesus, who lives and reigns with you and the Holy Spirit, one God, for ever and ever. Amen.

GOD, NEIGHBOR, SELF

Mark 12:28-34

Scripture: One of the scribes... asked him (Jesus), "Which is the first of all the commandments?" Jesus replied, "The first is this: 'Hear, O Israel! The Lord our God is Lord alone! You shall love the Lord your God with all your heart, with all your soul, with all your mind, and with all your strength.' The second is this: 'You shall love your neighbor as yourself.' There is no other commandment greater than these" (Mark 12:28-31).

Reflection: The greatest commandment section (12:28-34) of Mark's Gospel is the fifth of six debates that take place in the Temple after Jesus had triumphantly entered Jerusalem. In this section, the author is interested in preserving the link between Judaism and Christianity; he does not want to write to his community about the beginning of a new religion, but strives to show how Christianity is the fulfillment or completion of God's promises made to Israel.

In the editorial comment that introduces the question by the scribe, Mark informs the reader that "he came forward and heard them (Pharisees, Herodians, Sadducees) disputing and saw how well he had answered them" (12:28). The question, "Which is the first of all the commandments?" (12:28) was one that was frequently asked within Judaism. It was a legitimate question in light of the 613 laws; the rabbis sought to determine which commandment outweighed all the others. Jesus answers the question by quoting the shema, the prayer recited by every Jewish man in the morning and in the evening: "Hear, O Israel! The Lord our God is Lord alone! You shall love the Lord your God with all your heart, with all your soul, with all your mind, and with all your strength" (12:29-30; Deuteronomy 6:4-5). No problem here.

But before a good breath can be taken, Jesus declares, "The second is this: 'You shall love your neighbor as yourself'" (13:31; cf. Leviticus 19:18). The scribe had asked for "the first of all the commandments" (12:28), but he got not only the first but the second too. Here Jesus welds the love of God, the love of neighbor, and the love of self together. He identifies the love of God with the love of neighbor and the love of self.

Then, he declares, "There is no other commandment greater than these" (12:31). In other words, there are not two commandments, but there is only one — and it involves God, neighbor, and self. At this point, Mark has moved away from Judaism and toward Christianity, while maintaining some Jewish roots.

The scribe's reply to Jesus is peculiar to Mark's Gospel. The author uses the reply to further refine Jesus' remarks. He says, "You are right in saying, 'He is the One and there is no other than He.' And to 'love him with all your heart, with all your understanding, with all your strength, and to love your neighbor as yourself' is worth more than all burnt offerings and sacrifices" (12:32-33). Authentic love of God and authentic love of others is more important than the Temple cult, which by the time of Mark's writing had been destroyed.

Because of the insight of the scribe's answer, Jesus tells him, "You are not far from the kingdom of God" (12:34). Nowhere else in any of the Gospels does a scribe emerge with such praise. Why? Because he represents Mark's position — the community of the followers of Jesus are bound together by love of God, neighbor and self. Such community love surpasses "all burnt offerings and sacrifices" (12:33) of the past.

Meditation: In which ways do the members of your community (parish, church) keep the greatest commandment — the love of God, neighbor, and self?

Prayer: God of love, you have called your people to love you with all their heart, with all their soul, with all their mind, and with all their strength and to love their neighbor as they love themselves. Because of your great love, you sent Jesus to us to demonstrate that there are no boundaries to love. Help us to imitate his love and to do your will that we may come to share the joys of the kingdom, where you live and reign with him and the Holy Spirit, one God, for ever and ever. Amen.

COME DOWN QUICKLY

Luke 19:1-10

Scripture: A man named Zacchaeus… a chief tax collector and also a wealthy man, was trying to see who Jesus was…. He ran ahead and climbed a sycamore tree in order to see him…. Jesus looked up and said to him, "Zacchaeus, hurry on down, for today I must stay at your house…. Today salvation has come to this house because this man too is a descendant of Abraham" (Luke 19:2-5, 9).

Reflection: The story about Zacchaeus the tax collector (Luke 19:1-10) is unique to Luke's Gospel. It is the second to last story before the account of Jesus' triumphal entry into Jerusalem. The story's placement within the Gospel as well as the point of the story serve to highlight some of this author's interests which have been woven throughout the Gospel. The story is situated in Jericho. Another important story was already located in Jericho — the parable of the Good Samaritan (cf. 10:29-37). In the latter case, a most unlikely person turns out to be the one to be imitated. Likewise, Zacchaeus, another unlikely person (a chief tax collector and a wealthy man!), is held up by Jesus as one to be imitated.

The structure of this story is similar to that of the call of Levi, another tax collector (cf. 5:27-32). A tax collector was a Jew who worked for the Roman occupation forces. He made his living by raising the set amount of the tax, asking whatever he liked, and

213

pocketing the difference. He was considered to be an apostate by his fellow Jews. After Levi is called, he hosts a banquet for Jesus. After Zacchaeus is called, Jesus goes to stay at his house. In both stories, there are present those people who grumble and complain about Jesus' table fellowship with persons who are outside of the law.

Zacchaeus is called "a wealthy man" (19:2). Throughout his Gospel, the author has worked off of a theme that places wealth within the context of the community. His understanding is that everything a person has comes from God. Riches are given to some people to be shared with all people. There is only so much wealth available; the only way those who have no riches will ever get any is if those who have wealth share it with them.

The parable of the rich man and Lazarus (16:19-31) served to illustrate the fate of those who refuse to share their wealth with others. The boundaries drawn in this life will be drawn in the next. Wealth, according to Luke, is not a sign of God's blessing for a single person; it is a sign of one's responsibility to share the goods of the earth with others.

Zacchaeus declares, "Behold, half of my possessions, Lord, I shall give to the poor, and if I have cheated anyone of anything I shall repay it four times over" (19:8). Thus, Luke demonstrates how a rich man can be saved — by accepting Jesus' offer of table fellowship, by repenting of any injustice he may have done, by giving to the poor, and by welcoming Jesus to his home.

In the end, Jesus declares, "Today salvation has come to this house because this man too is a descendant of Abraham" (19:9). For Luke, a true descendant of Abraham, one who is heir to the promises of God in the Old Testament, is one who accepts Jesus as the Messiah, the Savior, "the Son of Man [who] has come to seek and save what was lost" (19:10). Through Jesus' declaration, Zacchaeus, who was considered an apostate Jew, is restored to his former position. For Luke, Jesus' role as Savior is seeking out and saving the lost.

On this level the story is about conversion in a post-resurrectional setting. Jesus draws people to himself. Then, he goes to them and offers them forgiveness; he lives in them. Finally, he confirms that a transition has been made in the life of the one who was called and responded with repentance.

Meditation: In which ways has Jesus sought you out, come to you, and saved you?

Prayer: God our savior, you sent Jesus, the Son of Man, to seek out and to save your people who were lost. He called tax collectors and sinners to repent and to return to you. Give us the spirit of Zacchaeus that we might respond to Jesus' passing through our lives. Give us the grace to repent and to accept his offer of salvation. We ask this through our Lord Jesus Christ, your Son, who lives and reigns with you and the Holy Spirit, one God, for ever and ever. Amen.

WHO'S INVITED?

Luke 14:12-14

Scripture: "When you give a banquet, invite the poor, the crippled, the lame, the blind and you will be blessed, because they won't have anything with which to repay you" (Luke 14:13).

Reflection: The third section (14:12-14) of Jesus' four-part instruction in Luke concerning table fellowship is addressed to his host, "one of the leading Pharisees" (14:1). Just as the places of honor and embarrassment are reversed in the first section (14:7-11), now Jesus reverses the order of those who are to be invited.

In this uniquely Lucan section of the Gospel, Jesus tells his host, "When you give a lunch or a dinner, do not invite your friends or your brothers or your relatives or your wealthy neighbors, lest they also invite you in turn and thus repay you" (14:12). If these people, those of the same class, are invited to a meal, they will most likely reciprocate and invite the host to a similar meal. Thus, he will be repaid.

Reversing the usual social custom, Jesus declares, "When you give a banquet, invite the poor, the crippled, the lame, the blind and you will be blessed, because they won't have anything with which to repay you" (14:14). Those persons to be invited to one's lunch or dinner are the outcasts, the downtrodden, the oppressed, the afflicted, the forgotten, the neglected.

This statement represents a particular Lucan theme — concern for the poor. It reminds the reader of the parable of the rich fool (12:16-21) and the ensuing exhortation, "Make for yourselves purses that don't wear out, an inexhaustible treasure in heaven where no thief approaches nor moth destroys. For where your treasure is, there will your heart be too" (12:33-34).

The poor are Luke's "inexhaustible treasure." Those who have wealth and are able to provide a lunch or dinner do so for the poor, so that they can share in the riches. Money is given to people so that it can be given away — that is, shared with those who have none.

Repayment for sharing what God has given one in this life cannot be the true host's concern. That is why he is "blessed" if he invites people who are unable to repay him with a like invitation. The host's concern, according to Jesus in this passage, should be the "resurrection of the righteous" (14:14). The host who has invited the outcasts, those who have no riches, to his lunch or dinner, will discover that he has "inexhaustible treasure in heaven" (12:33).

Meditation: Whom do you invite to lunch or dinner? Do they represent treasure in heaven or treasure on earth?

Prayer: God of the banquet hall, you invite the poor, the crippled, the lame, and the blind to your feast. You command that those who have received a surplus of your riches are to share them with those who have received a smaller portion. Open our eyes to see the needs of our brothers and sisters. Make us responsive to these needs once we see them that we may be declared blessed at the resurrection of the righteous. We ask this through Christ our Lord. Amen.

THE GREAT DINNER
Luke 14:15-24

Scripture: "A man gave a big dinner to which he invited many. When the time came for the dinner, he sent his servant to say to those invited, 'Come, everything is ready now.' But one by one, they all began to excuse themselves.... The master of the house was furious and said to his servant, 'Go out quickly into the streets and alleys of the town and bring in here the poor and the crippled, the blind and the lame.... I tell you, not one of those men I invited will taste my dinner'" (Luke 14:16-18, 21, 24).

Reflection: The last (14:15-24) of the four-part instruction concerning table fellowship most probably comes from Q (cf. Matthew 22:1-10) and begins with a beatitude-like response from one of the guests at the meal with Jesus: "Blessed is the one who eats bread in the kingdom of God" (14:15). Little does the guest who spoke those words realize the truth in them, for by the end of the allegorized story, which Jesus tells in response to these words, the speaker will realize that he will not taste the dinner!

The allegory is easy to understand. The man who gives the "big dinner" (14:16), a metaphor for the messianic banquet, is God. Those who are invited (Israel) "excuse themselves" (14:18), when the servant (prophets) delivers the invitation to them.

The invited are too preoccupied with daily concerns. One has "purchased a field and must go to examine it" (14:18). A second has "purchased five yoke of oxen" and he is on his "way to evaluate them" (14:19). A third excuses himself by saying, "I have just gotten married, and therefore I cannot come" (14:20).

These people who make the excuses are not Luke's primary concern, however. He is interested in those whom the master invites to the dinner after the originally invited guests refuse to come. Those who respond to the second and third rounds of invitations are the "blessed... in the kingdom of God" (14:15).

Who is "in the kingdom of God"? "The poor and the crippled, the blind and the lame" (14:21), the first group to be rounded up from the "streets and alleys of the town" (14:21), are "in the kingdom of God." These are the same people that Jesus earlier told his host to invite to his dinner (cf. 14:13). The poor are a particular concern of this author.

However, even all of these do not fill the banqueting hall. So the master "said to the servant, 'Go out along the highways and hedgerows and force them to come in so that my house may be filled'" (14:23). This second recruitment of people for the kingdom represents the Gentile mission, which will be further developed in Luke's second volume, the Acts of the Apostles.

The final sentence of the allegory summarizes Luke's view of salvation history: "Not one of those men I invited will taste my dinner" (14:24). In the context of the story, these are the "scholars of the law and Pharisees" (14:3).

Yes, "Blessed is the one who eats bread in the kingdom of God" (14:15); it will not be the one who reclined "at table in the place of honor" (14:8), but rather the one who took "the lowest place" (14:10). All is reversed around God's banquet table in his kingdom.

Meditation: In which ways have you accepted the invitation from God to his great feast?

Prayer: Master of the house, you invite all people to come to your home and share the great dinner which you have prepared. When we become preoccupied with other things, remind us that everything is ready. Help us to make a faithful response. Gather all your people together that your home may be filled with banqueters. Count us among the elect in the kingdom, where you live and reign with Jesus, your Son, and the Holy Spirit, one God, for ever and ever. Amen.

DETACHMENT

Luke 14:25-33

Scripture: "If anyone comes to me and doesn't hate his own father and mother, wife and children, brothers and sisters, and even his own life, he cannot be my disciple. Whoever doesn't carry his own cross and follow me cannot be my disciple.... No one who doesn't renounce all his possessions can be my disciple" (Luke 14:26-27, 33).

Reflection: The parable of the great feast (14:15-24) in Luke's Gospel is followed by a collection of sayings concerning discipleship (14:25-33). The sayings focus on the total dedication which is necessary for one to embrace discipleship and deal with issues such as attachment to family, persecution, realistic assessment and possessions.

This section of the Gospel is addressed to the "great crowds" (14:25) who are traveling with Jesus. The whole section reflects the author's emphasis on what it takes to be an authentic follower of Jesus in the world after the resurrection.

The first saying is from Q (cf. Matthew 10:37): "If anyone comes to me and doesn't hate his own father and mother, wife and children, brothers and sisters, and even his own life, he [or she] cannot be my disciple" (14:26). The most striking word in this saying is "hate." However, this word does not refer to a loathing of one's family but, rather, is a Semitic way of expressing absolute and total detachment from. Luke is saying that the family of a follower of Jesus takes second place to Jesus. A disciple's loyalty is first of all to Jesus. Otherwise, one falls into the category of the would-be followers of Jesus (cf. 9:57-62).

The second saying is from Q (cf. Matthew 10:38; 16:24) and Mark (cf. 8:34): "Whoever doesn't carry his [or her] own cross and follow me cannot be my disciple" (14:27). This saying is similar to the one found in 9:23. In both cases the emphasis is on making a choice between one's own life and following Jesus. Just as one must be detached from one's family, so must a disciple be detached from his or her own life. A person's commitment to Jesus must be more important even than devotion to his or her own life. Discipleship demands that a person carry the cross — which for Luke's community was a real possibility — and put Jesus first in one's own life.

Such a commitment to Jesus' way involves careful calculation; a person must realistically assess discipleship before embracing it. This should be done in the same way as a farmer who prepares to build a tower. "Wouldn't any one of you who wanted to build a tower first sit down and figure out the cost to see if you had enough to complete it? Otherwise, after laying the foundation and finding yourself unable to finish it, the onlookers would make fun of you and say, 'This one began to build but he couldn't finish'" (14:28-30).

This example is unique to Luke's Gospel. It emphasizes the importance of calculating the cost of discipleship. To decide to follow Jesus before carefully evaluating all that is involved might cause one to be embarrassed because of not being able to follow through with what one has begun.

The second example, that of two kings going to war, further emphasizes the importance of careful calculation. In this parable, unique to this Gospel, Jesus asks, "Wouldn't a king marching into battle first sit down and determine whether with ten thousand troops he can successfully oppose another king advancing upon him with twenty thousand troops? But if he can't, while the enemy is still far away, he will send a delegation to ask the terms for peace" (14:31-32).

Luke is exhorting the members of his community to sit down and reckon their chances of remaining faithful followers of Jesus before they go into the world and bear witness to Jesus. A king does this to avoid subjection to alien rule. A Christian does this in order to determine who the real king of the world is and to evaluate his or her commitment to this king.

The final saying of this section emphasizes a particular Lucan theme dealing with complete detachment from material possessions: "No one who doesn't renounce all his possessions can be my disciple" (14:33). As the reader has discovered so many times before, Luke believes that wealth is given to some people so that they can share what they have with others. Authentic discipleship demands that those who have riches are always sharing what they have with those who have none. This demonstrates one's detachment from material possessions and is what the Giver of all good gifts wills that his people do.

The simile of salt (14:34-35), which is omitted from the daily cycle of readings, concludes this section of the Gospel by further indicating the importance of total dedication to discipleship. The non-committed disciple is like salt that has lost its taste; "It is fit neither for the soil nor for the manure pile; it is thrown out" (14:35). Therefore, "Whoever has ears to hear, let them hear" (14:35).

Meditation: In which ways do you think that as a disciple of Jesus you are detached from your family, ready to accept persecution (the cross), have calculated the cost of discipleship, and renounced all your possessions?

Prayer: God of discipleship, from those who profess their faith in Jesus, your Son, you demand absolute commitment to his way of life. Mold us into the image of Jesus: Remove our earthly attachments to family and possessions. Give us the wisdom to calculate the cost of authentic discipleship that we might be willing to carry the cross all the way to the kingdom, where you live and reign with Jesus and the Holy Spirit, one God, for ever and ever. Amen.

LOST SHEEP AND COIN

Luke 15:1-10

Scripture: "What woman having ten coins and losing one would not light a lamp and sweep the house, searching carefully until she finds it? And when she does find it, she calls together her friends and neighbors and says to them, 'Rejoice with me because I have found the coin that I lost'" (Luke 15:8-9).

Reflection: Chapter 15 of Luke's Gospel contains three parables which all deal with loss — a lost sheep, a lost coin, and a lost son. The parable of the lost son (usually called the prodigal son) is omitted in the weekday cycle of readings. Luke's source for the parable of the lost sheep (15:1-7) is Q (cf. Matthew 18:12-14), while the parable of the lost coin (15:8-10) comes from his own special material.

Both of these parables, as well as that of the lost son, are applied to the theme of repentance by the author.

As Luke sets the stage for the telling of these parables, the author declares, "The tax collectors and sinners were all drawing near to listen to him (Jesus), but the Pharisees and scribes began to complain, saying, 'This man welcomes sinners and eats with them'" (15:1-2). The tax collectors and sinners, those considered social outcasts — the lost — listen (that is, hear the word and act on it, repent) to Jesus, while the Pharisees and scribes, those considered righteous — the found — fail to hear and act on the word; they do not repent.

The first parable begins with a question: "What man among you having a hundred sheep and losing one of them would not leave the ninety-nine in the desert and go after the lost one until he finds it?" (15:4). The logical answer to the question is never given: No shepherd would leave 99 sheep in the desert and go look for a stupid lost one! Ninety-nine sheep are more valuable than one sheep. The question recalls the prophet Ezekiel, who records, "Thus says the Lord God: I myself will look after and tend my sheep. As a shepherd tends his flock when he finds himself among his scattered sheep, so will I tend my sheep. I will rescue them from every place where they were scattered…. The lost I will seek out, the strayed I will bring back" (Ezekiel 34:11-12, 16).

God does what no shepherd would do; he seeks out the lost — tax collectors and sinners, those who were considered to be of no value. "And when he does find it, he sets it on his shoulders with great joy and, upon his arrival home, he calls together his friends and neighbors and says to them, 'Rejoice with me because I have found my lost sheep'" (15:56). For Luke, Jesus is the shepherd who goes out looking for the lost sheep; he "welcomes sinners and eats with them" (15:2). In the kingdom of God, the tax collectors and sinners sit at the table!

Then, Luke makes an application of the parable: "I tell you, in just the same way there will be more joy in heaven over one sinner who repents than over ninety-nine righteous people who have no need of repentance" (15:7). The tax collectors and sinners, the lost, respond to Jesus throughout Luke's Gospel. The Pharisees and scribes fail to respond, as they consider themselves already righteous. Jesus' address asks them to join him in rejoicing over the finding of one who was lost and to consider the lost, now found, one to be of great value.

This will mean that the Pharisees and scribes must relinquish their presupposition concerning their own righteousness. Repentance is not something that people do on their own; God makes the first move by seeking out the lost and calling them to respond (repent). Everyone is lost and needs to be found, Luke is saying. Some people, however, do not recognize the fact that they are lost.

The second parable about a woman who loses one of ten coins (15:8-10) makes the same point. Typical of Luke's style, the owner of the lost sheep is a man, while the owner of the lost coin is a woman.

The lost coin is one of ten coins; each coin was of little value. The answer to the question, "What woman having ten coins and losing one would not light a lamp and sweep the house, searching carefully until she finds it?" (15:8), is never answered because the logical answer is "No one!" However, the parable identifies the lost coin with tax collectors and sinners. What is of no value to people is of great value to God.

The emphasis of this parable is the celebration which follows the finding of the lost coin. "When she does find it, she calls together her friends and neighbors and says to them, 'Rejoice with me because I have found the coin that I lost'" (15:9). In the kingdom, God rejoices over the finding of one lost sinner. "There will be rejoicing among the angels of God over one sinner who repents" (15:10).

The agent of the search for the lost coin is a woman! It is not a man, a king, a landowner, but a woman. Thus, the author compares God's ruling activity to a woman, who searches for tax collectors and sinners — what is considered of little value.

Both parables conclude with fullness. The man finds the lost sheep and again has 100 sheep. The woman finds the lost coin and again has ten coins. Likewise, the father in the parable of the prodigal son has two sons. According to Luke, in the kingdom God intends to have everyone — in distinction to those who think that God is only interested in the righteous.

Meditation: When have you been lost and found by God? What is your response to God?

Prayer: God of the lost, you will that no one should be excluded from your kingdom. When we stray like sheep from your presence, come and find us. When we are lost like a coin, come and seek us out. Guide us to repentance through the gift of your Holy Spirit. Count us among those who repent that we might share the joy of your angels in heaven, where you live and reign with Jesus, your Son, and the Holy Spirit, one God, for ever and ever. Amen.

COMMENDATION FOR DISHONESTY!

Luke 16:1-8

Scripture: "There was a rich man who had a steward, and a report came to him that this man had been squandering his possessions.... The steward said to himself, 'What can I do? — my master is taking the stewardship away from me.' He called in his master's debtors one by one. To the first he said, 'How much do you owe my master?' He replied, 'Eight hundred gallons of olive oil.' He said to him, 'Take your bills, sit down, and quickly write one for four hundred.' Next he said to another, 'And you, how much do you owe?' He replied, 'A thousand bushels of wheat.' He said to him, 'Take your bills and write eight hundred.' And the master commended the steward for his wrongdoing because he'd acted wisely" (Luke 16:1, 3, 5-8).

Reflection: Luke's unique parable about the dishonest steward (16:1-8) begins a chapter of the Gospel which is concerned with the use and misuse of wealth. On one level, Luke employs the parable to teach his church about the prudent use of wealth in the light of an imminent crisis, such as the coming of the kingdom of God or the coming of the Son of Man.

In the ancient world, rich men were few, while peasants were many. Upon hearing that this parable is about a rich man whose steward has been squandering his master's money, the peasant audience would immediately side with the steward; he was about to lose his job.

When the steward begins to think, "What can I do? — my

master is taking the stewardship away from me. I can't dig and I'm ashamed to beg" (16:3), the audience is drawn closer to him, but it also recognizes that he is beginning to act like the rich man; he is taking matters into his own hands.

The steward's course of action is to insure that others will welcome him into their homes once the stewardship is removed from him. However, what he does is immoral. He calls in his master's debtors and reduces what they owe his master.

At this point the audience must call his actions into question. They feel that he has a right to his job, but can they agree to his cheating his master? To agree with the reduction of his master's debtors' bills is to take a moral holiday and to sanction the getting even of the steward with his master. The hearers of this parable are left in a quandary!

What is more important is the response of the master: "The master commended the steward for his wrongdoing because he had acted wisely" (16:8). All of a sudden the presupposition that the master is a bad man is reversed, just as the presupposition that the steward was a good man had been reversed when he began to act like his master. All of a sudden the parable turns the world up-side down!

The rich man was considered to have power, and, because of his power, the capacity to execute justice. His steward was squandering his property; with his power he could justly fire the steward. By praising his dishonest steward, however, he forfeits his power. In so doing, he becomes vulnerable to his steward. Instead of possessing power, the rich man now possesses vulnerability. In the kingdom of God masters and stewards do not get even with each other; they are vulnerable to each other.

The parable does not foster or condone dishonesty. The master praises his dishonest steward for his prudence, for looking ahead and planning appropriately. The steward was finally functioning as a steward and managing his master's affairs.

The parable declares that rich masters are not always cruel and powerful and that stewards are not right in getting even with them. In the kingdom of God, all people are equally vulnerable; therefore, everyone should act prudently if he or she intends to enter the kingdom.

Meditation: In which ways have you experienced the kingdom of God in moments of vulnerability?

Prayer: God of masters and stewards, you reverse the presuppositions of your people and you declare that in your kingdom things are not the same as they are on earth. Rich men are not necessarily cruel and powerful, and stewards are not right in getting even. Help us to recognize our common vulnerability. Make us prudent in our use of the goods of this world that we may come to share the joys of the next world, where you live and reign with Jesus, your Son, and the Holy Spirit, one God, for ever and ever. Amen.

GOD OR MAMMON?
Luke 16:9-15

Saturday
of Week

31

Scripture: "No servant can serve two masters. He will either hate one and love the other, or be devoted to one and despise the other. You cannot serve God and Mammon" (Luke 16:13-14).

Reflection: Following the parable of the dishonest steward (16:1-8), Luke gathers together a number of originally independent sayings of Jesus and uses them to make applications of the parable (16:8-13). Two verses (16:14-15) which consist of a saying against money-loving Pharisees are also included in this section; these verses serve to shift the audience from the disciples to the Pharisees.

The first application of the parable that Luke makes compares the prudent action of the dishonest steward to the children of this world. "The children of this world are more prudent in dealing with their own generation than are the children of light" (16:8). Luke is telling his Christian audience to use wisely the wealth which it has under its control.

One way to do this is to "make friends... with dishonest wealth, so that when it fails, you will be welcomed into eternal dwellings" (16:9). "Dishonest wealth" does not refer to possessions which have been acquired dishonestly; rather, it refers to that in which wealthy people trust — money. Such trust has a tendency to lead one to dishonesty.

233

According to Luke, those who have money should use it to make friends, like the steward did in the parable. In the back of his mind, Luke is probably re-emphasizing one of his favorite themes: wealth is given to people to be shared with those who have none. Christians should use their wealth (by giving alms?), so that when it is all used up, they will be welcomed into heaven. The wise use of one's money, according to this author, will gain the person a welcome into heaven.

In the second application, Luke explains that "the person who is trustworthy in very small matters is also trustworthy in great ones; and the person who is dishonest in small matters is also dishonest in great ones" (16:10). Those who are in positions of authority must be faithful in their use of wealth.

If someone is "not trustworthy with dishonest wealth, who will trust" that person "with true wealth?" (16:11). In other words, if one cannot use riches to make friends in this world, then how can God trust that person with the wealth of the kingdom of heaven? Jesus asks, "If you are not trustworthy with what belongs to another, who will give you what is his own?" (16:12). If a person is not trustworthy with earthly wealth which is on loan from God, how can he or she expect to share in eternal life? The answer is: "One cannot!" People are stewards of whatever God gives them.

The third application of the parable of the dishonest steward makes it clear that "no servant can serve two masters" (16:13). The two masters are God and wealth. Whichever master a person chooses to serve indicates upon whom or what he or she depends. According to Jesus, a true follower of his is dependent on God alone. A person "cannot serve God and mammon" (16:13).

"The Pharisees, who loved money, heard all these things and sneered at him (Jesus)" (16:14). The Pharisees held that wealth was a sign of God's special love. Prosperity was an indication of righteousness.

According to Jesus, however, it is not the outer appearance, riches, that is important; what is in the heart is what is really important. To the Pharisees Jesus declares, "You justify yourselves in the sight of others, but God knows your hearts; for what is of human esteem is an abomination in the sight of God" (16:15).

Luke is calling attention to the hypocrisy of the Pharisees, who look like they are serving God but are, in effect, servants of mammon. They are examples of the preceding saying of Jesus: "You cannot serve God and mammon" (16:13). What looks good to others on the exterior is not in harmony with what is in a person's heart. God knows the heart.

Wealth, according to Luke, is not necessarily a sign of God's blessing or righteousness. Only an investigation of the heart can reveal authentic righteousness. Nevertheless, those with wealth have an obligation to share what they have with those who have none. In this way they serve one master, God, and provide for their being welcomed into his kingdom.

Meditation: In which ways does your use of wealth reflect the fact that you serve God and that you are a steward of earthly riches?

Prayer: God of the heart, once you finished the creation of the earth and everything on it, you fashioned man and woman in your image and likeness and made them stewards of your many gifts. Everything of any value comes from you and is loaned to us out of your generosity. Make us trustworthy servants. Teach us to share your generosity with all our brothers and sisters in need. Help us to keep our eyes fixed on serving you, the real Master, who lives and reigns with Jesus and the Holy Spirit, one God, for ever and ever. Amen.

THE BRIDEGROOM IS HERE!
Matthew 25:1-13

Scripture: "The kingdom of heaven will be like ten virgins who took their lamps and went out to meet the bridegroom. Five of them were foolish and five were wise. The foolish ones, when taking their lamps, brought no oil with them, but the wise brought flasks of oil with their lamps" (Matthew 25:1-3).

Reflection: The parable of the ten virgins (Matthew 25:1-13), which is unique to this author, is part of the fifth sermon, sometimes called the eschatological discourse, of Jesus in Matthew's Gospel. The whole sermon deals with the coming of the new age and how followers of Jesus are to conduct themselves while waiting for its fullness.

The parable of the ten virgins is typically more an allegory than a parable for Matthew. The bridegroom is the Lord, whose coming as judge in glory the Church was eagerly awaiting. There is no mention of a bride in the allegory. The author felt it necessary to teach his community (the bride?) about watching, waiting, being prepared, and judgment.

The first point is watching. Matthew wants to emphasize that even though "the bridegroom was long delayed" (25:5), the members of his community should not give up hope concerning Jesus' return. The hope for Jesus' coming was beginning to wane, and Matthew wanted to make sure that it was kept alive.

The author's second point is waiting. While waiting for the coming of Jesus in glory, members of the Church should be doing good deeds. The foolish virgins are contrasted to the wise ones, much as the foolish man, who built his house on sand, is

237

contrasted to the wise one, who built his house on rock (cf. 7:24-27). The word of God is to be heard and acted upon while we wait for Jesus to come.

Being prepared is the third point. When the bridegroom finally arrives, members of the Church are to be ready like the five wise virgins, who took flasks of oil with their lamps. Each person must take care to be prepared, Matthew emphasizes. When the foolish virgins ask the wise ones for oil for their lamps, the wise ones reply, "No, for there may not be enough for both you and us" (25:9). Preparation cannot be shared. While the foolish virgins went off to buy oil, "the bridegroom came and those who were ready went into the wedding feast with him. Then the door was locked" (25:10).

The fourth point which interests Matthew is judgment. Jesus will function as judge when he comes. Simply acknowledging him as "Lord" (25:11) is not enough. One must have heard the word and put it into practice; that is, a person must have watched, waited, and been prepared. Otherwise, the bridegroom-judge will declare, "Amen, I say to you, I do not know you" (25:12). The five foolish virgins are not recognized by the bridegroom.

The moral added to the allegory, "Stay awake, for you know neither the day nor the hour" (25:13), is not about not sleeping, since all ten of the virgins "became drowsy and fell asleep" (25:5). The "stay awake" admonition means that members of the community should be adequately equipped for their task of being followers of Jesus. Their lives should be characterized by watching, waiting, and preparation for the coming of Jesus as judge.

Meditation: In which ways do you watch, wait, and prepare for the coming of Jesus as judge?

Prayer: Father of the bridegroom, once you sent your Son, Jesus, to teach your people how to hear your word and to act on it. After his death and resurrection, you promised that he would come again in glory as judge. Do not let us become drowsy in listening to your word and doing good deeds. Keep us watchful. Give us patience in waiting. Prepare us with lamps burning with virtue that we might go out to meet the bridegroom when he comes and be counted among those ready to enter into the wedding feast. We ask this through our Lord Jesus Christ, your Son, the bridegroom, who lives and reigns with you and the Holy Spirit, one God, for ever and ever. Amen.

A CONTRIBUTION FROM POVERTY

Mark 12:38-44

Scripture: One poor widow... came and threw [into the treasury] two small coins worth a few cents. Calling his disciples to himself, he (Jesus) said to them, "Amen, I say to you, this poor widow put in more than all the others who threw money into the offering box — they all contributed from their surplus wealth, but she, from her poverty, has contributed all she had, her whole livelihood" (Mark 12:42-44).

Reflection: The denunciation of the scribes (Mark 12:38-40) and the narrative about the poor widow's contribution to the Temple treasury (12:41-44) bring to a conclusion a series of debates between Jesus and various opponents. These two sections of Mark's Gospel also precede Jesus' eschatological discourse, sometimes referred to as the little apocalypse (13:1-37).

The denunciation of the scribes echoes a Marcan theme, which concerns appropriate behavior for Christians. Jesus teaches, "Beware of the scribes, who like to go around in long robes and accept greetings in the marketplaces, seats of honor in synagogues, and places of honor at banquets. They devour the houses of widows and, as a pretext, recite lengthy prayers" (12:38-40).

The behavior of the scribes is inappropriate for a member of Mark's community. The clothes they wear, the way they act, the honor they seek is not in line with the dependency on God

239

that characterizes an authentic follower of Jesus. Christians who imitate the scribes, Mark is warning, "will receive a very severe condemnation" (12:40).

The widow represents dependency upon God. Marks sets the stage with Jesus sitting "down opposite the treasury" and observing "how the crowd put money into the treasury" (12:41).

The author declares, "Many rich people put in large sums. A poor widow also came and put in two small coins worth a few cents" (12:41-42). A widow, a woman without a husband, in the ancient world was one who had lost her source of livelihood; she stood as an example of powerlessness. The widow in this story is so powerless that all she has are two copper coins, an insignificant amount.

However, using hyperbolic language, Jesus declares oxymoronically, "This poor widow put in more than all the others who threw money into the offering box — they all contributed from their surplus wealth, but she, from her poverty, has contributed all she had, her whole livelihood" (12:43-44).

The widow is held up as an example of a true follower of Jesus. She, who was dependent, is even more dependent after she gives away the only two coins she had. Dependency and powerlessness are characteristics of authentic followers of Jesus, according to Mark. She stands in stark contrast to the self-sufficient scribes in the previous section.

Meditation: In which ways are you like the self-sufficient scribes? In which ways are you like the dependent and powerless widow?

Prayer: God of widows, you reversed the values of this world and held up the dependent and powerless as examples of authentic followers of your Son, Jesus. When our behavior mirrors that of the scribes, remind us that this is not the way of discipleship. Help us to imitate Jesus in dependency and powerlessness that we might share in the life he lives with you and the Holy Spirit, one God, for ever and ever. Amen.

RESURRECTION?

Luke 20:27-38

Scripture: "The children of this age marry and are given in marriage, but those deemed worthy of the coming age and resurrection from the dead neither marry nor are given in marriage. Like the angels, they are no longer able to die — they are children of God since they have attained resurrection" (Luke 20:34-36).

Reflection: The section of Luke's Gospel which raises the question about the resurrection (Luke 20:27-38) comes from Mark's Gospel (cf. 12:18-27). Luke has maintained the Marcan setting in the Temple following the triumphant entry into Jerusalem and the cleansing of the Temple. The question about the resurrection is one of a series of debates between Jesus and his adversaries, who try to discredit him.

The question about resurrection is posed by "some Sadducees, those who deny that there is a resurrection" (20:27). The Sadducees, a priestly aristocratic group, accepted only the first five books of the Old Testament (Pentateuch) as Scripture. They followed only the letter of the law and rejected all oral legal traditions and teaching not found in the Pentateuch, such as the resurrection of the dead. Therefore, they loved to pose resurrection riddles.

The question the Sadducees ask of Jesus is based on the law of levirate marriage as found in the book of Deuteronomy (25:5-

10). The law states that if a brother died without having produced a child, his surviving brother was to beget a child with his widow. The child would not be considered the heir of the surviving brother but of his dead brother. The name of the dead brother would be given to the child.

"Now there were seven brothers; the first married a woman but died childless. Then the second and the third married her, and likewise all the seven died childless. Finally the woman also died. Now at the resurrection whose wife will that woman be? For all seven had been married to her" (20:29-33).

Jesus answers the question/problem/riddle in two ways. First, he declares that the problem fails to take into account the difference between life on earth and life in heaven. "The children of this age marry and are given in marriage, but those deemed worthy of the coming age and resurrection from the dead neither marry nor are given in marriage. Like the angels, they are no longer able to die — they are children of God since they have attained resurrection" (Luke 20:34-36).

On earth people marry in order to guarantee the continuation of the human race. This is not necessary in the coming age of the resurrection because people "like the angels, are no longer able to die — they are children of God since they have attained resurrection" (20:36). The law concerning marriage on earth does not apply and is not appropriate in the life of the coming age of the resurrection.

Indirectly, Jesus is declaring that the Sadducees, who were supposed to know the mind of God from the law, should know this difference. Life in the age to come will not be like life on earth. The person who knows the mind of God would know this.

In the second answer to the question/problem/riddle, Jesus argues that the separation between this life and the life of the world to come implied by the question is inaccurate because it fails to consider the continuing relationship between God and his people. Using the law (Exodus 3:6) that the Sadducees so firmly adhered to, Jesus explains that death does not break a person's relationship with God.

"That the dead will rise even Moses made known in the passage about the bush, when he called 'Lord' the God of Abraham, the God of Isaac, and the God of Jacob. Now he is not God of the dead, but of the living, for to him they are all alive" (20:37-38). By the time of Moses, Abraham, Isaac, and Jacob had been dead a long time. Therefore, they must be alive in God if Moses refers to God as the God of the patriarchs. Death cannot destroy the relationship between God and his faithful people.

The question of the resurrection is one Luke was answering for his own community of believers. The Sadducees represent members of his community who were questioning the validity of the resurrection. This scene answers their question and assures them of the authenticity of their faith in the resurrection.

Meditation: Today, what do you consider to be valid reasons for believing in the resurrection of the dead?

Prayer: God of Abraham, Isaac, and Jacob, death does not separate you from your faithful people. When the broken body of your Son, Jesus, was overcome by death, you raised him to the fullness of life with you. Strengthen our faith in his resurrection and bring us to the kingdom, where you live and reign with Jesus and the Holy Spirit, one God, for ever and ever. Amen.

I AM SORRY

Luke 17:1-6

Scripture: "If your brother sins, rebuke him; and if he repents, forgive him. And if he wrongs you seven times in
one day and returns to you seven times saying, 'I'm sorry,'
you should forgive him" (Luke 17:3-4).

Reflection: This section (Luke 17:1-6) of Luke's Gospel consists
of three originally independent sayings of Jesus addressed to the
disciples. These sayings follow a series of sayings about the law
(16:16-17), about divorce (16:18), and the parable of the rich man
and Lazarus (16:19-31), all of which are omitted from the daily
cycle of selections from Luke's Gospel. The sayings deal with
what disciples of Jesus are to do and how they can do it.

The first saying (17:1-2) is concerned with Christian influence. Luke's source is Mark (9:42). "Scandal is inevitable, but
woe to the one through whom it comes. It would be better for
him to have a millstone placed around his neck and be thrown
into the sea than for him to cause one of these little ones to sin"
(17:1-2).

Luke accepts the inevitable fact of sin in his community.
However, using hyperbolic language, he warns those who lead
others to sin through scandal. "Little ones" represent the powerless — children, the poor, widows, etc. Those with any amount
of status in the community have a serious responsibility not to
scandalize anyone else. It would be better to be sealed in cement
and tossed into the river than to lead a powerless person to sin!
Luke hopes that this warning by Jesus will deter members of his
community from influencing weaker Christians in the wrong way.

The second saying (17:3-4), which comes from Q (cf. Matthew 18:15, 21-22), is concerned with a call to repentance and forgiveness. Members of the community are to rebuke the sinner in the hope of fostering his or her repentance. "If your brother [or sister] sins, rebuke him [or her]; and if he [or she] repents, forgive him [or her]" (17:3). This call to repentance is part of the lifestyle of a Christian for Luke.

Also, a Christian in Luke's community must be willing to forgive as often as the sinner repents. If a brother or a sister "wrongs you seven times in one day and returns to you seven times saying, 'I'm sorry,' you should forgive him [or her]" (17:4). Followers of Jesus in the Lucan community are called to a limitless forgiveness of those who sin against them and then repent.

Because of this responsibility to use their influence carefully and to forgive limitlessly, Christians need help; they are weak in faith. "The apostles said to the Lord, 'Increase our faith'" (17:5).

The third saying (17:5-6) is from Q (cf. Matthew 17:20). In this passage from Luke Jesus addresses the apostles, "If you have faith the size of a mustard seed, you could say to this mulberry tree, 'Be uprooted and planted in the sea,' and it would obey you" (17:6). The declaration here is that they already have some faith, which is sufficient to avoid improper influence of others and to forgive without limit. No matter if faith is only the size of a mustard seed — a very tiny seed — Luke is telling his community, it is sufficient to adhere to a Christian way of life.

The section which follows (17:7-11) further develops this idea.

Meditation: In which ways does your Christian way of life influence others? Whom have you forgiven limitlessly because he or she continues to repent?

Prayer: Faithful God, you never abandon your people. When sin entered the world, you immediately promised liberation and forgiveness. You sent Jesus, your Son, to rescue us from slavery to sin. He taught us that by our lifestyles we would influence others. He called us to repentance and offered us unlimited forgiveness. Send the Holy Spirit to direct our lives and prompt us to forgive those who sin against us. Make us strong in the faith we profess in Jesus the Christ, who lives and reigns with you and the Holy Spirit, one God, for ever and ever. Amen.

UNPROFITABLE SERVANTS

Luke 17:7-10

Scripture: "When you have done all you have been commanded, say, 'We are unprofitable servants; we have only
done what we should have done'" (Luke 17:10).

Reflection: After presenting three sayings about Christian influence, unlimited forgiveness, and faith (17:1-6), Luke presents a
section (17:7-10) which further explores the meaning of faith.
Here, Luke reminds the members of his community that they are
servants, who have no claim on God's graciousness. They are
exhorted by Jesus to do their duty as his followers.

The section begins with a question: "Who among you would
say to your servant who has just come in from plowing or tending sheep in the field, 'Come here immediately and take your
place at table'?" (17:7). The answer is, of course, no one. A person who had a servant, who functioned both as a farm hand and
as a shepherd, employed the servant to wait on him. The name
"servant" appropriately designates a role.

The appropriate response made by one who has such a servant is this: "Prepare something for me to eat. Put on your apron
and wait on me while I eat and drink. You may eat and drink
when I am finished" (17:8). This is what a servant is supposed to
do — serve the person for whom he works.

"The servant is owed no thanks, is he, because he did what

247

he was commanded?" (17:9). The obvious answer is, "Of course not." The servant is fulfilling his role as a servant.

The Lucan application to his Christian community follows: "So should it be with you. When you have done all you have been commanded, say, 'We are unprofitable servants; we have only done what we should have done'" (17:10). The amount of faith that God has given is sufficient to do what God asks. God gives enough faith to a person to fulfill his or her role as servant.

However, a servant is not able to do more than is required. There is no room for any type of moral superiority. God gives the gift of faith, which enables people (servants) to influence others properly and to forgive unlimitedly. Everyone, however, is reduced to the same equal status — that of servant. No servant can ever go beyond what God expects.

Meditation: When did you last experience yourself as a servant who received enough faith from God to do what you were obliged to do?

Prayer: God of servants, long ago you called the first man and first woman to serve you by giving them dominion over all the earth. When they turned away from your face, you called the patriarchs and judges to serve you and you made your people as numerous as the stars in the sky. The prophets, who proclaimed your word, were your servants. In our own time, you have sent Jesus, your Servant and your Son, who not only taught us how to be faithful servants, but died serving your will. Guide our footsteps in his paths, for he is Lord for ever and ever. Amen.

THE FOREIGNER RETURNED

Luke 17:11-19

Scripture: "Ten [lepers] were cleansed, were they not? Where are the other nine? Has none but this foreigner returned to give thanks to God?" (Luke 17:17-18)

Reflection: Luke's unique story about the cleansing of ten lepers (17:11-19) continues the author's discussion about faith, which he began in the previous section (17:5-10). At the conclusion of the ten lepers account, Jesus tells the one leper who returned, "Stand up and go; your faith has saved you" (17:19). The distinction to be made in this story, then, is between faith, salvation, and healing.

The setting of the encounter between Jesus and the ten lepers is somewhere around the border of "Samaria and Galilee" (17:11). Leprosy in the ancient world was considered to be any type of skin infection. Those who contracted it were sent out of the community until their healing, if it took place, could be verified by one of the Jewish priests, according to Leviticus 14:2-9. Until such verification, however, the lepers had to keep a distance between themselves and others who did not have leprosy.

The ten lepers in Luke's narrative "stood at a distance from him (Jesus) and raised their voice, saying, 'Jesus, Master! Have pity on us!'" (17:13). They request pity — healing, mercy, compassion. It is important to note that in a previous section of the Gospel Luke portrays a scholar of the law answering Jesus' question about who was neighbor to the man who fell victim to robbers as "the one who treated him with mercy" (10:37). This "one" was a Samaritan.

Jesus, now, plays the role of the Good Samaritan. He tells the ten lepers, "Go show yourselves to the priests" (17:14). No details of how the healing took place are given, since Luke is not interested in a healing-miracle account. He has other purposes in mind.

One of Luke's purposes is to hold up the Samaritan as an example of a person who accepts God's gift of faith and, then, responds appropriately with thanks and praise. One of the lepers, "realizing he had been healed, returned, glorifying God in a loud voice; and he fell at the feet of Jesus and thanked him. He was a Samaritan" (17:15-16). Just as in a previous instance (10:29-37) Jesus held up a non-Jew as an example of a person who responds to God's gift of faith, here another Samaritan is uplifted before the eyes of Jesus' Jewish contemporaries.

For Luke, salvation is present now. All a person needs to do is to respond to God's offer, as did the Samaritan. Jesus' two questions, "Ten were cleansed, were they not? Where are the other nine?" (17:17), ask about the other Jewish lepers who did not respond in faith to the gift of salvation offered by God. None but the "foreigner returned to give thanks to God" (17:18), yet all ten were cleansed.

The experience of healing for the other nine lepers did not save them. Their healing was God's first move in their lives. A response was needed; they needed to acknowledge what God had done for them through Jesus and praise and thank God for this gift.

Healing can usher in salvation, as it did for the Samaritan. However, God's initiative demands a response of faith so that a relationship develops between God and the person. This is salvation.

Luke's story is based on a similar account found in 2 Kings 5. There, Naaman the Syrian, a leper and a foreigner goes to the

Jordan River and plunges into it seven times in obedience to the prophet Elisha's command. He at first resisted such a simple procedure for his cure. After he realizes that he has been healed, however, he returns to Elisha and praises the God of Israel. He demonstrates that he has responded with faith to God's initiative in his life.

Naaman the Syrian is contrasted with the people of Israel and their lack of faith. The one Samaritan leper in Luke's story is contrasted with nine Jews and their non-acceptance of God's offer of salvation. For Luke, it is always the most unlikely people who respond to God's gracious gift. The author will develop this theme in the Acts of the Apostles.

Meditation: Identify one of God's initiatives in your life. How did your response of faith foster a relationship with God? In which ways did you glorify God and thank him?

Prayer: God of compassion, you always have pity on your people and unceasingly offer them your mercy. Pour out on us the gift of your Holy Spirit. When we cry out in need, help us to experience your saving power. Enable us to respond to your graciousness with a deeper faith and a stronger relationship with you. All glory and thanks be to you, Father, Son, and Holy Spirit, one God, who lives and reigns for ever and ever. Amen.

THE KINGDOM IS AMONG YOU

Luke 17:20-25

Thursday
of Week

32

Scripture: "The kingdom of God is not coming in a way that can be observed, and no one will announce, 'Look, here it is,' or, 'There it is.' For behold, the kingdom of God is in your midst" (Luke 17:20-21).

Reflection: Following the cleansing of the ten lepers account, Luke presents a pronouncement saying about the coming of the kingdom of God (17:20-21), which is followed by a discourse dealing with the Second Coming of Jesus (17:22- 37). Today, the weekday cycle of readings includes only the first four verses (17:25-27) of this discourse; the rest of the verses of the teaching (17:26-37) are read tomorrow.

Luke's primary source for this material is Q (cf. Matthew 24:23, 26-27) with one verse from Mark (13:21), although he has reworked his sources to fit the situation of his readers at the time he was writing this Gospel.

Luke uses the pronouncement about the coming of the kingdom of God to reject the notion that the time of the event could be calculated. The Pharisees are portrayed as asking Jesus "when the kingdom of God would come" (17:20).

The reply that Jesus gives reflects the author's perspective and his historical situation at the time he was writing this Gospel.

253

First, "The kingdom of God is not coming in a way that can be observed" (17:20). This response cancels out any possibility of observable phenomena preceding the coming of the kingdom. In other words, there will be no signs which indicate that the kingdom is coming.

Second, "No one will announce, 'Look, here it is,' or 'There it is'" (17:21). Just as there will be no visible signs, there will be no one who can locate the coming of the kingdom in a particular place. It has no boundaries.

In fact, "Behold, the kingdom of God is in your midst" (17:21). Thus, Luke shifts the popular notion of the time from an imminent observable coming of the kingdom to an emphasis on the presence of the kingdom in Jesus' ministry and the presence of the Holy Spirit in his ministry. The kingdom of God is present now.

But while the kingdom of God is present now, Luke cautions his community against an over-emphasis on its presence now to the exclusion of the Second Coming of Jesus. "The days will come when you will long to see one of the days of the Son of Man, but you will not see it" (17:22).

There were also those in Luke's church who thought that it was possible to experience the Second Coming of Jesus in the present in a secret way. Jesus addresses these people, "There will be those who will say to you, 'Look, it's here,' or 'Look, it's there.' Do not go off, do not run in pursuit" (17:23). Just as the kingdom cannot be located spatially (cf. 17:21), so the Second Coming of Jesus cannot be spatially restricted. "For just as lightning flashes and lights up the sky from one side to the other, so will it be in the day of the Son of Man" (17:24). The event will be universal and instantaneous.

The Second Coming of Jesus, of course, will not take place until after his rejection, suffering, and death. Therefore, Jesus adds, "But first he [the Son of Man] must suffer greatly and be rejected by this generation" (17:25).

Meditation: In which ways have you experienced the presence of the kingdom of God?

Prayer: God of the kingdom, from the first day of creation you have established your rule upon the earth. Through the patriarchs and matriarchs, judges and prophets, and kings and queens you have established your presence with your people. Jesus, your Son, proclaimed that your kingdom could not be observed but that it was among us. Awaken us to this presence. Keep us from running in pursuit of earthly kingdoms. Teach us to wait for the Second Coming of Jesus, which will be as lightning flashes and lights up the sky. He is Lord for ever and ever. Amen.

PREPARED DISCIPLES

Luke 17:26-37

Scripture: "Where the body is, there, too, will the vultures gather" (Luke 17:37).

Reflection: The second part of the discourse, which cautions the members of Luke's community against thinking that the Second Coming of Jesus has already taken place, focuses on the time and the place of his coming (17:26-37). Luke's source for this material is Q (cf. Matthew 10:39; 16:25; 24:17-18, 28, 37-41) and Mark (Mark 8:35; 13:15-16). The author has woven his sources together to form a discourse which addresses the concerns of his audience.

The Second Coming of Jesus, according to Luke, will take place while people are occupied with the daily events of life — eating, drinking, marrying, buying, selling, planting, building. Two examples of people of the past who were not prepared for an intervention of God into history are given.

First, "just as it happened in the days of Noah, so it will be in the days of the Son of Man. They ate and drank, married and were given in marriage up to the day that Noah entered the ark, and the deluge came and destroyed them all" (17:26-27).

Second, "as it was in the days of Lot: they ate and drank, bought and sold, planted and built; but on the day when Lot left Sodom, fire and brimstone rained from the sky and destroyed

257

them all. So will it be on the day the Son of Man is revealed" (17:28-30).

Noah and Lot represent those who are prepared for the day of the Second Coming of Jesus. Around Noah and Lot were others who were not prepared for the flood and the destruction; these perished in the midst of their concern over earthly affairs. According to Luke, the attitude of Christians must be that of indifference toward things of the earth while waiting for the coming in glory of Jesus.

When this day comes, it will demand an immediate response, and only those who are detached from earthly affairs and prepared for the day will be able to make the necessary reply. "On that day, a person who is on the housetop and whose belongings are in the house must not go down to get them, and likewise a person in the field must not return to what was left behind" (17:31). There can be no turning back. "Remember the wife of Lot" (17:32). She turned back and was destroyed.

What will really matter to Jesus will be the fact that people have followed his journey of rejection, suffering, and death. "Whoever tries to save his life will lose it, while whoever loses it will save his life" (17:33). A great divide will be created by his coming — not based on earthly values.

"On that night there will be two people in one bed; one will be taken, the other left. And there will be two women grinding meal together; one will be taken, the other left" (17:34-35). The criteria for being taken are two: preparedness and discipleship.

"Where, Lord?" (17:37) the disciples ask Jesus. For Luke, this sets the scene to teach his community that no time can be given. The First Coming of Jesus has taken place; now, disciples prepare themselves for his Second Coming, which has not yet taken place, while they live out the demands of discipleship.

When the Second Coming of Jesus does take place, it will be obvious to all. "Where the body is, there also the vultures will gather" (17:37). In other words, just as a person can determine where a dead body is in the desert by observing the vultures overhead, so will a prepared and committed Christian be able to identify the coming in glory of Jesus. There will be no need to ask where such an event will take place; it will be obvious.

Meditation: In which ways are you prepared for Jesus' Second Coming in glory?

Prayer: God of Noah and Lot, you promised the people of the past that you would send a Savior, who, when he came, promised them that he would one day come again in glory. Do not let us grow impatient or complacent this day. Keep us prepared for the day of the Son of Man, whose Second Coming we await. We ask this through our Lord Jesus Christ, your Son, who lives and reigns with you and the Holy Spirit, one God, for ever and ever. Amen.

DON'T LOSE HEART

Luke 18:1-8

Scripture: "There was a judge in a certain city who neither feared God nor felt shame before any human being.
Now there was a widow in that city who kept coming to
him and saying, 'Do me justice against my adversary.' For
a while the judge was unwilling, but eventually he thought,
'While it is true that I neither fear God nor feel shame
before any human being, because of the way this widow
keeps bothering me, I'll do her justice so she won't keep
coming and end by doing me violence'" (Luke 18:2-5).

Reflection: The parable of the persistent widow (18:1-8), which
follows Jesus' discourse concerning the Second Coming of the
Son of Man, functions as an exhortation to the members of the
Christian community to not lose heart while they wait for the Lord
to come. For years the Church had been praying to the Father
and saying, "Your kingdom come" (11:2), but it had not yet come
at the time Luke was writing nor, for that matter, has it come today! Is it possible to believe that God will some day "see to it
that justice is done" (18:8)? "When the Son of Man comes, will
he find faith on earth?" (18:8).

Faced with the delay of the Second Coming of Jesus, Luke
tells the members of his community "a parable about the necessity for them to pray always without becoming discouraged"
(18:1). The point of the parable, as Luke situates it in his narra-

tive, is that if a corrupt judge will grant a persistent widow the justice she demands, how much more will God "secure the rights of his chosen ones who call out to him day and night" (18:7). Therefore, Christians should remain steadfast in prayer and not lose heart. Persistent prayer will maintain faith. God will not abandon his faithful and prayerful people, who wait for Jesus to come in glory.

The parable, if removed from its Lucan function, presents an interesting metaphor for God and his kingdom. The judge in the parable functions as a negative metaphor for God! Jesus declares that the judge "neither feared God nor felt shame before any human being" (18:2). Later, the judge himself declares, "I neither fear God nor feel shame before any human being" (18:4).

The judge, by the fact that he is a judge belongs to the upper class of society. In the shame-honor culture of the time of Jesus, the judge would have received honor from the class of people to which he belonged. But this judge has separated himself both from God and human beings. He, therefore, is shameless and an outlaw judge.

The shameless judge is pitted against the shameless widow. A woman had no honor in the culture of Jesus' time; a widow was a woman who had even less than no honor! Her husband was dead, and this meant that she had no one to support her financially and no one to protect her.

The honorless widow continues to go to the shameless judge and says, "Do me justice against my adversary" (18:3). In other words, she pleads with the judge to defend her honor — which she doesn't have! The judge, then, becomes no longer a judge, but her opponent because "for a long time the judge was unwilling" (18:4).

Finally, the judge decides to defend the widow's honor. What is his reason? "Because of the way this widow keeps bothering me, I'll do her justice so she won't keep coming and end by doing me violence" (Luke 18:5). In other words, the judge decides for the widow out of convenience and out of fear of being struck by a defenseless woman! The judge, who neither fears God nor human beings, fears a widow, one of the weakest members of society!

It is because the widow continues to bother the judge that she finally receives justice. The kingdom of God is like the persistent widow; it keeps manifesting itself regardless of honor or shame. In this case, it does not come in the form of a just judge (an appropriate metaphor for God) but in the form of an unjust judge (not an appropriate metaphor for God). It does not come in the form of an honorable man (an appropriate metaphor for God) but in the form of a shameless widow (not an appropriate metaphor for God). The kingdom of God comes because God, like a shameless widow, bothers everyone!

Meditation: In which ways have you experienced the kingdom of God because you were persistent in prayer?

Prayer: God of widows, you teach your people to remain persistent in prayer in order to maintain their faith. Night and day we cry out to you: Bring justice to all people on the earth. Where there is discrimination, show us equality. Where there is economic imbalance, show us generosity. Where there is shame, show us human dignity. Keep us strong in faith until Jesus, the Son of Man, comes in glory; he is Lord for ever and ever. Amen.

ENTRUSTED WITH GOD'S GIFTS

Matthew 25:14-30

Scripture: "It (the kingdom of heaven) is like a man who was leaving on a journey who called in his servants and entrusted his possessions to them. To one he gave five talents; to another, two; to a third, one — to each according to his ability. Then he went away" (Matthew 25:14-15).

Reflection: The parable of the talents (Matthew 25:14-30), follows the parable of the ten virgins and precedes the judgment of the nations in the fifth discourse of Jesus in Matthew's Gospel. Matthew's source is Q (cf. Luke 19:12-27).

Throughout this sermon (24:1-25:46) the author deals with the coming of the new age and how disciples are to conduct themselves while waiting for the day of judgment. The parable of the talents focuses on the wise and faithful use of one's gifts while waiting for the return of the man (Jesus) "who was… on a journey" (25:14).

In its Matthean setting, the parable explains how disciples are to use their "talents," while waiting for the day of judgment when the Son of Man will come in glory. Matthew exhorts the members of his church to act boldly like the first servant, "who received five talents" and "immediately… went and traded with them, and made another five" (25:16); and like the second servant, "who received two" and "made another two" (25:17).

When, "after a long time the master of those servants" (25:19) comes back and settles accounts, he will declare, "Well done, my good and faithful servant. Since you were faithful in small matters, I will give you greater responsibilities. Come, share your master's joy" (25:21). It is important to note that the master does not think that five and two talents comprise a great responsibility, but only small matters! Faithful disciples will receive greater responsibilities.

The servant who received one talent is the real focus of the parable. After being given his one talent, he "went off and dug a hole in the ground and buried his master's money" (25:18). Thus, he insured a verdict from his master that would pronounce him responsible, since he did not risk trading the money like the first two servants, and he followed an acceptable, prudent, and trustworthy action of the time.

However, when he comes forward to present his one talent and fulfill his obligations, he reveals his presuppositions about his master — viz., that the absentee landlord was known to be "a demanding person, harvesting where he did not plant and gathering where he did not scatter" (25:24). It was "out of fear" that this servant "went off and buried the talent in the ground" (25:25).

The master, however, tells this servant that his actions do not correspond with the servant's image of the master: "So, you knew that I harvest where I did not plant and gather where I did not scatter? Should you not then have put my money in the bank so that I could have got it back with interest on my return?" (25:26-27). The obvious answer is, of course, "Yes." So, the third servant has created his own trap! While waiting for the day of judgment, Matthew exhorts the members of his church to use their gifts wisely and boldly; otherwise, they will discover themselves with the "wicked, lazy servant" (25:26) "in the darkness outside, where there will be wailing and gnashing of teeth" (25:30).

But there is more. Matthew is also interested in the image of the master. The third servant characterized him as "demanding" (25:24), that is, ruthless. But is he? To his servants he gave generous portions of his wealth. When the third servant wanted to return the one talent, he refused to take it and "gave it to the one with ten" (25:28). Is the master a demanding person or a generous one?

Matthew is presenting two images of God, the master. As he unravels the story, he invites the members of his church to examine their presuppositions about God. If they imagine God to be generous, then they will not be afraid to act boldly with the gifts that God has entrusted to them. If, on the other hand, they image God to be a stern judge, then they will act out of fear and not use their God-given talents.

While waiting for the future coming of Jesus, members of Matthew's church are told to choose how they will live: in freedom, like the first two servants, or in fear, like the third servant. One's choice mirrors one's image of who God is and how God acts.

Meditation: What is your image of God? How does this image influence the way you live?

Prayer: Gracious God, from the first day of creation you have ceaselessly entrusted countless gifts to your people and asked them to use their talents according to their abilities. Guide us into a responsible use of these gifts. Enable us to act boldly and wisely and not out of fear. May our hands be full of good deeds on the day of judgment, that we may be counted among your good and faithful servants who share your joy. We ask this through our Lord Jesus Christ, your Son, who lives and reigns with you and the Holy Spirit, one God, for ever and ever. Amen.

SUMMER IS NEAR

Mark 13:24-32

Scripture: "Learn a lesson from the fig tree. When its branch becomes tender and sprouts leaves, you know that summer is near" (Mark 13:28).

Reflection: The last selection from Mark's Gospel during Cycle B (13:24-32) is taken from the author's apocalyptic chapter. Apocalyptic literature usually comes into existence during a period of cultural collapse. It is characterized by dualism; the good God is removed from the evil world, small forces of good battle huge forces of evil.

Apocalyptic writing divides time between the present age and the age to come, when God will bring an end to the battle and a final solution. Those who live during the present age are exhorted by the author to remain faithful. Mark employs this type of literature to discuss the Second Coming of Jesus and to exhort the members of his community to remain faithful while they wait for this great event to take place.

Borrowing Old Testament apocalyptic images from Ezekiel (32:7), Joel (2:10), and Isaiah (13:10), Mark describes the Second Coming of Jesus: "The sun will be darkened, and the moon will not give its light, and the stars will be falling from the sky, and the powers in the heavens will be shaken. And they will see 'the Son of Man coming in the clouds' with great power and glory" (13:24-26).

From Mark's perspective, Jesus will come as the divine judge. "Coming in the clouds" indicates his divinity (cf. Exodus 34:5, Leviticus 16:2, and Numbers 11:25). Jesus looks "like a son of man coming on the clouds of heaven," who, "when he reached the Ancient One and was presented before him... received dominion, glory and kingship" (Daniel 7:13-14). Thus, the Old Testament apocalyptic images are applied to Jesus by Mark.

When will this final intervention into and triumph of God in history take place? "As for that day or hour, no one knows — not the angels in heaven, nor the Son, but only the Father" (13:32). The author believes in an imminent Second Coming, but he does not speculate when it will take place.

All his readers can do is to "learn a lesson from the fig tree. When its branches become tender and sprout leaves, [they] know that summer is near" (13:28). In Israelite culture the presence of the fig tree represents blessing, while its absence represents curse.

In this "lesson," Jesus erases all time. The story goes from spring (sprouting leaves) immediately to summer. What happens takes place in the present. In other words, for Mark, the end is near. The present is the time of blessing for those who see these things happening (13:29); they "know that he is near, at the very gates.... This generation will not pass away until all these things come to pass. Heaven and earth will pass away, but my words will not pass away" (13:29-31). In other words, the author of Mark's Gospel firmly believes in an imminent Second Coming of Jesus.

He, like Jesus, does not know when this will happen. But he knows that he must warn his readers. "Be watchful! Be alert!" (13:33) he says. "You do not know when the time will come" (13:33). The final triumph of good is about to take place in the present.

Meditation: How do you discover yourself to be apocalyptic in your thinking and speaking?

Prayer: Almighty God, you teach us to learn a lesson from the fig tree; the power and glory of your grace is always near. Keep us watchful and alert for the times you triumph in our lives. Make us worthy to stand in the presence of the Son of Man, our Lord Jesus Christ, when he comes in the clouds with great power and glory; he lives and reigns with you and the Holy Spirit, one God, for ever and ever. Amen.

NOT A STONE LEFT

Luke 21:5-19

Scripture: While some people were talking about how the Temple was adorned with costly stones and votive offerings, he (Jesus) said, "These things you see here — the days will come in which not a stone will be left upon another stone that will not be torn down" (Luke 21:5-6).

Reflection: The entire apocalyptic discourse found in Luke is modeled after Mark (13:1-37), although the author of the third Gospel has reshaped his Marcan material to conform to his own views concerning eschatology (the end things). The section begins with a prophecy concerning the destruction of the Temple (21:5-6) and is followed by Jesus' instruction concerning the signs of the end (21:7-11) and imminent persecution (21:12-19). It is important to note that Luke has separated the destruction of the Temple from the Second Coming of Jesus.

The admiration of the Temple by some people prompts Jesus to speak of its destruction. By the time that Luke was writing this Gospel (ca. 85 A.D.), the Temple had long been destroyed by the Romans in 70 A.D. He can freely portray Jesus as predicting its destruction within the Gospel because, historically, it has already been destroyed.

The prediction of the Temple's destruction leads to the next section, which sets the tearing down of the Temple within the context of other events. This gives the author the opportunity to

271

explain what behavior is proper to the members of his community as they engage in the daily following of Jesus and wait for
his delayed coming in glory.

In order that they not be led astray, Jesus tells his disciples,
"Do not be deceived, for many will come in my name, saying, 'I
am he,' and 'The time has come.' Do not follow them!" (21:8).
Mark's teaching concerning the imminent end of the age rings
false for Luke. He views the time in-between Jesus' First and his
Second Coming to be much longer than Mark anticipated; this
in-between time is for the missionary work of the community.

The end is not at hand. The war and insurrection surrounding the destruction of the Temple was not a historical sign of the
end, according to Luke. "Nation will rise against nation, and kingdom against kingdom. There will be powerful earthquakes, and
famines and plagues in various places. There will be dreadful
sights and great signs from the skies" (21:10-11). All of these
events are part of the course of world events for Luke, and they
do not herald the end.

Even persecution, a real possibility for the members of
Luke's community, does not bring the end nearer. People had
been seized and persecuted, handed over to synagogues and put
in prisons. Some of them had been handed over by members of
their own families — "parents, brothers, relatives, and friends"
(21:16). Some had been put to death. Whoever follows Jesus is
"hated by all because of [his] name" (21:17).

The purpose of such suffering, according to Luke is this: "It
will lead to your giving testimony" (21:13). Witnessing or giving
testimony is an important theme for Luke; it is fully developed in
his second volume, the Acts of the Apostles. There, before his
Ascension, Jesus instructs his disciples, "You will be my witnesses
in Jerusalem, throughout Judea and Samaria, and to the ends of
the earth" (Acts 1:8).

Those who are persecuted can rest assured that they will
receive "a wisdom in speaking that all... adversaries will be powerless to resist or refute" (21:15). For Luke, this is the wisdom of

the Holy Spirit, who has guided all of the author's characters in the Gospel and will continue to do so in the Acts of the Apostles.

Christians are not to worry about the end of the age. Their principal concern is to witness to Jesus. "Not a hair on [their] heads will be destroyed" (21:18). It is by their perseverance that they will secure their lives (cf. 21:19). Perseverance allows people to witness. God will secure their lives and bring them to eternal life.

Meditation: In which ways do you witness in this time in-between the First Coming of Jesus and his Second Coming in glory?

Prayer: God of the faithful, you protect your people from deception and you preserve them from false prophets. Do not let us be terrified by the daily course of world events. When we are persecuted, guide us with your Holy Spirit in giving testimony to our faith. Give us wisdom is speaking that others are powerless to resist or refute. Enable us to persevere that we may share in the kingdom, where you live and reign with Jesus, your Son, and the Holy Spirit, one God, for ever and ever. Amen.

HAVE SIGHT!

Luke 18:35-43

Scripture: As he (Jesus) was approaching Jericho a blind man was seated by the roadside begging. When he heard the crowds going by, he asked what was going on. They told him, "Jesus of Nazareth is passing by." So he cried out and said, "Jesus, Son of David, have mercy on me!" (Luke 18:35-38).

Reflection: Other than the parable of the persistent widow (18:1-8) and the account of the healing of the blind beggar (18:35-43), the daily cycle of readings omits the rest of chapter 18 of Luke's Gospel — the parable of the Pharisee and the tax collector, the saying about children and the kingdom, the account of the rich official, the saying about riches and renunciation, and the third prediction of the passion (18:9-34).

Luke's account of the healing of the blind beggar (18:35-43) is modeled after Mark's story of the healing of the blind beggar Bartimaeus (cf. Mark 9:46-52). Luke uses the story to contrast the faith of the blind man to the lack of understanding of the Twelve. In the verse preceding the beginning of the blind man account, the author editorializes, "They (the Twelve) understood none of this (the third prediction of the passion); the saying was kept hidden from them and they failed to comprehend what he (Jesus) said" (18:34). Luke also uses the blind man story as an example of the appropriate human response to the gift of salvation brought by Jesus. The blind man's actions represent the appropriate approach to salvation and conversion for members of Luke's community.

First, the blind man hears the word about Jesus of Nazareth passing by. After hearing the word, he immediately responds by shouting, "Jesus, Son of David, have mercy on me" (18:38). "Son of David" indicates Jesus' role as Messiah, the Anointed One, the expected royal leader from David's line who would restore the kingdom of Israel. For Luke, Jesus is the One who brings salvation for all people and preaches the establishment of the kingdom of God. The blind man, then, after hearing the word, asks for salvation.

Second, the blind man addresses Jesus as "Lord" (18:41), which for Luke indicates the risen Lord. The blind man has faith; that is, he has sight. "Have sight; your faith has saved you" (18:42), Jesus tells him. His response of faith to the word has enabled him to see and to be saved. Throughout Luke's Gospel, healing is a manifestation of the kingdom of God and the gift of salvation. Sight is a metaphor for faith in the risen Lord.

Third, the response to the gift of salvation is to give "glory to God" (18:43). Like the one cleansed leper, who returned to Jesus "glorifying God in a loud voice" (17:15), the blind man demonstrates that conversion elicits praise of God. God makes the first move by offering the gift of salvation; people respond by giving thanks to God for this undeserved gift.

Fourth, acceptance of the gift of salvation and praise of God leads to discipleship. Once he receives his sight, the blind man immediately follows Jesus (cf. 18:43) on his journey "to Jerusalem" where "all the things written by the prophets about the Son of Man will be fulfilled. He will be handed over to the Gentiles and he will be mocked and insulted and spat upon; and after they have scourged him they will put him to death, and on the third day he will rise" (18:31-33).

Authentic discipleship involves a willingness to be rejected, to suffer, to die, and to rise with Jesus.

Meditation: Name an instant in your life when you heard the word, responded with faith in the risen Lord, praised God for this gift, and found yourself a more committed disciple.

Prayer: God of Jesus, have pity on us. Speak the word of your kingdom to us. Order us to come closer to you that we might believe more fully in the name of your Risen One, Jesus, the Lord, and become authentic disciples. Open our eyes to see the marvels of your wisdom and power, so that we might always praise you. All glory is yours, Father, Son, and Holy Spirit, one God, for ever and ever. Amen.

A TALL SHORT MAN

Luke 19:1-10

Scripture: A man... named Zacchaeus, who was a chief tax collector and also a wealthy man, was trying to see who Jesus was; but he wasn't able because of the crowd, for he was short in stature. So he ran on ahead and climbed a sycamore tree in order to see him, because he was about to pass that way. When Jesus reached the place, he looked up and said to him, "Zacchaeus, hurry on down, for to-day I must stay at your house" (Luke 19:2-5).

Reflection: The narrative about Zacchaeus the tax collector (19:1-10), unique to Luke's Gospel, reflects the horizontal dimension of a response to Jesus' offer of salvation, just as the previous account of the healing of the blind beggar (18:35-43) demonstrates the vertical aspect of the human response to conversion. The reader needs to remember that the story is written from a post-resurrectional perspective and, thus, demonstrates how people respond (or should respond) to the risen Lord, according to this author.

There is some quality that draws people to the risen Lord as Luke demonstrates in Zacchaeus' action of climbing a sycamore tree "in order to see Jesus" (19:4). Before Zacchaeus seeks to see who Jesus is, God has already offered to him the gift of salvation. Zacchaeus' action demonstrates his acceptance of the gift.

When Jesus spies the tax collector in the tree, he tells him, "Zacchaeus, hurry on down, for today I must stay at your house"

(19:5). The risen Lord comes as a person to a sinner's house, into a sinner's life. "Today salvation has come to this house" (19:9). The tax collector's response is to come down quickly and receive salvation with joy (cf. 19:6). The horizontal dimension of conversion enters into the picture when Zacchaeus declares to Jesus, "Look, Lord, I am giving half of my possessions to the poor, and if I have cheated anyone of anything I shall repay it four times over" (19:8). In other words, the man has accepted the gift of salvation, repented of any injustice, and promises to share his wealth with the poor, who occupy a place of particular importance in this Gospel. Such a response is what it means to be "a descendant of Abraham" (19:9), an heir to the promises of God.

Such a declaration causes problems for those who observe this course of events. A tax collector, such as Zacchaeus, was considered to be an apostate, that is, one who had abandoned Judaism. He worked for the Roman occupation and made his living by raising the tax and pocketing the difference. From a Jewish perspective, he had forfeited his right to God's promises. He was a sinner.

Luke's point is that God is interested in sinners. Those who are righteous have no need of God. Only sinners need salvation. "The Son of Man has come to seek and to save what was lost" (19:10), Jesus declares. One who is not lost does not need to be found. Zacchaeus, the tax collector/sinner, is a host to salvation.

By identifying Zacchaeus as "a wealthy man" (19:2), Luke also makes an important point about riches, which he believes are given to people to be shared with others. Zacchaeus is contrasted to the rich official, who could not detach himself from his possessions in order to follow Jesus (cf. 18:18-23).

Riches cannot guarantee eternal life, according to Jesus. Only complete dependence on God can do that (cf. 18:24-27). It is possible for a rich man, like Zacchaeus, to be saved, if he responds to God's offer of salvation and shares his wealth with others. By doing this, his life is even more transformed.

Meditation: In what recent experience have you been drawn toward Jesus, found yourself making a radical response to him, and discovered salvation?

Prayer: God of sinners, you sent your Son, Jesus, to seek out and to save your lost people. We acknowledge our sin; we know that we need Jesus to pass through our lives and to call us down from our sycamore trees of selfishness. Give us the grace of conversion that we, like Zacchaeus, may respond with faith to your gracious offer of salvation and be counted among the elect in the kingdom, where you live and reign with Jesus and the Holy Spirit, one God, for ever and ever. Amen.

ENGAGE IN TRADE

Luke 19:11-22

Scripture: Now after they had listened to these things, [Jesus] proceeded to tell them a parable because he was near Jerusalem and they thought that the kingdom of God would appear there immediately. So he said, "A nobleman went off to a distant country to obtain a kingship for himself and then return. He called ten of his servants and gave them ten gold coins and told them, 'Trade with these until I return'" (Luke 19:11-12).

Reflection: Luke's parable of the ten gold coins (19:11-28) follows the narrative about Zacchaeus the tax collector (19:1-10), which is located in Jericho, and it immediately precedes Jesus' triumphant entry into Jerusalem (19:29-40), which is omitted from the weekday cycle of readings. Luke's source for the parable is Q (cf. Matthew 25:14-28), which he combines with his own unique story about a rejected king. The parable's location in the Gospel serves a number of purposes.

First, this post-resurrectional author corrects a problem which has developed in his community — namely, that the events which took place in Jerusalem (the rejection, suffering, death, and resurrection of Jesus) represent the end of the age. There is no better place to deal with this misunderstanding than immediately before Jesus triumphantly enters Jerusalem, where he will be rejected, suffer, be put to death, and rise on the third day.

Luke deals with this problem a number of times. After the resurrection he portrays the two disciples on the road to Emmaus as telling Jesus, "We were hoping that he would be the one to liberate Israel" (24:21). Again, in the Acts of the Apostles, before describing Jesus' Ascension, the disciples ask, "Lord, are you going to restore the kingdom to Israel at this time?" (Acts 1:6).

Luke's response to those who "thought that the kingdom of God would appear there immediately" (19:11) is a simple "Not yet." The end of the age did not come with the Christ-events in Jerusalem. Luke makes this clear in the Acts of the Apostles, when Jesus tells his disciples, "It is not for you to know the times or seasons that the Father has established by his own authority" (Acts 1:7). Therefore, followers of Jesus are to be faithful and productive servants while they wait for the fullness of the kingdom of God to appear and the end of the age to come.

Second, Luke reminds the members of his community that they are accountable during the interim between Jesus' Ascension and his return in glory. Followers of Jesus are stewards, who have been given a variety of resources.

The parable states that the nobleman "called ten of his servants and gave them ten gold coins" (19:13). However, once the nobleman returns from his journey, the parable refers to only three servants and their reports of their stewardship.

The first servant, by trading his gold coin, has earned ten more. The nobleman, who has obtained a kingship for himself, declares that the servant is "faithful in this very small matter" (19:17) and gives him the responsibility of ten cities.

Likewise, the second servant reports that he has earned five more coins. He is given the charge of five cities by the nobleman-become-king.

The focus of the parable is on the third servant, who declares to the king, "Sir, here is your gold coin; I kept it stored away in a handkerchief, for I was afraid of you, because you are a stern man; you take up what you did not set down and you reap what you did not plant" (19:20-21). This servant, unlike the first two, presupposes that the king is demanding and dishonest, but he does not act on his presupposition. Therefore, with his own words he condemns himself.

Had he acted on his own words, he would have put the king's money in a bank so that on his return he would have collected it with interest (cf. 19:22-23). This servant is a contradiction to himself. His fear of the king immobilized him. His gold coin was taken away and given to the servant who had successfully traded his coin for ten more gold pieces.

The parable calls into question the image of Jesus as a kingly judge. The allegorical trait of the parable is clear: Jesus is the nobleman who "went off to a distant country to obtain the kingship for himself and then to return" (19:12).

The distant country is heaven after the Ascension. The kingship is received upon his return, which will take place at the end of the age, the day of judgment and accountability. On that day, whenever it takes place, followers of Jesus will be judged not only on their stewardship, but on how their actions correspond to their presuppositions about the king. The parable declares that the nobleman's "fellow citizens… despised him and sent a delegation after him to announce, 'We do not want this man to be our king'" (19:14).

Those who do not accept the nobleman's kingship end up slain before him (cf. 19:27). These are those who refuse to accept the kingdom of God as proclaimed by Jesus.

But the question which is raised is this: Is the nobleman-turned-king a harsh judge or not? Two servants do not presuppose him to be severe. One servant judges him to be demanding and accuses him of being a thief. Which of the servants is correct? This is difficult to answer since the king gives the first servant ten cities and the second servant five cities. Furthermore, he does not take back the third servant's coin but gives it to the first servant.

The answer to the question is not given in the parable. Luke's third point is that every follower of Jesus must act according to his or her presuppositions concerning either the graciousness or harshness of the king. While waiting for the king's return, can followers of Jesus remain passive and still be faithful? The answer to the question is left to the reader.

Luke, obviously, believes that a person cannot remain passive and still be counted a faithful follower of Jesus, but he never explicitly states it in the parable. Rather Jesus declares, "To everyone who has, more will be given, but from the one who has not, even what he has will be taken away" (19:26). Jesus' return in glory as king is not imminent according to Luke. However, it will take place, and, when it does, each person will be judged according to his or her stewardship, which will be based on his or her presuppositions about the graciousness or harshness of the king.

Fourth, Luke uses this parable to bring to a close his journey to Jerusalem section. As Jesus enters Jerusalem, the crowds proclaim, "Blessed is the king who comes in the name of the Lord" (19:33). Jesus does not enter the city to receive kingly power but to be rejected, suffer, die and be raised from the dead. The kingship will be bestowed on him after he goes away (Ascension) and returns from the "distant country" (19:12) of heaven.

Meditation: How do your presuppositions about Jesus as king and judge influence your image of responsible stewardship?

Prayer: Kingly God, you have entrusted the gold coins of your creation to your people to be used wisely in the spread of your kingdom. Guide us in the ways of responsible stewardship. Send your Holy Spirit with the fire of the mission of Jesus that we might be counted among your faithful servants. Give us patience as we wait for the glorious return of your Son, our Lord Jesus Christ, who lives and reigns with you and the Holy Spirit, one God, for ever and ever. Amen.

JERUSALEM DESTROYED

Luke 19:41-44

Scripture: When (Jesus) drew near and caught sight of the city [Jerusalem], he wept over it saying, "If only you had realized on this day what makes for peace — but now it is hidden from your eyes" (Luke 19:41-42).

Reflection: Following Luke's account of Jesus' journey up to Jerusalem (19:28) but while only drawing near (cf. 19:41), the author records a unique lament over the city (19:41-42) and a prediction concerning its destruction (19:43-44), which is probably borrowed from Mark's Gospel (cf. Mark 13:2). Both the lament and the prediction precede the cleansing of the Temple (19:45-48).

In this section of the Gospel, Luke is attempting to deal with the historical destruction of Jerusalem and the Temple after the Jewish-Roman war, which resulted in the leveling of the city and the Temple in 70 A.D. Luke ties the destruction of the city and the Temple to the rejection of Jesus by the Jews. Therefore, in this passage from Luke, Jesus states, "If only you [Jerusalem] had realized on this day what makes for peace — but now it is hidden from your eyes" (19:41-42).

In Jewish thought, the Temple in Jerusalem was the dwelling place of God on earth. The city should not have been destroyed, but it was. This fact sent a shock-wave throughout the world. Luke, then, writing long after the event, portrays Jesus as

287

saying, "Days will come upon you when your enemies will set up a siege wall around you; they will encircle you and hem you in on all sides. They will level you to the ground and your children within you, and they will not leave one stone upon another within you" (19:43-44).

According to Luke, in Jesus God had come to his people, but they did not recognize the time of their visitation. God was not recognized. When Jesus, the peaceable king entered the city to the cry of the crowd — "Peace in heaven and glory in the highest" (19:38) — the people chose rebellion and violence, which resulted in the destruction of the city of peace.

Meditation: When has God visited you and you failed to recognize his visitation?

Prayer: God of peace, your Son, Jesus, entered your holy city, Jerusalem, proclaiming peace and the establishment of your kingdom, but he found only rejection, suffering, and death. By raising him from the dead, you founded a new Jerusalem, which is not built of brick and mortar but of human, living stones. Keep us faithful throughout our pilgrimage of life. Enable us to recognize the time of your visitation that we might share in the kingdom, where you live with Jesus and the Holy Spirit, one God, for ever and ever. Amen.

HOUSE OF PRAYER

Luke 19:45-48

Scripture: Jesus entered the Temple area and proceeded to drive out those who were selling things, saying to them, "It is written, 'My house shall be a house of prayer, but you have made it a den of thieves'" (Luke 19:45-46).

Reflection: Immediately after predicting the destruction of the city of Jerusalem, Jesus enters the Temple area and begins to cleanse it (19:45-48) in preparation for his teaching ministry in Jerusalem (20:1-21:38). Luke's source for this section is Mark's Gospel (cf. Mark 11:15-19).

By cleansing the Temple of "those who were selling things" (19:45), Jesus demonstrates his authority, which will be questioned immediately after the incident (20:1-8). Also, his action echoes the prophet Malachi, who, speaking for God, declares, "Lo, I am sending my messenger to prepare the way before me; and suddenly there will come to the Temple the Lord whom you seek, and the messenger of the covenant whom you desire. Yes, he is coming, says the Lord of hosts. He will sit refining and purifying [silver], and he will purify the sons of Levi" (Malachi 3:1, 3).

Jesus' address to those in the Temple, "My house shall be a house of prayer, but you have made it a den of thieves" (19:46), echoes two Old Testament prophets: Isaiah (56:7) and Jeremiah (7:11). In Luke's view, Jesus indicts the religious leadership for permitting the Temple's true purpose to be perverted. In other

289

words, the religious leaders have not been faithful to what the Temple has meant; therefore, the Temple will be destroyed (cf. 19:43-44).

Because the religious leaders have not been faithful, Jesus must teach "in the Temple area every day" (19:47). Luke situates more of Jesus' teaching in the Temple than either of the other two synoptic writers. "The chief priests, the scribes, and the leaders of the people, meanwhile, were seeking to put him to death" (19:47) because of his teaching in and not because of his cleansing of the Temple.

However, because Luke has much more teaching material to present, Jesus' adversaries "could find no way to accomplish their purpose because all the people were hanging on his words" (19:48). Here, Luke is able to emphasize one of his principal themes — hearing the word of God and doing it.

Meditation: In which ways do you think that you sometimes forget the purpose of your local church building to be a house of prayer?

Prayer: Lord God, the entire world is your temple, wherein dwells your kingdom, power, and glory. From the stones of the earth we erect reminders of your constant presence. Come and dwell in our buildings and in our hearts that we might bow down in prayer before you. Through the teaching of your Son, Jesus, we have heard your word; help us to put it into practice. We ask this through our Lord Jesus Christ, who lives and reigns with you and the Holy Spirit, one God, for ever and ever. Amen.

GOD OF THE LIVING

Luke 20:27-40

Scripture: "The children of this age marry and are given in marriage; but those who are deemed worthy of the coming age and resurrection from the dead neither marry nor are given in marriage" (Luke 20:34-35).

Reflection: The daily cycle of selections from Luke's Gospel omits the questioning of Jesus' authority (20:1-8), the parable of the tenant farmers (20:9-19), and the question about paying taxes to the emperor (20:20-26), which contain Jesus' teaching in the Temple. Jesus' answer to the question about the resurrection (20:27-40) silences all his questioners and offers him the opportunity to ask a question (20:41-44) and to denounce the scribes (20:45-47), although these last two incidents are omitted from the daily cycle of readings.

The question about the resurrection, which comes from Mark (12:18-27), is raised by "some Sadducees, those who deny that there is a resurrection" (20:27), but more accurately reflects those persons in Luke's community who were questioning the resurrection. Historically, the Sadducees were the priestly aristocratic group, who accepted only the first five books of the Bible — the Pentateuch — and followed the law in these books to the letter. Also, they rejected oral legal tradition and the resurrection of the dead.

The riddle that Luke portrays them presenting to Jesus is

based on the law of levirate marriage, as found in Deuteronomy 25:5-10. Basically, the law states that if a man's brother dies without having fathered a child, the man is responsible for taking the widow and begetting a child for his dead brother. The child begotten as a result of this union was to bear the deceased man's name and be considered the deceased man's heir.

The Sadducees present this riddle to Jesus: "There were seven brothers, and the first, after taking a wife, died childless. The second and the third then married her, and likewise, the seven, too — all died childless. Finally the woman also died. Now at the resurrection whose wife will that woman be? All seven had been married to her" (20:29-33).

The riddle presupposes that the way of life in the world to come is the same as it is in the present world. In the case of the riddle, this would mean polyandry, which was unacceptable and excluded by the law of Moses.

Jesus corrects the basic presupposition that the present world and the world to come were identical. "The children of this age marry and are given in marriage; but those who are deemed worthy of the age to come and of resurrection from the dead neither marry nor are given in marriage" (20:34-35). Life in the present world is human and mortal; sexuality guarantees the continuance of the human race. In the world to come, sexuality will not be necessary because people do not die, "for they are like angels; they are children of God because they have attained the resurrection" (20:36).

Once the presupposition of the riddle is lost, the riddle itself is no longer a trap. Then, Jesus addresses the question of resurrection by appealing to the very same Scriptures that the Sadducees had appealed to in order to trap him.

He reminds them that in the Book of Exodus (3:6) Moses "called 'Lord' the God of Abraham, the God of Isaac, and the God of Jacob" (20:37). God is not the Lord of the dead but of the living. Therefore, the patriarchs must either be in some sense alive or they will be raised from the dead. To God "all are alive"

(20:38). Death does not terminate a person's relationship with God, Luke is telling his community. Once a relationship with God is established, it endures even beyond death.

Meditation: What is the one question about the resurrection that you would like to ask Jesus?

Prayer: God of Abraham, Isaac, and Jacob, you are the Lord of the living. To you all people are alive. Death is not the end of our relationship with you but only a door to the new life of your kingdom revealed by Jesus, your Son. Instill in us a fervent hope that on the day when our earthly bodies meet death we may share in the resurrection of our Lord Jesus Christ, who lives and reigns with you and the Holy Spirit, one God, for ever and ever. Amen.

SHEEP AND GOATS

Matthew 25:31-46

Scripture: "When the Son of Man comes in his glory, and all the angels with him, he will sit upon the throne of his glory, and all the nations will be gathered together before him. And he will separate them one from another, as a shepherd separates the sheep from the goats" (Matthew 25:31-32).

Reflection: The Matthean cycle of readings ends with the author's unique judgment of the nations scene (25:31-46), which also ends the fifth (or eschatological) sermon of Jesus dealing with the new age. The attentive reader has waited patiently for this narrative from the very beginning of the Gospel.

Throughout the work, Matthew has argued that members of his church are not to determine who will be in or who will be outside the kingdom of God. The weeds and the wheat grow together. The dragnet is large enough to hold everything (everyone).

The guide for correct behavior, according to Matthew is righteousness, doing the will of God. Joseph was the first person the author presented as a righteous man, one who had to break the law of God by taking Mary as his wife, even though she was with child before their marriage, in order to obey the will of God revealed to him through a dream.

The author of this Gospel also presented the beatitudes, a

series of statements naming blessed those who exhibit the socially reversed way of the reign of God. Echoing the themes of the beatitudes, Matthew presents a judgment scene which is already taking place and which is based on a person's behavior toward the "least ones" (24:40, 45).

Matthew reminds his church that the Son of Man will come in glory some day, and on that day, whenever it is, he will judge "all the nations" (25:32). Here, the author indicates his belief that the Gospel must be preached to "all nations" (28:19) before the final day takes place.

But before that final day, a daily judgment is taking place. This daily judgment is based on one's adherence to behavior patterns that have already been established — giving food to the hungry, giving drink to the thirsty, welcoming the stranger, clothing the naked, caring for the ill, visiting the imprisoned. This is the way that a person does God's will and is declared to be righteous.

However, according to Matthew's story, the motivation of those who behaved in these ways was not the fact that they knew that Jesus would identify himself with the poor and suffering, but they recognized their actions to be the behavior that God wanted. Only after having cared for the poor and the suffering did they discover that they were caring for Jesus. Only after caring for the poor and the suffering are they declared righteous, those who have done the will of God.

The righteous are contrasted with those who began with the wrong presupposition. They went out looking for Jesus, but they failed to see him in the poor and suffering. In not meeting the needs of the poor and the suffering, they failed to do the will of God, and they failed to recognize Jesus. By neglecting the obvious, they also neglected God's will. They "will go off to eternal punishment" (25:46).

By relating this scene, Matthew answers some questions that have dominated all the material preceding this section. To be watchful means to be able to recognize the Son of Man in those most in need. To be ready means to love those in need and care for them. To be faithful means to perform concrete deeds of mercy and service for those in need.

The righteous know this; but they will be surprised to discover that when they were ready, watchful, and faithful, they were ministering to Jesus, Emmanuel — God-with-us. The condemned also know what it means to be watchful, ready, and faithful, but they do not minister to those in need; they keep looking for Jesus, when he is very present to them. They must be held accountable for their free decision not to behave according to what God would have them do.

Doing the will of God, according to Matthew, is summarized in the dual commandment of love of God and neighbor as self (cf. 22:34-39). "The whole law and the prophets depend on these two commandments" (22:40). Entrance into the kingdom depends on keeping these two commandments of love — not because they are commandments, but because they represent the will of God.

Meditation: What is your motivation for meeting the needs of the poor and suffering?

Prayer: Father of Jesus, since the foundation of the world, you have prepared your kingdom for the righteous, those who have freely done your will. Keep us watchful, ready, and faithful. Give us the strength to care for our brothers and sisters in need. When the Son of Man comes in his glory, may he count us among those worthy to share eternal life with him, with you, Father, and with your Holy Spirit. You live and reign as one God, for ever and ever. Amen.

A KINGDOM NOT OF THIS WORLD

John 18:33-37

Scripture: Jesus answered [Pilate], "My kingdom is not of this world. If my kingdom were of this world, my attendants would fight to keep me from being handed over to the Jews. But as it is, my kingdom is not here." So Pilate said to him, "So you are a king?" Jesus answered, "You say that I am a king" (John 18:36-37).

Reflection: Because Mark's Gospel contains no scene which could be considered "kingly," the editors of the Sunday cycle of readings were forced to abandon Mark in favor of John for the final Sunday of Ordinary Time, the Solemnity of Christ the King. On this day the feast being celebrated dictates the choice of a Gospel selection.

Throughout his Gospel, John portrays Jesus as being in charge of every situation. He is fully aware of what is going to happen to him, and he takes the initiative in the events which lead to his death. During his trial before Pilate, the Roman governor asks Jesus, "Are you the king of the Jews?" (18:33). Jesus, fully in charge, does not answer the question, but poses one of his own to Pilate, "Do you say this on your own or have others told you about me?" (18:34).

While Jesus is ironically accused by Pilate to be a king, the fact of the matter is that he is king.

299

Again, Pilate poses a question to Jesus: "What have you done?" (18:35). Jesus does not answer but, rather, describes the origin, quality, and meaning of his kingship.

First, Jesus states, "My kingdom is not of this world" (18:36). In other words, Jesus' kingdom is not earthly. If it were, his attendants would be fighting to keep him from being handed over. But as it is, his kingdom is not here (cf. 18:36).

Second, Jesus expresses the quality of his kingship: "For this I was born and for this I came into the world, to bear witness to the truth" (18:37). Jesus reveals the truth about God in his own person, in his words, and in his actions.

Third, Jesus' kingship means that "everyone who is of the truth hears [his] voice" (18:37). They accept him as king of their lives. Jesus is the real king, whose power comes from above and is exercised over Pilate even as he proceeds to put Jesus to death. No human authority has any real power over "the king of the Jews" (18:33).

Meditation: In which ways does Jesus exercise his kingship in your life?

Prayer: God of the world, you made your Son, Jesus, the King of the universe, as he was preparing for his own suffering and death. Make us loyal, trustworthy, and faithful servants of Christ, our king. Enable us to testify to his truth and to listen to his voice, that we might one day share in the fullness of his kingdom, where he lives and reigns with you and the Holy Spirit, one God, for ever and ever. Amen.

JESUS, REMEMBER ME

Luke 23:35-43

Scripture: One of the criminals hanging there reviled Jesus, saying, "Are you not the Messiah? Save yourself and us." In response the other rebuked him, saying, "Have you no fear of God? — you're under the same sentence!" Then he said, "Jesus, remember me when you come into your kingdom" (Luke 23:39-40, 42).

Reflection: Luke's source for his crucifixion of Jesus narrative is Mark (15:26-32), but he has reworked the material to prepare for his own unique account of Jesus' dialogue with the two criminals, "one on his right, the other on his left" (23:33). The selection from the crucifixion account, which has been chosen for today's Gospel (23:35-43), includes the dialogue with the two criminals.

The way that Luke has organized his material in this section reflects a parallel with Jesus' threefold temptation in the desert after his baptism. First, the rulers tempt the crucified One by saying, "He saved others, let him save himself if he is the chosen one, the Messiah of God" (23:35). Second, the soldiers jeer and say, "If you are the King of the Jews, save yourself" (23:37). Third, "One of the criminals hanging there reviled Jesus, saying, 'Are you not the Messiah? Save yourself and us'" (23:39).

Jesus refused to use his divine power for his own benefit. Throughout the Gospel his mission has been to teach God's will and obedience to God's will. Jesus did not give in to the temptation in the wilderness to use his power for himself. Neither does he succumb to temptation while hanging on the cross. His power

301

has been used for the benefit of others. His obedience to death by martyrdom, demonstrates and perfects his obedience to God.

Luke presents the truth about Jesus through the irony of the threefold temptation. The "Messiah of God" (23:35) and "King of the Jews" (23:37) saves lives by giving away his own life in obedience to God.

Luke is exhorting his readers to avoid attachment to self-preservation, for such attachment is idolatrous. In the midst of the persecution and martyrdom of the members of Luke's community, other members are told not even to cling to life itself. Jesus did not hold onto life; he obeyed God. Neither can followers of Jesus cling to their lives; if obedience to God means martyrdom, then authentic discipleship must face it willingly.

The unique Lucan scene which depicts Jesus in dialogue with the two criminals serves another of the author's purposes. While the first criminal represents the final in a threefold series of temptations, the second criminal stands as an example of repentance. He acknowledges his own sin, accepts his punishment as justified, expresses his repentance, and pronounces Jesus to be innocent. In this way, he serves as a model of all that Jesus has taught, preached and done throughout the Gospel. This repentant criminal addresses Jesus, "Remember me when you come into your kingdom" (23:42). Jesus replies, "Amen, I say to you, today you will be with me in Paradise" (23:43). For Luke the kingdom is present in Jesus. Therefore, the repentant criminal rests "in the bosom of Abraham" (16:22) already. The destiny of every follower of Jesus is Paradise.

Meditation: In which ways do you experience the temptation to save your life instead of giving it in obedience to God?

Prayer: God of the Messiah, you sent your Son, the King of the Jews, to teach and to preach and to demonstrate how to live the way of your kingdom. When we are tempted to save our lives, make us obedient to your will. Help us to acknowledge our sin and repent of our idolatry. Enable us to be obedient to your will to death. Remember to bring us to Paradise that we might live with you, Jesus, and the Holy Spirit, who are one God, for ever and ever. Amen.

TOTALLY DEPENDENT ON GOD

Luke 21:1-4

Scripture: "This poor widow threw in more [into the Temple treasury] than all of them. All the others threw in offerings from their abundance, while she, from her want, threw in all the livelihood she had" (Luke 21:3-4).

Reflection: Jesus' denunciation of the scribes (20:45-47), which is omitted from the daily cycle of readings, prepares for the section concerning the poor widow's contribution to the Temple treasury (21:1-4). Jesus declares that the scribes "devour the houses of widows" (20:47). Then, he holds up a widow, who puts "two small coins" (21:2) into the treasury of the Temple, as an example of discipleship.

Luke's source for this story is Mark (12:41-44). Because of Luke's persistent interest in the poor and detachment from material possessions, this narrative serves his purpose of stressing the importance of complete dependence upon God.

In the culture of the time, a widow — a woman whose husband had died — was powerless. Her source of livelihood, her husband, was gone. Therefore, she was totally dependent upon others to care for her.

The powerless widow in Luke's story is contrasted to the "rich throwing their offerings into the treasury" (21:1). The wealthy are the powerful. They make their offerings "from their abundance" (21:4).

The powerless widow makes herself even more powerless by "throwing in two small coins... all the livelihood she had" (21:4). In other words, if she was dependent before, she is totally dependent now. She can only trust in and depend upon God, whereas the wealthy can trust in and depend upon themselves.

Luke holds up the widow is an example of authentic discipleship. Her gift of herself, "all the livelihood she had" (21:4) is "more than all of them" (21:3). Her action is to be imitated — not the actions of the scribes, who "will receive a very severe condemnation" (20:47). The widow makes her gift "from her want" (21:4), which is a hyperbolic way of stating that she gives away what she does not have!

Her action fits one of Luke's major themes — wealth is given to some people in order to be shared with others. The author of this Gospel has emphasized this point in the parable of the rich fool (12:16-21) and in Jesus' discourse on the importance of dependence upon God (12:22-34) which follows it, in the parable of the rich man and Lazarus (16:19-31), in the narrative about the rich official (18:18-23) and the discourse on riches and renunciation (18:24-30) which follows it, and in the story about Zacchaeus the tax collector (19:1-10).

Meditation: In which ways do you experience yourself to be totally dependent upon God? In which ways do you experience yourself totally dependent upon your wealth?

Prayer: God of widows, you raise up the poor and make them rich in your sight. You give riches to your people that they might share their abundance with those who have nothing. Fill us with the spirit of generosity and awaken us to the realization that every good gift comes from your hand. Enable us to give back to you what you have freely given to us. We ask this through our Lord Jesus Christ, your Son, who lives and reigns with you and the Holy Spirit, one God, for ever and ever. Amen.

WHAT NOT TO LOOK FOR

Luke 21:5-11

Scripture: "See that you're not led astray, for many will come in my name, saying, 'I am he,' and 'The time has come.' Do not follow them!" (Luke 21:8).

Reflection: By the time that Luke wrote his Gospel (ca. 80-90 A.D.), the Jerusalem Temple had already been destroyed by the Romans 10-20 years earlier. The destruction of the Temple sent a shock-wave through early Christianity; it was one of those events which should not have happened but did happen. Jews and Jewish-Christians believed that God lived in the Temple; therefore, how could the mighty God permit his house, his dwelling place on earth, to be destroyed by pagan Romans?

Before Luke, the author of Mark's Gospel had to wrestle with this question. His answer portrayed Jesus predicting the destruction of the Temple as a sign of the coming of the age. Since Mark believed that the Second Coming of Jesus was imminent, this answer worked for a number of years.

However, by the time of Luke, the belief in the imminence of Jesus' Second Coming was waning. Therefore, Luke had to deal with the problem of the destruction of the Temple in a different way. This author chooses to separate the destruction of the Temple from the signs of the Second Coming of Jesus and create a period which he calls "The times of the Gentiles" (21:24). During this time between the destruction of the Temple and the

305

Second Coming of Jesus, followers of Jesus are to be witnesses to all that Jesus said and did.

Because of the historicity of the toppling of the Jerusalem Temple, Luke preserves Jesus' prediction of its destruction (cf. Mark 13:1-2); he has to in order to preserve his own credibility as a writer. Jesus' prophecy echoes that of Micah (3:12) and Jeremiah (22:5).

Luke's organization of this material leads to two ensuing questions about "When will this happen?" (21:7) and "What will be the sign that they are about to happen?" (21:7). In other words, the foretelling of the destruction of the Temple prepares for Luke's version of Jesus' (eschatological) discourse about the last things.

Today's selection (21:5-11) contains the prediction of the destruction of the Temple and the first half of the answer to the first question about when this will happen. Because Luke is interested in maintaining his middle period of witnessing, he warns the members of his community, "See that you are not led astray, for many will come in my name, saying, 'I am he,' and 'The time has come.' Do not follow them!" (21:8). The imminent end of the age and the Second Coming of Jesus have been pushed back into the indefinite future. Even the proclamation of the imminent end of the age and the coming of Jesus has become a false teaching for the author of this Gospel. Anyone making such an announcement is to be considered a false messiah.

The end of the age and the Second Coming of Jesus will not be preceded by rumors "of wars and insurrections" (21:9). Again, Luke warns his readers, "When you hear of wars and insurrections, do not be terrified; for such things must happen first, but it will not immediately be the end" (21:9). Political upheavals will continue as part of the course of world events; these do not indicate that the world is coming to an end or that Jesus is returning in glory. "Nation will rise against nation, and kingdom against kingdom" (21:10).

Not even cosmic disturbances can be considered as indicators of the end of the world. For Luke, these are natural occurrences with no other value. "There will be powerful earthquakes, famines, and plagues in various places; there will be dreadful sights and great signs in the skies" (21:11).

So far, then, Luke has not yet answered the questions. He has not indicated when the end will come because he does not know, and, while he wants to preserve the expectation of the Second Coming of Jesus, he significantly modifies the imminent hope for Jesus' return in glory. Furthermore, Luke has only told the reader what not to look for as signs of the end — false messiahs, wars, insurrections, cosmic disturbances.

Meditation: Today, how do you expect the Second Coming of Jesus in glory?

Prayer: God of the Temple, once you established your dwelling place in a tent, and you traveled with your people. Later, your kings built a house in which you came to live. In the fullness of time, you came to live with your people in the person of Jesus, your Son. Send your Holy Spirit to come and dwell in our hearts. Make us temples of your presence. Keep us faithful until Jesus comes in glory; he is Lord for ever and ever. Amen.

GIVE TESTIMONY
Luke 21:12-19

Scripture: "But before all this, they'll lay hands on you and persecute you, handing you over to the synagogues and prisons, having you brought before kings and governors because of my name" (Luke 21:12).

Reflection: This section (21:12-19) of Luke's Gospel continues Jesus' (eschatological) discourse about the last things. However, this unit focuses on Luke's period in between the destruction of the Temple and the Second Coming of Jesus in glory — the period of witnessing or testimony.

Before there are signs of the end of the age, there will be plenty of time for followers of Jesus to bear witness to what he said and did. As had already happened in Luke's community, some disciples had been seized and persecuted; they had been handed over to synagogues and prisons; they were led before kings and governors. And there was going to be a lot more seizures, persecutions, imprisonments, and trials, as Luke develops in his second volume, the Acts of the Apostles. All of these trials "lead to your giving witness" (21:13).

In giving witness, Luke urges his readers to remember "not to prepare ahead of time how to defend yourselves" for Jesus himself "shall give [them] an eloquence and wisdom which all those opposing [them] will not be able to resist or refute" (21:14-15). This guidance will come from the Holy Spirit, who, even though he has been active throughout the Gospel, will be received by Jesus' followers in a dramatic way in the Acts of the Apostles.

While standing firm, "by… perseverance" (21:19) followers of Jesus "will save [their] lives" (21:19), even when their own relatives hand each other over to death. Jesus had already prepared for this when he said, "I tell you [I have come] for division" (12:51). In Luke's community, there were "parents, brothers, relatives, and friends" (21:16), who betrayed their Christian relatives.

But there is hope in the midst of persecution. "You will be hated by all because of my name, yet not a hair on your head will be destroyed" (21:18). Luke slips into hyperbole in order to stress that witness, testimony, leads to dependence upon God. Jesus has already instructed his followers to seek his Father's kingdom first and all other things would be given to them (cf. 12:22-34). The "Father is pleased to give you the kingdom" (12:32). Now is the time to bear witness that this is true.

Meditation: In which ways do you experience persecution because you witness, give testimony, about Jesus?

Prayer: Faithful God, throughout history your people have suffered persecution because they trusted in your benevolent care. When we are tried because of our faith, give us wisdom in speaking that our adversaries may be powerless to resist or to refute us. Keep us faithful when members of our own families abandon us. Help us to persevere until the coming of Jesus in glory. He lives and reigns with you and the Holy Spirit, one God, for ever and ever. Amen.

THE TIMES OF THE GENTILES

Luke 21:20-28

Scripture: "When you see Jerusalem surrounded by an army, know that its desolation is at hand.... Jerusalem will be trampled underfoot by the Gentiles until the times of the Gentiles are fulfilled.... Then they will see the Son of Man coming on a cloud with power and great glory" (Luke 21:20, 24, 27).

Reflection: Earlier in this (eschatological) discourse on the last things, Jesus foretold the destruction of the Temple. In today's section (21:20-28) he speaks about the destruction of Jerusalem and the coming of the Son of Man.

Historically, Jerusalem was destroyed by the Roman army in 70 A.D. after a three-year war with the Jews. Jesus' prediction of the fall of Jerusalem is a literary device which Luke uses to justify the prediction of Jesus' coming in glory as the Son of Man. At the time of Luke's writing (80-90 A.D.), Jerusalem had already been destroyed for 10-20 years.

Therefore, Jesus can accurately say, "When you see Jerusalem surrounded by an army, know that its desolation is at hand. Then let those in Judea flee to the mountains. Let those inside [the city] leave it, and let those in the countryside not go into it" (21:20-21). Now, the question which was asked earlier is answered: "What will be the sign that all these things are about to

311

happen?" (21:7). The answer is the presence of troops surrounding Jerusalem.

Luke understands the historical destruction of the city as "the time of retribution when all that has been written is fulfilled" (21:22) and as "a wrathful judgment upon this people" (21:23). In other words, Jerusalem will "be trampled underfoot by the Gentiles until the times of the Gentiles are fulfilled" (21:24). The "times of the Gentiles" is Luke's period of undetermined length between the destruction of the Temple and Jerusalem and the coming of Jesus in glory. The Gentiles will prevail; they will be converted, as Luke explains throughout the Acts of the Apostles.

The destruction of Jerusalem is not viewed as the beginning of the end by Luke, but as an assurance that just as Jesus was accurate in predicting the destruction of the Temple and Jerusalem, so is he accurate in predicting his coming in glory. Using typical apocalyptic imagery, Jesus states, "There will be signs in the sun, the moon, and the stars, and distress among nations on earth in despair at the roaring of the sea and the waves, people fainting in fear and foreboding over what is coming upon the world, for the powers of the heavens will be shaken" (21:25-26).

These are the signs which indicate that the Son of Man is "coming on a cloud with power and great glory" (21:27).

When "these signs begin to happen," Jesus states, "stand erect and raise your heads because your deliverance is at hand" (21:28). Luke believed that everything else in the apocalyptic timetable (destruction of the Temple and Jerusalem) had already taken place. All that remained was the Second Coming of Jesus.

However, while he believed that this was all that remained, he didn't think that it would happen quickly. Yes, Jesus would come in glory, but not yet. The "times of the Gentiles" had to be fulfilled. The author's second volume, the Acts of the Apostles, had to be written. There would be a delay in Jesus' coming. Luke could never have realized that after almost 2,000 years Christians are still waiting for the coming of the Son of Man.

Meditation: How has the destruction of something in your life been the sign of a new beginning for you?

Prayer: Creator God, you have given us the sun, the moon, and the stars as signs of your enduring presence. You have made the roaring of the sea and the waves signs of your power. When destruction envelops our lives, help us to stand firm in hope. Keep us watchful and ready that we might stand erect, raise our heads, know that our redemption is at hand, and see the Son of Man, our Lord Jesus Christ, coming on a cloud with power and great glory. He lives and reigns with you and the Holy Spirit, one God, for ever and ever. Amen.

THE KINGDOM IS NEAR

Luke 21:29-33

Scripture: "Consider the fig tree and all the other trees. When their buds burst open, you see for yourselves and know that summer is now near. So, too, when you see these things happening, you will know that the kingdom of God is near" (Luke 21:29-31).

Reflection: Luke's version of the lesson of the fig tree, which is part of Jesus' (eschatological) discourse about the last things, comes from Mark's Gospel (13:29-31), but the author has made some significant changes.

No longer is the lesson about a fig tree; now it includes "all the other trees" (21:29). In the ancient world, the fig tree's presence was a sign of blessing; its absence was a sign of being cursed. Luke, and before him Mark, understands "the fig tree and all the other trees" (21:29) to be signs "that the kingdom of God is near" (29:31). This means that the presence of the fig tree heralds not only the presence and the blessing of the kingdom of God now, but it also points toward the fullness of the kingdom at the end of the age.

Time is collapsed in the lesson. "When their [the trees'] buds burst open, you see for yourselves and know that summer is now near" (29:30). What happened to spring? Buds are a sign of spring — not of summer. Summer, however, represents the end of time. Thus, Luke declares that at the present moment the kingdom of

315

God exists; God's kingdom is always near. There is no need to look forward to some glorious future; in the present is the future for Luke.

Therefore, "this generation will not pass away until all these things have taken place" (21:32). "This generation" is a reference to the human race, which will remain until the coming of Jesus in glory. Also, the human race participates in the kingdom of God now.

Likewise, "heaven and earth will pass away, but my [Jesus'] words will not pass away" (21:33). The belief that Jesus will come again endures to the present day.

For Luke, the fig tree and all the other trees serve as reminders of both the presence of the kingdom of God now and the fullness that waits to be realized when Jesus comes in glory. The author has adapted Mark's lesson of the fig tree to suit his perspective of the in-between period of time, which has been set aside for witnessing and giving testimony.

Meditation: Make a list of the lessons that you have learned from observing trees.

Prayer: God of the trees, you have created the world in all its wonder and entrusted its care to the human race. Jesus declared that the trees were signs of your blessing upon and presence with your people. Help us to learn the lesson of the trees that we might know the nearness of your kingdom, while we wait in joyful hope for the coming in glory of Jesus, who lives and reigns with you and the Holy Spirit, one God, for ever and ever. Amen.

BE VIGILANT

Luke 21:34-36

Scripture: "Be alert at all times and pray that you will have the strength to escape all these things that are going to happen, and to stand before the Son of Man" (Luke 21:36).

Reflection: The exhortation to vigilance (21:34-36) concludes Jesus' (eschatological) discourse about the last things. Vigilance means two things for Luke. First, the person who follows Jesus while waiting for his return in glory must "take care" that his or her heart does not "get weighed down with dissipation and drunkenness and the cares of everyday life" and, as a result, "that day come upon [him or her] unexpectedly, like a trap" (21:34-35). Nothing should distract a person from his or her primary concern — the return of the Son of Man.

Dissipation and drunkenness can be summarized in one word, sensuality, which is escapism. According to Luke, Christians are not to immerse themselves into sensuality in order to escape "the cares of everyday life" (21:34). Furthermore, "the cares of everyday life" are not to preoccupy their time. The day Jesus comes in glory will confront "everyone who lives on the face of the earth" (21:35). The Christian stance, then, is not to let their hearts "get weighed down" (21:34); they are to be alert at all times, or, in other words, to stay awake.

Second, for Luke vigilance means prayer. Throughout the Gospel, the author has indicated that prayer is the opposite of losing heart, of giving up. Prayer intensifies persistence. Prayer gives a person "strength to escape all these things that are going to happen, and to stand before the Son of Man" (21:36).

While he has separated the destruction of Jerusalem and the Temple from the Second Coming of Jesus, Luke has accomplished two other important moves in this discourse. First, he has pushed the Second Coming of Jesus into the indefinite future. Second, he has preserved the belief that Jesus will come again.

The liturgical year ends with the Christian standing in Luke's in-between time. His or her responsibility is to witness, or give testimony, to the words and deeds of Jesus, not to be caught up in sensuality and daily cares, to pray, and to watch for the day of the Son of Man.

Meditation: In which ways do you keep a daily vigil for the coming in glory of Jesus?

Prayer: God of all who wait, you strengthen your people in faithfulness through your gift of the Holy Spirit. Preserve our hearts from lethargy and sensuality. Keep us free of all daily anxieties. Inspire us to be vigilant at all times. We ask you to move us to prayer for strength that we might be prepared for the day of the Son of Man, the coming in glory of your Son, our Lord Jesus Christ, who lives and reigns with you and the Holy Spirit, one God, for ever and ever. Amen.

LIFTED UP

John 3:13-17

September 14

Scripture: "Just as Moses lifted up the serpent in the desert, so must the Son of Man be lifted up, so that everyone who believes in him may have eternal life" (John 3:14-15).

Reflection: The discourse about the Son of Man being lifted up, just as Moses lifted up the serpent in the desert (3:13-17), is part of a response to a question asked by Nicodemus, a Pharisee and ruler of the Jews who came to Jesus at night. Both Nicodemus' question and Jesus' answer are part of a larger section composed of statements, questions, and answers between the same two people.

In a post-resurrectional context, Jesus' statement, "No one has gone up to heaven except the one who has come down from heaven, the Son of Man" (3:13) makes more sense. The pre-existent Word, the Son, has always been with God from the beginning. He became flesh and made his dwelling on the earth. Therefore, he is the one who came down from heaven. Through the glory of his suffering, death, and resurrection, he has returned to heaven in the Johannine perspective.

His suffering and lifting up in death on a cross have the power to heal all humankind, just as the serpent mounted on the pole healed any of the Israelites who looked upon it (cf. Numbers 21:9). Jesus was exalted through his cross and resurrection and became the source of healing for all people. This is the same as eternal life for all who believe in Jesus, God's gift to the world in the incarnation and again in the crucifixion and resurrection. "God so loved the world that he gave his only Son, so that everyone who believes in him might not perish but might have eternal life" (John 3:16). The person who believes in Jesus will share in eternal life, the fullness of life.

God's purpose in giving Jesus to the world and lifting him up in glory was not "to condemn the world, but that the world might be saved through him" (3:17). Jesus' purpose was to save everyone who would believe in him; everyone who looks upon his cross is healed.

Meditation: What healing effects has the cross of Jesus had on your life?

Prayer: God of eternal life, when your people sinned you punished them with saraph serpents, but you saved them by instructing your servant, Moses, to mount a serpent on a pole so that whoever looked at it would recover. Your Son, Jesus Christ, was lifted up on the pole of the cross for the salvation of the world. The instrument of death, however, also became the throne of glorification, for you lifted him up in the triumph of the resurrection. Strengthen our faith in him that we might be worthy of eternal life. We ask this through Christ our Lord. Amen.

BLESSED ARE YOU

Matthew 5:1-12

Scripture: "Blessed are you when they insult you and per-secute you and utter every sort of evil thing against you because of me. Rejoice and be glad, for your reward will be great in heaven" (Matthew 5:11-12).

Reflection: The first of five sermons in Matthew's Gospel is com-monly called the Sermon on the Mount (5:1-7:29). It begins with the beatitudes (5:1-12), sayings of Jesus derived from Q (cf. Luke 6:20-23). However, some of the Matthean beatitudes are unique to this author.

The entire sermon is addressed to "the crowds" who fol-low Jesus "up the mountain" (5:1), where he teaches them like a rabbi — sitting down. His position on the mountain also recalls the reception of the law by Moses on Mount Sinai. Since Mat-thew conceives of Jesus as a new Moses (found in the parallel between the five sermons and the five books of Moses), this set-ting serves to reveal his theological perspective concerning Jesus.

Matthew records nine beatitudes, each of which begins with the word "blessed." Blessedness is the characteristic of those who have achieved everything and now resemble God. To be blessed, according to Matthew, is to share in the characteristics of God. In its basic understanding, blessedness means "happiness," that which puts a person at ease. In each beatitude there is woven an inherent contradiction between blessedness and the state of the person described.

"Blessed are the poor in spirit, for theirs is the kingdom of heaven" (5:3), is the first beatitude. This beatitude has a parallel in Luke 6:20; however, Matthew has added "poor in spirit" to the original version. The hyperbole and contradiction comes through more readily, if the reader understands the beatitude in this fashion: Happy are the depressed, for they now experience the presence of God!

The second beatitude states, "Blessed are they who mourn, for they will be comforted" (5:4). This beatitude might be rendered in this way: Happy are they who cry because of the death of a loved one; their comfort will come through their mourning. Also, when in tears, they are like God!

"Blessed are the meek, for they will inherit the land" (5:5) might be rendered in this way: Happy are those who endure injury without resentment and with patience; they are like God. One day, they will be given the kingdom of heaven.

The fourth of the nine beatitudes deals with a particularly Matthean theme — righteousness. "Blessed are they who hunger and thirst for righteousness, for they will be satisfied" (5:6). To be righteous means that a person behaves according to God's will. One who is righteous does the will of God. Happy are they who are hungry and thirsty for knowledge of God's will — no matter what it may mean (even death, as for Jesus); these people will get that for which they hunger and thirst!

"Blessed are the merciful, for they will be shown mercy" (5:7). In this beatitude, mercy means unlimited compassion. It might be best understood in this way: "Happy are those who are always compassionate; through their compassion they demonstrate that they are like God, who is unlimited in compassion. They will receive compassion through their own demonstration of it."

The sixth beatitude declares, "Blessed are the clean of heart, for they will see God" (5:8). The clean of heart were those who were permitted to worship in the Temple. Here, however, Jesus states, "Happy are those who can approach God; they will see God's face." If one remembers that no one could see the face of God and live, the contradictory nature of this beatitude becomes clear.

"Blessed are the peacemakers, for they will be called children of God" (5:9), states the seventh beatitude. They who make peace are like God. However, those who make peace will not be declared great or held up as examples. Rather, they will be called children of God. A child was one who was powerless. As children of God, peacemakers are the powerless in a culture that looks to the powerful to make peace!

The eighth beatitude re-echoes Matthew's righteousness theme: "Blessed are they who are persecuted for the sake of righteousness, for theirs is the kingdom of heaven" (5:10). This one might best be understood in this way: Happy are those who are made to suffer because they do God's will; in their suffering and doing God's will, they share now in his kingdom. In a culture in which suffering or persecution was understood as punishment by God for sin, this beatitude was certainly contradictory.

The final beatitude is spoken directly to the reader: "Blessed are you when they insult you and persecute you and utter every sort of evil thing against you because of me. Rejoice and be glad, for you reward will be great in heaven" (Matthew 5:11-12). Matthew is telling his church: Happy are you when you are insulted, persecuted, and defamed because you faithfully follow Jesus. It is contradictory for one to be happy in the midst of insults, persecution, and defamatory remarks, let alone to "rejoice and be glad" (5:12)!

The reward promised for being happy in the midst of insults and persecution is not to be understood as something earned. In Matthew's understanding, reward is the underserved gift of God because a person sought out God's will and did it. Getting a reward is not sufficient motivation for doing God's will; one does it because it is what God wants a person to do. Because one has been motivated to do the will of God because one knows it to be what God wants, this person will inherit the kingdom of heaven.

Persecution should not be a deterrent in doing God's will. Those who are persecuted stand in line with the prophets, who did God's will and suffered because of it. According to Matthew, "Thus, they persecuted the prophets who were before you" (5:12). Since the prophets share in the kingdom of heaven, those who imitate them will likewise share in it.

Meditation: In which ways are you blessed? That is, in which ways do you share in the characteristics of God now, as presented by the beatitudes?

Prayer: Blessed are you, God of heaven and earth. You revealed your law through Moses, and, when your people sinned, you called them back to your covenant through the prophets. Help us to realize that in your eyes it is the poor in spirit, the mourning, the meek, those who hunger and thirst for righteousness, the merciful, the clean of heart, the peacemakers, and the persecuted who are welcomed into your kingdom. Teach us always to rejoice and be glad in Jesus, your Son, who lives and reigns with you and the Holy Spirit, one God, for ever and ever. Amen.

A GRAIN OF WHEAT
John 12:23-28

ALL
SOULS

November 2

Scripture: "The hour has come for the Son of Man to be glorified. Amen, amen, I say to you, if the grain of wheat that falls to the ground does not die, it remains just a grain of wheat; but if it dies, it produces much fruit" (John 12:23-24).

Reflection: After the anointing at Bethany and the triumphant entry into Jerusalem (12:1-19), John portrays Jesus as involved in a dialogue with Andrew and Philip about the hour for his glorification (12:20-36). This section (12:23-28) is part of this dialogue.

Throughout his Gospel, John has made reference to Jesus' "hour," that is his suffering, death, and resurrection. Now, Jesus, who is in control of everything throughout the Gospel, declares, "The hour has come for the Son of Man to be glorified" (12:23). For John, Jesus' glorification is his lifting up on the cross (cf. 3:14-15) and his being lifted up by the Father in his resurrection.

It is through Jesus' death and resurrection, his "hour," that he will become accessible to all people. He is the grain of wheat that must fall to the ground and die in order to produce much fruit (cf. 12:24-24). A single grain of wheat dies in order to produce a stalk with many more grains of wheat. Likewise, Jesus' death will produce many believers.

This is stated in a different way in the next verse, in which Jesus says, "Whoever loves his life loses it, and whoever hates his life in this world will preserve it for eternal life" (12:25). Real life is not earthly life. Therefore, whoever loves earthly life will end up losing eternal life, but whoever is unconcerned with earthly life will discover real life with Jesus.

"If anyone would serve me let him follow me, and where I am, there also will my servant be" (12:26), Jesus declares. In other words, those who claim to be disciples must be willing to suffer, die, and be raised, just like Jesus. Authentic followers of Jesus will be in the same place where Jesus is — on the cross! "The Father will honor anyone who serves" Jesus (12:26).

While one is undergoing suffering, death, and resurrection, he or she may feel like Jesus: "I am troubled now. Yet what should I say? 'Father, save me from this hour'?" (12:27) And of course the answer to this is, "It was for this purpose that I came to this hour" (12:27). Every follower of Jesus will have to face his or her "hour," according to Jesus. The challenge is to remain faithful, as Jesus remained faithful.

"Father, glorify your name" (12:28), Jesus prays. He asks God to give praise to himself through what is about to happen to Jesus — suffering, death, and resurrection. John portrays God's response as a voice from heaven which says, "I have glorified it and will glorify it again" (12:28). In the faithful life of Jesus and in the faithful lives of every one of his followers, God has the opportunity to receive praise from every person's suffering, death, and resurrection.

Contrary to popular belief, then, suffering, death, and resurrection are not evils to be avoided. Rather, they are vehicles of the Father's glory to be freely embraced. They represent the "hour" of glorification for every human being who believes in and trusts in Jesus, the one who has already been glorified through his own suffering, death, and resurrection.

Meditation: In which events of your life have you already experienced the "hour" that gives glory to the Father?

Prayer: Father, you glorified your Son through his suffering, death, and resurrection. When his hour came, you lifted him up in death and in new life. Like the grain of wheat, he fell to the earth and died and produced much fruit. When we are faced with and troubled by our hour, may we glorify your name through our suffering, death, and resurrection. Make us faithful servants of Jesus, who lives and reigns with you and the Holy Spirit, one God, for ever and ever. Amen.

THE TEMPLE OF THE BODY
John 2:13-22

FEAST of the
DEDICATION of
ST. JOHN
LATERAN

November 14

Scripture: Jesus answered and said to them, "Destroy this temple and in three days I will raise it up." The Jews said, "This Temple has been under construction for forty-six years, and you claim you will raise it up in three days?" But he was speaking about the temple of his body (John 2:19-21).

Reflection: In John's Gospel the cleansing of the Temple (2:13-22) occurs immediately after the wedding at Cana narrative. Thus, unlike the Synoptic Gospels (Mark, Matthew, and Luke), which place this scene much later in the gospel — after the triumphant entry into Jerusalem — John portrays the scene as taking place very early in the ministry of Jesus. Cleaning out the Temple would not be considered the best way to begin a public career, unless, of course, one understands Johannine theology.

John tells the reader that "the Passover of the Jews was near" and "Jesus went up to Jerusalem" (2:13). Passover is the yearly celebration of the escape of Israel from Egyptian slavery. For John, however, Passover is also a metaphor for Jesus, who dies on the cross while the passover lambs are being sacrificed in the Temple and whose body is treated as a passover victim (cf. 19:31-37). Jesus passes over from death to life.

In light of this understanding, Jesus' words about the destruction of the Temple, which is framed in apocalyptic language in the Synoptics, makes sense. "Destroy this temple and in three days I will raise it up" (2:19) is a Johannine reference to Jesus and his resurrection. John makes it clear in an editorial comment which follows the dialogue, "He was speaking about the temple of his body. Therefore, when he was raised from the dead, his disciples remembered that he had said this, and they came to believe the Scripture and the word Jesus had spoken" (2:21-22).

The driving out of those "who sold oxen, sheep, and doves" (2:14), which were used for the Temple sacrifices, and the spilling of "the coins of the money-changers" and overturning of "their tables" (2:15), which contained the coins for the Temple tax, illustrate that the old ways have been eliminated by Jesus, according to John. In making "a whip out of cords" and driving "them all out of the Temple area, with the sheep and oxen" (2:15), Jesus declares that those who are members of his body no longer have need of the Temple.

The new Temple, the new dwelling place of God, is in the incarnation, the body and blood of Jesus, and in those who form the body of the Church. "Get them [oxen, sheep, doves, and money-changers] out of here, and stop making my Father's house a marketplace" (2:16). God is not interested in temples, according to John; God is interested in those who form the temple of the body of Christ, believers.

Those who believe know that they worship the Father by their faith in his only Son. Those who do not believe ask, "What sign can you show us to justify your doing these things?" (2:18). The sign has already been given — the suffering, death, and resurrection of Jesus. Some, however, do not understand and ask, "This Temple has been under construction for forty-six years, and you claim you will raise it up in three days?" (2:20)

Later, when speaking with the Samaritan woman, Jesus will tell her, "The hour is coming, and is now here, when true worshippers will worship the Father in Spirit and truth; and indeed the Father seeks such people to worship him. God is Spirit, and those who worship him must worship in Spirit and truth" (4:23-24).

Meditation: As a member of the body of Christ, the new temple of Jesus, how do you worship the Father in Spirit and in truth?

Prayer: God of Spirit and truth, when your only Son slept in death on the cross, you awakened him to the glory of the resurrection and established the community of his followers as his body. Through the waters of baptism we have been initiated into this new temple. Keep us faithful. Make our worship authentic. Bring about in our lives the passover of Jesus so that we might share his glory with you, who live and reign with the Holy Spirit, one God, for ever and ever. Amen.